CONTEMPORARY
IMAGES
OF CHRISTIAN
MINISTRY

CONTEMPORARY IMAGES OF CHRISTIAN MINISTRY

Donald E. Messer

ABINGDON PRESS
Nashville

CONTEMPORARY IMAGES OF CHRISTIAN MINISTRY

Library of Congress Cataloging-in-Publication Data

MESSER, DONALD E.
  Contemporary images of Christian ministry.
  Bibliography: p.
  Includes index.
  1. Clergy—Office. I. Title.
  BV660.2.M45 1989   262'.1   88-24173
            ISBN 0-687-09505-0 (pbk.: alk. paper)

Scripture quotations, unless otherwise noted, are from the Revised Standard
Version of the Bible, copyright 1946, 1952, 1971 by the Division of Christian
Education of the National Council of Churches of Christ in the USA. Used by
permission. Those noted NEB are from *The New English Bible.* © The
Delegates of the Oxford University Press and the Syndics of the Cambridge
University Press 1961, 1970. Used by permission.

The author gratefully acknowledges the following:

Amnesty International USA for the excerpt from *Matchbox*, October 1983. For
more information about Amnesty International, write to: AIUSA 322 Eighth
Avenue, New York, NY 10001.

The Christian Century Foundation for excerpts from "The Divine Madness of
Ministry" by Gary Charles, which first appeared in *The Christian Century*, April
20, 1983. Copyright © 1983 by The Christian Century Foundation.

The Christian Century Foundation for "The Scandal of Vocation" Beverly
Roberts Gaventa, which first appeared in *The Christian Ministry*, July 1983.
Copyright © 1983 by The Christian Century Foundation.

MANUFACTURED BY THE PARTHENON PRESS AT
NASHVILLE, TENNESSEE, UNITED STATES OF AMERICA

In Love with Gratitude

to

George M. and Grace A. Messer

and

Owen V. and Wanita J. Nagel

Contents

Foreword

Thousands of young people, both men and women, are entering theological seminaries, dreaming of serving the Church and, through the Church, humankind. They are full of enthusiasm, ready to submit themselves to rigorous intellectual discipline. They dream of following the footsteps of the great ministers of yesteryear. A few years later, some of them will be frustrated or will have reduced their expectations and dreams to an ongoing bureaucratic reality. But many will be enabled to carry on courageous ministries in rural areas or in big cities, in small communities or in big congregations, enjoying the excitement of relating God's vision to daily and concrete human realities.

Donald Messer presents readers—pastors and theological students—with a series of challenging images that picture afresh the potential of this vocation. These images provide the encouragement that is necessary to persevere to meaningful and relevant ministry. While books on pastoral theology are abundant, it is the particular merit of the present volume to open avenues for our imagination through images and symbols that, while building on experience, discover new possibilities, new excitement, and new ventures.

Donald Messer writes out of sincere empathy for pastors. He is one among them; he hopes with them; he confesses sins and shortcomings with them. He works with them for the fulfillment not only of a personal vocation but also of the vocation of the Church as the servant people of God in the world. I have found myself in this book: my days in the local parish, my days in the ecumenical movement, my temptations, my doubts, my researches, my questions. It is a conversation among colleagues, but a conversation with one who has the capacity to provoke us to look more widely and to look beyond. The collage of images offers different entry points for our imagination and provides an overall picture of the pastoral vocation that is full of excitement and the experience of new generations of students in theological training. But it also offers a vast amount of reading, revealed on almost every page by quotations that enlarge the frame of reference for the reader.

The issue is a vital one. Religious renewal is taking place worldwide with manifestations of spiritual power and inspiration for justice, but it is also accompanied by sectarianism and irrationalism. More than ever, a new generation of pastors is needed who will be able to project dimensions of spirituality in the service of a praxis for a more just and human society. A new generation of pastors, "inspired by the vision of the prophetic and priestly service that the Christian Church is called to provide to the whole of society," will become salt and leaven inside parishes that will be transformed into salt and leaven for the whole of the human society.

For all of us for whom the pastoral ministry is our personal vocation and for all who cherish memories of pastors who have been a blessing to their lives, this book is a sober, brilliant, and imaginative approach to this vocation. It is also an invitation to young people to consider, through the symbols, images and passion of this book, the calling to the ministry as God's standing invitation.

EMILIO CASTRO
GENERAL SECRETARY
WORLD COUNCIL OF CHURCHES

Introduction

Just as a friend was completing a pastoral visit, he was confronted by a somewhat less than friendly dog. Though the young clergyman tried to step away, the mutt sank its teeth into his leg. Belatedly from the doorway a parishioner hollered, "Oh! Don't bite him—he's the minister!"

This incident, more humorous for others than for the wounded preacher, gives cause to reflect on this layperson's remark. Was the concern directed primarily toward the pastor or to the animal? Was it a fear of food poisoning for the dog or fright that God might unleash divine revenge on a favorite pet? Perhaps the dog was permitted to bite anyone but the minister—clergy need not only special purchasing discounts but also complete dog-bite exemptions. Or it might have been a rabies scare; you never know when a pastor might bite back!

Misunderstandings of the meanings of Christian ministry not only exist but they flourish as well. The stereotypical portrait of a pastor as a "holy person," a breed apart, oddly different from the rest of humanity, needing special care and treatment, is a traditional heresy. Likewise, the sketch of a pastor as a second-class citizen, deprived of political rights and responsibilities, often emerges. Some even seek to paint all pastors alike—colorless, joyless, sexless creatures—as if God used the seminary machinery to create human photocopies.

In Herman Melville's novel *Moby Dick*, there is an episode in which the chaplain addresses the crew: "Shipmates, God has laid but one hand upon you; both his hands press down upon me." Such a declaration adds drama but substitutes fiction for fact. God places different, but equal, demands on clergy and laity. Double standards of morality or ministry are unsupportable. Both laity and clergy are called to exercise Christ's ministry in Church and society. Each of us must find the locus of service to humanity in our own vocation.[1]

Rethinking the Image of Ministry

A need exists for rethinking the image of ministry in our time, reappropriating the central biblical and theological understandings in contemporary metaphors appropriate to the age. This is not to downgrade in any way the traditional images of priest, prophet, or shepherd, but rather to recognize that throughout the centuries the Christian church has altered its images in light of the times and circumstances. Fresh ways of picturing ministry sometimes break the old stereotypes and capture anew the dimensions that have been lost or, at least, somewhat obscured or diminished.

Since biblical days, many provocative and profound images of ministry have enlivened the imagination and empowered the people of God. Over the centuries, symbols of priest, prophet, pastor, servant, and shepherd have been metaphors of ministry without parallel in terms of their influence and impact on Christian communities in a variety of cultures. In recent decades more secular models have accented creative dimensions of ministry—counselor, administrator, pastoral director, professional, midwife, player coach, and enabler to name but a few.

However, each generation must review and reappropriate these portraits of ministry, finding its own contemporary images that project motivation and meaning. In this book, a series of somewhat paradoxical paradigms of ministry will be explored in the belief that they offer perspectives essential to the art of ministry in our time.

Doing so does not imply that the traditional images of ministry no longer have authority or relevance for the Christian community. It neither suggests that these metaphors can be understood without reference to the more historic self-understandings of ministry, nor should it be interpreted to mean that each contemporary image has equal merit and meaning for every individual. Faithful discipleship does not look the same on every person. Likewise, it is assumed that dominant images may change for persons, depending on their own life experiences, places and stages of ministry. A twenty-five-year-old seminary graduate may find it difficult, for example, to become a "wounded healer" if life has spared him or her from any serious setbacks or brutal blows. Just as many a seminary student cannot fully appreciate the value of studying patristics or church administration, often it takes the developing lessons of life to clarify the importance or significance of particular propositions or truths.

14

These contemporary images should be viewed, therefore, as supplementing, not supplanting, such traditional concepts as priest, pastor, and prophet. It is hoped that these metaphors will give new meaning to the traditional roles of ministry—namely that of administrator, organizer, preacher, liturgist, teacher, and counselor.[2] By complementing the more biblical and historical prototypes, it is hoped that new vision and vitality may be experienced by those who accept the call and challenge of Christian ministry.

In the chapters that follow, ministry is viewed as not simply the professional preserve of the ordained but as an expression of the total church, both clergy and lay. What has been written relates both to clergy and lay, though certain sections (such as the problem of stereotypes and ordination) apply more specifically to the clergy.

It is quite impossible to explore the contemporary images of Christian ministry without first understanding the art of imaging and its function within the life of the Christian community. A brief review of the history of ministerial images through the centuries is provided to enable the reader to grasp the richness of the heritage as well as to underscore how different conceptions of ministry have dominated certain eras. An overview of certain contemporary misunderstandings of ministry is analyzed in an effort to move to renewed understandings appropriate for the church today.

Fundamental to appropriating anew the nature and task of ministry is to reaffirm certain central theological convictions. In a section underscoring a theology of ministry, eight propositions are shared, which affect significantly how Christian ministry is conceived and embodied.

Laity and clergy in ministry often experience a loneliness and competitiveness in part because ministry is often viewed as individualistic acts of service rather than as an expression of God's gift of grace to the community of faith. We imagine ourselves to be religious entrepreneurs, self-sufficient in our sawdust evangelism or prophetic thundering or pastoral counseling or whatever. Instead of acknowledging our common status as sinners, we are sometimes unwilling to admit our own vulnerability and need for others. We are not private practitioners, but representatives called by God, confirmed by the church, and in covenant with colleagues. Being a minister is to move beyond professionalism to accept the servant nature of Christian ministry.

In the light of these pivotal perspectives, five contemporary images of Christian ministry are set forth, not in juxtaposition to one another but as images being juggled in order to maximize the many dimensions of ministry in our time. Readers are invited to step inside these images to test their value and vitality. The metaphors are independent of ordination, so laypersons may test their possible authenticity and potential actualization. Seminarians seeking a model for ministry will want to measure their conceptions against these paradoxical images. Established clergy may be willing to open their imaginations anew and serendipitously discover fresh insights and visions.

The last chapter provides an opportunity to integrate these images by sharing a vision of what it might mean to have a public ministry in a global village. The stress is on how social and political action can be integral parts of one's ministry, linking lay and clergy together in common bonds of faithfulness and effectiveness.

Ecumenical and Inclusive

By design, this book seeks to be ecumenical in its understanding of the church's mission and ministry. Particular traditions and denominations would accent different syllables in the language of faith or would feel more at home speaking one dialect over another. Another value of speaking in terms of "images" or "metaphors" is that they can be applied by persons in their own setting, be it inner city, rural, or suburban. Each, conscious of his or her own theological stance and cultural setting, must determine which images can be appropriated and can have normative status in witness and work.

Since no person speaks theoretically value free or writes from a theological vacuum, it is self-evident that my own life experiences and Protestant background as a United Methodist pastor in the United States affect my thinking. My own background includes ministry in small, rural churches in South Dakota, a black inner-city church in Boston, Massachusetts, as well as larger membership city and suburban churches. During the past eighteen years, as president first of Dakota Wesleyan University for ten years and now The Iliff School of Theology, it has been my privilege to work closely with innumerable Christian laypersons and pastors and to preach in hundreds of local church settings, conferences, and retreats. Though my work has been primarily administrative, I have attempted to be faithful to my ordination vows and to bring a pastoral perspective to my work with colleagues, trustees, students, donors, and others. It is out of my own spiritual journey and my relationships with the church that this book on contemporary images of Christian ministry emerges. The images presented, however, do not pretend to be original creations but rather reflect a widespread spectrum of Catholic and Protestant thought. The reader, by critical reflection, should seek to eliminate unnecessary autobiographical bias and discover the appropriate balance for his or her own ministry in the church and in the world.

In recognition of what Barbara Hargrove has called "the new wind of the Spirit" blowing in the church, this writing conscientiously seeks to be inclusive in language about both the human and the divine. The images presented seek to be appropriate to both women and men. It is quite impossible, however, to completely rid the text of masculine and patriarchal conceptions, since they have been so pervasive in the historic literature and thinking of the church regarding ministry. Quotations from others are shared as originally stated; to do otherwise would do violence to accurate historical scholarship. I affirm the Christian ministry, be it for ordained or for laypersons, as God's gift to all persons.

Words of Gratitude

No manuscript is ever produced without the substantial assistance and encouragement of others. This book, far from being the exception, rather illustrates the principle. When one writes about the church and its ministry, one stands in debt to so many persons who have touched one's life from earliest childhood to the present day. One literally benefits from an "endless line of splendor," persons who have generously shared their lives and faith. It is quite impossible to cite them all by name, but I live with a sense of deep gratitude for this special "cloud of witnesses" who have made an impact on my life.

Special appreciation must be expressed to the Board of Trustees of The Iliff School of Theology for the three-month study leave they provided me in late 1984. Without this special time for research, reflection, and writing, this book would not have been possible. Had it not been for my colleagues in administration, H. Edward Everding, John F. Willson, James R. Sutherland, and Barbara G. Bartholomew, who carried additional work responsibilities during my leave, I could never have left the office for time in my study. Special thanks are due to my daughter, Christine Messer, and my student assistants—Kip Roozen, Donna Schmauch, and Donn Grinager—for their research help. To Virginia Dorjahn, whose typing and editorial skills were indispensable, no words of gratitude can ever match her labor of love.

In the course of this project, I have benefited from consultation and conversations with innumerable persons who themselves are engaged in Christian ministry. Opportunities to teach in Iliff-at-Aspen seminars and to lead retreats in Wyoming, Washington, Colorado, North Dakota, Idaho, and California provided chances for the presentation of these ideas and yielded important critiques. For example, a clergywoman in Washington particularly questioned me for making ministry far too individualistic and overlooking the corporate church. Since then I have consciously sought to rethink my own perspectives, remembering that one's vision of the church is indeed pivotal to one's image of ministry. In particular, Emilio Castro, Delwin Brown, A. James Armstrong, Paul Murphy, John Blinn, and Bonnie J. Messer are to be thanked for reading all or portions of this document and offering thoughtful criticisms and suggestions. Obviously, no one but myself is responsible for the final version.

Over the years I have come to understand most fully the meaning of Luther's "priesthood of all believers" by the ministry of love I have experienced from my own family. My wife, Bonnie, and our children, Christine and Kent, have been central channels of grace in my life. My parents, George and Grace Messer, first shared the meaning of the faith and demonstrated "the ministry of the laity" for me. My parents-in-law, Owen and Wanita Nagel, for almost twenty-five years have shown me how Christian love can be incarnated in daily living. Thus it is to them—parents-in-love and in law—that I dedicate this book.

Chapter One

THE ART OF IMAGING

Truth lies in the imagination. This may be only half a truth, but it is the half we most often forget.

—SALLIE McFAGUE, *Metaphorical Theology*

Someone once remarked that the trouble with each new generation is that we haven't taken the time to read the minutes of the last meeting! We make assumptions about the past that are not verifiable. We are all time bound and experience based and tend to make judgments based on limited understandings. One value of studying history is that it helps us break through these personal prisons and cultural cocoons, freeing us to view life from a broader perspective and context.

It is not uncommon, for instance, for persons to perceive Christian ministry from very narrow perspectives rather than through the rainbow prism of possibilities that exist. We tend to forget that there are a variety of angles by which ministry can be viewed biblically, theologically, and sociologically. Historically, there have been many models of ministry, with certain of these images being more predominant in one era than in another. While each denominational house has tended to claim it has the best view, in reality there have always been competing, conflicting, and complementing ways of imaging Christian ministry. Catholic scholar Avery Dulles has noted that the New Testament does not prescribe a single understanding of Christian ministry. Hierarchical and other distinctions are human inventions and may be altered. Revisioning Christian ministry, as Dulles insists, must "be something more than a reflection of the contemporary *Zeitgeist*." The biblical and theological roots of ministry and the special mission of the church must be normative.[1]

In this chapter the importance of images for understanding

Christian ministry will be explored. In the next chapter, the changing historical images will be traced in synoptic form down through the centuries. It is beyond the scope of this book to attempt to recreate all the notable nuances emerging worldwide in the first two millennia of Christianity. This brief historical treatment does not pretend to duplicate, for example, the in-depth analysis presented in *The Ministry in Historical Perspectives*, edited by H. Richard Niebuhr and Daniel D. Williams. Rather, the purpose is to highlight how particular images of ministry seem to have come to the forefront during certain ages of the life of the church. In essence, they were the "contemporary images" during that slice of human history. Understanding these changing historical images of Christian ministry can lead to deeper and richer metaphors for persons practicing the art of ministry today.

Ministry is the gift of God to the whole people of God. The Bible does not designate ministry as the prerogative of the ordained clergy. The gifts of ministry are given not just to individuals but to all who are baptized in Jesus Christ, the corporate body of the church. The contemporary images of ministry outlined in this book are not the sole property of the ordained clergy and other religious professionals. Even though the examples and illustrations tend to focus more often on the clergy, almost all the images and their implications are applicable to laypersons as well. Certain dimensions, clearly delineated, are more oriented to the meaning of ordination.

The Importance of Images

Attempting to define words with precision can be equivalent to trying to walk through quicksand. It is important to write with clarity, but stretching terms too thin can become a ridiculous exercise in the extreme. Some writers have presented cogent arguments distinguishing words like *image* from *metaphor* and *model*.[2]

Actually, the term *metaphor* (which is less common in vernacular speech) has a richer dimension in that it implies a comparison between differing things in order to suggest a likeness between the two. Thus "wounded healer" or "enslaved liberator" could be properly listed as metaphors in contrast to "preacher" or "prophet," which would be in the category of *image*. Such splitting of fine hairs does not significantly aid the discussion; therefore, for general purposes, the terms will be treated synonymously.

Imaging in this book attempts to blend the concepts of generalized mental portraits, self-understandings (the view one has of oneself), and inner attempts to objectify what one seeks to be and to do in ministry. The stress is on envisioning contemporary images of Christian ministry that are more than functional (what one is trying to accomplish) but also relational and personal (emphasizing what one is trying to be or to become). It is not a contribution to the image industry, now listed in metropolitan phone books, that sometimes urges individuals and institutions to reshape public perception, saying, "Fake it till you make it."

Conceptual language should not be understood as being the opposite of imaging. Both stand on the same continuum; they are complementary, not contradictory. Conceptual thinking always strives for precision and clarity, while the world of imagination always includes an element of the poetic and the ambiguous. The symbiotic relationship between the two types of expression has been best explored by Sallie McFague in her presentation of the need for metaphorical theology in our day. She argues that

> images "feed" concepts; concepts "discipline" images. Images without concepts are blind; concepts without images are sterile . . . there is no suggestion of hierarchy among metaphors, models, and concepts; concepts are not higher, better, or more necessary than images, or vice versa. . . . The task of conceptual thought is to generalize . . . to criticize images, to raise questions of their meaning and truth in explicit ways.[3]

Part of the problem with some of the more popular contemporary images of Christian ministry is that they are far too conceptual and lack the poetic imagination of envisioning and challenging. Images like *facilitator* or even *professional* are sterile terms, unlikely to give birth to new forms of spiritual strength or new energies of motivation during times of crisis.

Just as ninety-six different images of the church can be identified in the New Testament, so also there exist a plethora of contemporary images of ministry in today's Christian literature. This book, however, will focus only on five major metaphors that have a dialectical or paradoxical quality, believing these models of ministry have the most promise for engaging the mind of the church and empowering its leadership. Some might be included to suggest that phrases such as "servant leader" or "political mystic" or "practical theologian" should be divorced on the grounds of incompatibility; on the contrary, I shall attempt to demonstrate that the inherent tension or seeming polarity are actually dialectical truths that dare not be collapsed or synthesized.

All life is paradoxical. Our rationalistic tendency is to seek to flatten every mystery into a neat concept. Doing so is important for enhancing communications and ensuring consistency. Simultaneously, however, this process often squeezes out the richness of the original meaning. Poetry reduced to prose is no longer poetic. People and events are not easily quantifiable, but are rather a curious combination of contradictions and ambiguities. As Leonard I. Sweet observes:

> The architecture of truth is like a gateway arch. The secret of the gateway arch is that paradoxically all its component stones are trying simultaneously to fall. It is the same way with truth. Each component truth, taken alone, will fall to the ground and break. A single truth cannot bear the weight of life. But put truths together in the form of a gateway arch, and they will carry any load.[4]

Imagery in Theology and Science

Paul Minear, in his classic study *Images of the Church in the New Testament*, suggests that images are a way to explore realities that cannot be fully investigated or explored by objective study or measurement. Minear claims "a reality that is inherently a mystery will demand for its perception an awakening of the imagination."[5] Christian ministry is inherently a mystery, not easily studied, measured, or quantified by social science instruments. The language and literature of the New Testament are rich with incredibly vivid images that break through the limits of our imagination.

Jesus could hardly be termed a systematic theologian; he did not use words with the precision and consistency and clarity that conceptual thinkers would appreciate. Rather, his most characteristic style of teaching was with the use of stories, parables that were either so surprising, shocking, or obscure that often the disciples had to ask for explanations. Jesus was a communicator of ideas through the art of imaging *par excellence*. His parables of the prodigal son, a lost coin, wayward sheep, hidden treasures, and so forth, have continued to live from age to age, while the conceptual interpreters of his word and work have found their own understandings petrified in particular cultural eras. A metaphorical thinker, Jesus knew the serendipitous art of creating the new by transforming the old. As F. W. Dillistone noted, Jesus brought "into creative relationship the apparently opposite and contrary," gaining treasure both for language and for life.[6]

Contemporary theology manifests an increased awareness of the importance of images, metaphors, and stories that question theological perspectives too dependent on rationalistic analysis and devoid of imaginative abstractions. James H. Cone says, "White theologians built logical systems; black folk told tales." Liberating truth, says Cone, is best told in story, even personal anecdote.[7] Similarly, Susan Brooks Thistlethwaite reports that

> women have learned through consciousness-raising efforts that the truest understanding often comes not from division, but from integration of otherwise seemingly disconnected ideas in order to imagine new possibilities. . . . Theological discourse today needs to recognize the continuum between image and concept, and to take more account of the imagistic basis of all thought.[8]

Increasingly, we are realizing the significance of probing our own personal autobiographies for clues as to God's presence and power. A "story theologian" like John Shea argues that whenever "our biographies are deeply probed, a root metaphor appears, a myth which gives meaning to our lives.[9] Douglas Bland, writing about storytelling in grief ministry, says:

> To probe our biographies for root metaphors—those images and incidents that point beyond themselves toward a life-giving myth—and to use storytelling as a way to speak of God is to assume that God is with us to be encountered at the depths of our lives. As long as the biblical witness and our lives are seen as separate entities, all our energy will be spent building bridges over gulfs that do not necessarily exist. If God is really incarnate, then probing for metaphors and telling stories may be the best way to discover and share God.[10]

Imagistic thinking is not confined to the realms of theology or poetry but is critical to the worlds of the natural and social sciences. Metaphors are pervasive in everyday life and language, thought and action. The ubiquitous nature of images means they appear universally among all peoples and can be found in the earliest human cultural expressions. From the earliest ages, children learn and construct their world through metaphors. Ideas in science are often derived from images. A philosopher of science, Jacob Bronowski, argues that "the whole of science is shot through and through with metaphors, which transfer and link one part of our experience to another, and find likenesses between the parts. All our ideas derive from and embody such metaphorical likenesses."[11] From Darwin's theory of the survival of the fittest to Einstein's theory of relativity, one can see scientists probing the mysteries and complexities of the universe with the aid of imagistic methods.

All too often, however, religion has squashed the imagination, insisting on doctrinal tests, pretending to have captured the truth in some particular symbol or dogma. Likewise, ministerial images have been too often reduced to tasks—teaching, counseling, administering, or preaching—eliminating the emotive and empowering portrait that feeds the functions. How you teach, counsel, administrate or preach is significantly affected by your own imagistic self-understanding, whether you see yourself as a "super saint" versus a "wounded healer" or as a "hired hand" versus a "political mystic"—just to cite a couple of options.

To speak, therefore, of contemporary images of Christian ministry is not to speak abstractly for its own sake or necessarily to forsake traditional titles, but rather to search for current language and understandings that might expand our imaginations and empower our ministries. Some models may border on "dead metaphors," once appropriate and vital, but now less alive with meaning and energy. In a culture in which the verb *preach* has negative connotations of judgmental moralizing and a lack of genuine dialogue, the traditional portrait of a "preacher" is more problematic. The "shepherd" image, as precious as it is to most Christians historically, may have lost some of its communicative power in a time when persons are no longer so agrarian. Additionally, few contemporary congregations care to be characterized as "sheep," for that comparison evokes a degree of "dumbness" and passivity not prized. Using images and metaphors is not an attempt to escape the process of critical reasoning or the responsibility of clear expression. Rather it is to affirm, with theologian Sallie McFague, that "far from being an esoteric or ornamental rhetorical device superimposed *on* ordinary language, metaphor *is* ordinary language. It is the way we think."[12]

Images have a way of affecting human behavior at a deeper, subliminal level. A paradox has an evocative power that not only captures the imagination but also elicits new personal responses. In the depths of one's psyche a meaningful metaphor can transform perspectives, touch attitudes, transcend loyalties, and trigger powerful feelings that may explode into new aspirations and actions. With Susan Brooks Thistlethwaite, I am persuaded that

> metaphor is thought in action. Metaphor reveals the deepest experiences of human beings and impels them to act in new ways. Metaphor has frequently been employed by Christians in the history of the church both to describe their communal experience ,and to motivate themselves to repentance and change.[13]

Readers, lay and clergy, are invited to "try on" these contemporary paradoxical portraits of ministry to see if they "fit," not simply for the sake of new fashions or trends, but in the hope that they provide a new style of motivation and sustenance for those who seek to represent Christ's love in the world.

Reasons for Seeking Contemporary Images

This discussion underscores the importance of imaging for the Christian church and ministry. I am convinced that an essential part of our problems within the church and its leadership today stems from a need to discover and appropriate contemporary images of ministry faithful to the gospel of Jesus Christ.

Three reasons especially can be cited for seeking contemporary images of Christian ministry. *First, images can inflame the imagination and provide us identities beyond simply filling offices or fulfilling role expectations.* All of us need periodically to take stock of who and "whose" we are. The initial excitement of seminary graduation and the first appointment can wear thin when clergy find themselves among the ambiguities and compromises of the parish. It is easy to despair if one is uncertain of one's calling, limited in one's professionalism, and lacking a sense of support from colleagues and ecclesiastical supervisors. Likewise, for the layperson, the fresh enthusiasm of "new birth" or renewed church membership can be dampened by a host of problems ranging from home dilemmas (as one mid-life Ph.D. told me, "I believe God is calling me into ministry, but my spouse doesn't hear that message at all") to stubborn social systems resistant to individual Christian change efforts to an unsupportive church environment, more inclined to the *status quo* or church politics as usual.

Those clergy who are able to tolerate the ambiguities and

disappointments of the local church without losing their sense of eagerness and expectancy about what might happen are usually those persons who have been able to develop a clarity and assurance about their own calling or vocation. For those who lack such clarity and assurance, the most fortunate are those who have a mentor who can model for them other images or who is willing to help them rethink or reexamine their call to parish ministry. Episcopal leaders and other types of church supervisors may be these mentors, or if "authority hang-ups" seem to prohibit this relationship, whenever possible leadership should be used to encourage mentor possibilities and the development of support groups.

Similar relationships and structures are needed for laypersons, linking lawyers with lawyers, business persons with business persons, farmers with farmers, and so on, as well as appropriately creating mixed settings in which people of many backgrounds may share regarding the ministry of the laity. In life's journey, everyone needs an opportunity to share his or her story. For every storyteller there must be a listener. The listener need not be a guru but simply rise to the needs of the moment. Sheldon B. Kopp reports that "there is an old saying that whenever two Jews meet, if one has a problem, the other automatically becomes a rabbi."[14]

Demonstrating an openness to hear another's problem, to discuss questions related to another's call or motivating image of ministry, may stimulate and sustain persons facing crises in life. Ministry is more than just a call to do something; it is a challenge to be someone who loves and cares. Beyond the functional roles of preaching, administrating, leading worship, and such, ministers are called to symbolize the holy amid the profane, to represent a vision larger than parochial self-interest, and to stand at the helm of leadership while reaching out to heal the wounds of the broken.

The Christian ministry of clergy and laity is far more than roles and functions and tasks. For identity's sake, one must drink deeply of something stronger than titles like "senior minister," "associate pastor," or even "layperson." It is dangerous to define oneself solely by what one does. We dare not confuse functional roles with the issue of who we are as persons. Basing one's self on success or failure in job roles can be like sinking in sand. Who we are ultimately is a gift of grace, not a work of merit. There is a personal, imaging dimension crucial for our identities. What McFague has suggested about our thinking regarding God can apply equally to our understanding of

Christian ministry: "*Many* metaphors and models are necessary . . . a piling of images is essential, both to avoid idolatry and to
attempt to express the richness and variety of the divine-human
relationship."[15]

*A second reason for encouraging the search for contemporary images
is the hope of recovering a sense of urgency.* Halford Luccock, in his
sermon "Bell, Book, and Candle," told how the pastor had strictly
instructed the secretary not to interrupt the time set aside for sermon
study and preparation. One day a fire broke out in the Yale Chapel.
With some hesitation, the secretary politely went to the door and
declared: "I'm awfully sorry to disturb you, but I think the building is
on fire." Somehow, we in the ministry need to realize that there is a
fire, but this time it's not the chapel—it's planet Earth that's burning!

In an age of unparalleled military growth and arms escalation—a
time that sees Jonathan Schell speak of nuclear annihilation leaving
us with a "republic of insects and grass" and in which scientists, such
as Carl Sagan, speculate on "nuclear winters"—laity and clergy dare
not do business as usual but need to be ministers of peace in a world at
war. Politics is not an either/or option but an ethical obligation.[16] As
the Reverend Andrew Young, mayor of Atlanta and former
ambassador to the United Nations, once declared, "There comes a
time in a democratic society when you have to do more than just
preach . . . you have to see that the Kingdom of God becomes
incarnate in the life of society. And that means politics."

As most theological educators painfully realize, many clergy
colleagues are not locked in their studies meditating or preparing
sermons while persons and nations are smoldering in flames. In fact,
one might speculate that the demise of a learned clergy can be traced
to the day when churches started speaking of the pastor's "office"
instead of calling it a "study." We fear that Fred B. Craddock perhaps
has diagnosed a broader constituency than simply students when he
points to those who "comb through bibliographies seeking not the best
books but those with the fewest pages and largest print, who live by the
eleventh commandment, Thou shalt barely get by."[17] Barely getting
by may be the maxim of many clergy, but hardly by those who feel a
deep sense of calling regardless of circumstance or who have found for
themselves the equivalent to the Aldersgate experience of John
Wesley: "a heart strangely warmed." Many of the problems faced in
scattered, small, and struggling parishes may indeed be systemic and
structural, but until the church has clergy who "burn" with the

spirit of commitment and are "on fire" with a competence to match, then the ministry of the laity is unlikely to have the dimension of urgency so desperately needed.

Third, the search for contemporary images of Christian ministry may also enable us to find a sense of direction or organizing motif for our communities of faith in the world. One contribution that black Baptist preacher Jesse Jackson has brought to politics is his insistence that the question facing America is not one of "new ideas" so much as of "new directions." Likewise, the issue facing our churches is not that we lack a consensus on major ideas or theology; we suffer not so much from confusion, but from infidelity to that which we as Christians affirm.

Beverly Roberts Gaventa tells of a friend who is the pastor of a new congregation. What he is doing in terms of calling on people and organizing new events is quite significant. She says that he has been engaged in this task with enthusiasm and integrity. Yet after Martin Luther King Jr.'s birthday celebration, her friend began to talk not only of his admiration for King, but also of how inadequate he felt in his own ministry, for it certainly lacked the visibility and impact of King's. Others, overhearing, joined in the chorus of frustration until someone finally spoke up, noting how the concept of vocation was being overlooked. "The question is not if we have the impact of a King, but whether or not we are clear about *our* tasks and are faithful to them." Gaventa further argues:

> Without a clear understanding of our own particular vocation, we flounder about, subject to every claim from the outside and capable of no focused, sustained effort in any direction. As Alice learns from the Cheshire Cat, if you don't know where you're going, any road will take you there. The scandal is not that we cannot do everything, but that we do not recognize the particular thing given to us to do.[18]

New Testament Images of Christian Ministry

Ministry is a generic term that is not *per se* the exclusive language of the Christian community. John McNeill, in his *History of the Cure of Souls*, saw Socrates and Confucius as early exemplars of this form of addressing human need. The Greek word for ministry is *diakonia* and is inclusive of both laity and clergy. The basic English definition of the word is simply "service."

The first usage of the term in the New Testament is found in the writings of Paul. In I Corinthians 12:4-30, he speaks of the "varieties of service," outlining various functions—healers, administrators, workers of miracles, speakers in tongues, and others—being performed by persons in the early church. At other points, Paul speaks of himself and others as "ministers of a new covenant" (II Cor. 3:6), "servants of Christ" (II Cor. 11:23), and "faithful minister(s)" (Col. 1:47; 4:7), engaged in "the ministry of reconciliation" (II Cor. 5:18). In the letter to the Ephesians, reference is made that "some should be apostles, some prophets, some evangelists, some pastors and teachers, to equip the saints for the work of ministry, for building up the body of Christ" (Eph. 4:11-12). The apostles are referred to in Acts 1:17 as a *diakonia*, the same term for ministry or service as noted in Ephesians 4:11-12.

The term *diakonia* later became identified with the office of "deacon" in the life of the church, but its inclusive sense was never totally obscured. First Timothy 3:8-13 outlines some of the characteristics of qualifications Paul considered imperative for a person holding the office of a deacon ("must be serious, not double-tongued, not addicted to much wine, not greedy for gain . . . the husband of one wife"). To the deacon Timothy he declares: "Always be steady, endure suffering, do the work of an evangelist, fulfil your ministry" (II Tim. 4:5).

A more ancient usage of the term *diakonos* meant "waiter," leading to speculation that the earliest use of the term may have stemmed from those who "waited on" or "served" the tables in the early Christian communities. Another frequently used term in the New Testament, referring to Christian workers, was *doulos* or "slave." This language, which today is so foreign and repugnant to us, meant to convey a status or relationship—one belonged as property to the master—while the term *diakonos* was more functional, with an implied status, describing what one does for others. The frequent biblical interchangeability of these terms is perhaps best seen in the saying of Jesus: "But whoever would be great among you must be your servant [*diakonos*], and whoever would be first among you must be slave [*doulos*] of all" (Mark 10:43-44).

One term not in the New Testament, but certainly traditional in the Christian community, is *priest* (*hiereus*), which was derived from the Greek and Latin for "elder" (*presbuteros* and *presbyter*). The latter, thought by some to be derived from the Jewish synagogue, was certainly used early in Christian history to designate a specialized religious worker or office. In the New Testament, reference is made to the priesthood of Christ and all who are baptized, but it is not applied to those set aside via ordination.

While the word *minister* has clear biblical roots, it is fruitless to suggest that one set of terms is more authentic or authoritative than the other. There is a great variety in the New Testament literature, and to make normative any single image or title is to perpetrate a hermeneutical injustice. Historically, terms like *priest* belonged more to the Roman Catholic, Anglican, and Orthodox traditions, while *pastor* was more Lutheran, *minister* more in the Reformed tradition, and *preacher* in frontier American churches. But the ecclesiastical vocabularies are more mixed now, so that even those distinctions do not always hold true. Underscoring this conclusion, Avery Dulles argues:

> The New Testament usage cannot be decisive for our terminology today, if only because the structure of ministry seems to have been different in different communities. In the Pauline letters (Romans, I Corinthians, and Ephesians) we learn of a great variety of services, functions, and charisms in the Body of Christ—but it is impossible to say which of these imply what we would call "offices." Paul speaks a great deal of ministers of the word, but much less of governmental offices. The Book of Acts gives considerable attention to presbyters and prophets. The Pastoral Letters, probably by a disciple of Paul, attach great importance to the office of bishop without, however, clearly distinguishing between bishops and presbyters. A curious fact about the New Testament is the absence of any precise indication as to whether there were officers specially designated for cultic functions. The term "priest" *(hiereus)* is not applied to any particular class of persons within the Christian community, though the entire Christian community is designated as a "priestly people" (1 Peter 2:9).[19]

There is, however, a movement to create a unity where there is not uniformity in scripture or in tradition. The World Council of Churches Faith and Order Commission has developed a remarkable document on *Baptism, Eucharist and Ministry* (BEM) as the result of some fifty years of study and consultation. A conference in Lima, Peru, where more than a hundred theologians of virtually all church traditions (including Eastern Orthodox, Roman Catholic, Baptist, Methodist, Pentecostal, Anglican, and Lutheran) unanimously recommended that this statement be submitted for official study and response by the churches. BEM seeks to overcome past doctrinal division and to find promising convergences in shared convictions and perspectives. Among its most controversial findings or recommendations is that, while the New Testament does not offer a single pattern of ministry as a blueprint or norm for the church, and even though it is clear that there have been a variety of forms of ministry in different places and times, the Holy Spirit helped create a tradition that should now be considered normative for the ordained clergy—namely, a hierarchical scheme of bishop, presbyter, and deacon. Though acknowledging problems with this particular pattern of church order, and even noting the need for reform due to lack of collegiality in leadership, the trivialization of the deacon's role, and other unanswered questions, the WCC document still insists that it "may serve today as an expression of the unity we seek and also as a means for achieving it."[20]

What will be the outcome of this important study and response is yet undetermined, but it is unlikely that the elusive unity unknown for nearly two thousand years in the Christian church will be quickly established in the closing years of the twentieth century. There is reason to rejoice, however, that even while persons quest for uniformity in ministerial orders, there is now a clear recognition that no one form was ordained exclusively by God and all others are heretical misunderstandings of divine will. What is crucial, of course, is not the terminology or even the structure, but rather that there be a renewed understanding of ministry for the sake of the church and the world.

The art of imaging is at the heart of the Christian gospel. Jesus' parables are extended metaphors, full of surprise, shock, and serendipity. By the use of story, Jesus makes an impact on our imaginations and subconscious in ways that abstract, conceptual thought seldom does. The New Testament writers offered multiple metaphors, attempting to express the mystery and meaning of the church. Likewise, no single image of Christian ministry was normative in scripture or tradition beyond the understanding of serving God by meeting human need. In our own times there is no set metaphor to best describe or fit the ecumenical church.

Historically, images have changed as the experiences of laity and clergy have evolved in the contexts of new cultural and political situations. Contemporary clergywomen, for example, are reshaping our images and understanding. Tradition is ever evolving and they are co-authoring a new tradition as they share their story of what God has done in their lives. They are envisioning new options. In Lynn N.

Rhodes' words, "They are called to co-author their tradition and co-create their future."[21] The construction of contemporary images requires both an appreciation of the church's heritage and an appropriation of its theological teachings regarding Christian ministry.

Chapter Two

SHIFTING
HISTORICAL IMAGES
OF MINISTRY

> *[A person] always looks for a model or an example to follow. What determines one's being human is the image one adopts.*
> ABRAHAM J. HESCHEL, *Who Is Man?*

Urban T. Holmes warns of the fallacy of following the "archaeological school" of pastoral theology, thinking we can unearth a "blueprint for contemporary ministry" by digging through hundreds of years of Christian history and literature. On the other hand, while there is no master model, there are truths to be regained and traditions to be recounted that can be creatively reappropriated in our contemporary understandings of the church, its ministry, and its mission.[1] What follows is a sketch of some of these dominant historical images or roles of ministry, which have so effectively permeated the imagination of the church and influenced so much of the implementation of the gospel message over the centuries.

Early Church Images of Ministry

Without question the apostles were the early spiritual leaders of the church. Clearly they had their authority from the early church's recognition that they had been called into this ministry by Jesus Christ, either before the crucifixion or just immediately after the resurrection. Paul, who counted himself in this category, underscored this theory when he wrote: "And God has appointed in the church first apostles" (I Cor. 12:28). This apostolic ministry was clearly understood as an extension of Jesus' own ministry.

From the writings of an early Christian apologist, Justin Martyr (c. 100–c. 165), it is possible to claim Christ wove together the three ancient Jewish charismatic offices of king, priest, and prophet into a new style of leadership for the church. These ministerial modes, though identifiably separate, are closely interrelated. The kingly and prophetic functions were always expressed by Jesus in ways that made the mutual relationship understandable.[2]

The language of "kingship" today tends to alienate many persons. The ring of patriarchal exclusiveness and hierarchical imperialism hardly sounds fitting to the ear of modern consciousness. The governance of God over the world, however, was the meaning the term sought to express, and it was interpreted in the church to justify the need for order and power, not as ends in themselves, but in order to achieve the kingdom of God on earth.

The prophetic dimension cannot be understood apart from the Jewish heritage of persons such as Amos, Hosea, Jeremiah, and countless others who spoke words of both judgment and hope in the name of God despite their own and their people's cultural captivity at the time. The priestly idea refers to one who performs or leads cultic, sacramental, or, at least, worshipful acts on behalf on the community. Further, it includes the pastoral, caring dimension critical to the formation and nurturing of persons in community.

It is possible to trace these ideas through various Christian thinkers, but let it suffice simply to demonstrate one way John Calvin interpreted these three modes of ministerial leadership. He assigned the office of kingship to the state and priesthood to the church, suggesting that the prophetic function most properly fit the academies of higher learning. The validity of this approach for our time is nonexistent, for if the church and its ministry are to be alive to its mission and responsibility, all the historic modes of ministry must be creatively present in a dynamic dialectic so each mode is expressed uniquely, yet as an integral part of the complete dimensions of ministry.

The Primacy of the Priesthood Image

The paramount image of ministry through most of the centuries has been that of priest *(hiereus)*. This term, as noted earlier in this chapter, is used in the New Testament to refer not to a specialized religious worker but only to Jesus Christ or to the *laos* of the whole church. The first clear written reference to calling a cleric a "priest" is from about A.D. 190, when Polycrates of Ephesus called John, the beloved of the Lord, a *hiereus* "who wore the sacerdotal tiara."[3] Yet very early in the life of Christendom, "priest" became the dominant image and the term adopted most universally to specify the religious professional.

While this was but one of the earliest types of ministry, it gradually became normative as the Eucharistic sacrament gained in significance. When the communion table was transformed into an altar, the priest's role ascended in authority. As liturgical celebrant, the priest gained power and prestige. The status of the charismatic prophet or teacher, as well as that of the deacon, declined with the increasing eminence of the priests and bishops of the church.[4] Church historian George H. Williams notes that in the process ordination, which had developed to set the clergy apart from the laity,

> acquired the significance of a kind of second baptism or a second penance in blotting out all but carnal sin . . . a step toward construing the clerical state as a superior stage of Christian achievement both morally and spiritually, and a step also toward the doctrine of the indelibility of ordination.[5]

The sacramental perspective became all pervasive and had an overwhelming impact on the church and its understanding of ministry. This should not be considered too surprising since, throughout the evolution of human societies, the office and functions of the priesthood have been differentiated from other positions and functions in society. In the Middle Ages a clear code of forbidden functions emerged for the clergy; they were not to be merchants, magistrates, or militiamen. Cultic ceremonies and rituals have generally required a separate set of persons whose duties were distinct from the responsibilities of others but which contributed to cultural legitimation and societal integration. Since the prophetic thrust, with its cries of justice and judgment, has tended to challenge both legitimation and integration, this dimension has seldom been encouraged in any culture or religion.

A consequence of this heightened sense of the sacrament was to separate the ministry of the clergy and the laity. What limited distinctions existed in the New Testament church evolved into a major disparity. In communion the priest stood, and the people kneeled; the priest was at the altar, and the people came to the altar rail. The priest took both the elements of bread and wine, but the laity received only the bread. The priest became a holy person, a *shaman* working the mysteries of God. Doctrines such as transubstantiation, claiming the real presence of Christ in the Eucharist, gave the priest tremendous power in the eyes of the common folk. The power to forgive sins and to excommunicate people from the only source of salvation added to the distance between clergy and laity.

Increasingly over the centuries the church gained political power. Partly this was due to intentional activities of certain leaders, but largely it was the result of social disorganization in Europe and the need for civilization and civility. The church kept aflame the light of learning during times when the darkness of anti-intellectualism prevailed in much of the West. Enormous gaps between the educated clergy and the uneducated laity developed. The Bible became the province of the priests, monks, and bishops as it was not translated into the vernacular, and the people were totally dependent upon the clergy's leadership for interpretation and understanding of the scriptures.

Success often breeds corruption, and the church is no exception. However, even attempts by the church to reform itself often led to distancing the clergy and laity. The monastic movement was an attempt to live at the level of poverty as did Jesus and the early apostles. But dedicated labor has a way of turning a profit, spawning institutional growth, increasing properties, and generating administrative problems and tasks. Even movements initiated by Francis and Dominic, who turned to begging, discovered their orders soon multiplying to the point where this got out of hand.

With the imposition of the standard of celibacy for the clergy, the gap widened. Earlier this had not been required. The Bishop of Mans openly had been married. As late as A.D. 966, Rutherius reported that all the clergy were married in his area, and some of them more than once. However, Roland H. Bainton reports that

> for centuries an incompatibility had been sensed between sexual relations and ministry at the altar and the married priest was enjoined to abstain during the period of his ministration. The Gregorian reform, partly for practical reasons to break up the system of hereditary bishoprics and partly for ascetic reasons because virginity was rated higher than marriage, undertook to make the reform universal.[6]

Legal imposition of prohibition does not always yield the desired results. Clergy refused to abandon their wives. Systems of clerical concubinage arose and were taxed by church officials. Even the papacy was not immune. In a time when clergy and state had become intermingled, with the church in the position of power, it perhaps was not surprising for a medieval prince-bishop to say that as a priest he was celibate but as a prince he had a large family![7]

Reformation Images of Ministry

Among the most striking effects of the Protestant Reformation was the revolutionary thinking brought to bear on the whole question of what was then the "contemporary" image of ministry in the church. Without question, while many priests (if not most) were living exemplary lives, true to their highest ideals and in keeping with their deepest commitments to Christ, it is also true that there was rampant clerical scandal and hypocrisy. Without the aid of retrospective social science instruments, measuring with computers degrees of fidelity and infidelity in the pre-Reformation church, let it suffice to presume that there was a legitimate need for reform, but that probably the Protestant reformers, like all radical change agents, had a tendency to spice their rhetoric with hyperbole in order to attract followers to their cause. The old Protestant tendency to equate evil with pre-Reformation Catholicism and goodness with the Protestant reformers simply will not stand the tests of history or truth. Life is far more ambiguous and the historical situation far more complex to justify such simplistic notions of good and evil.

A fundamental innovation introduced by Martin Luther was his insistence on the priesthood of all believers. Appealing to I Peter 2:9 ("But you are a chosen race, a royal priesthood, a holy nation, God's own people, that you may declare the wonderful deeds of him who called you out of darkness into his marvelous light"), Luther often reclaimed what was an essential New Testament understanding. His most famous appeal is in *The Babylonian Captivity of the Church*: "We are all priests, as many of us as are Christians. But the priests, as we call them, are ministers chosen from among us. All that they do is done in our name."[8] Ordination is rooted not in bishop's authority to ordain, but in the priesthood of all believers.

The dominant ministerial images of the Reformation are those of the "preacher" and the "pastor." The term *priest* was essentially set aside as a dead metaphor, because for the Protestants it simply had too many negative implications. Wilhelm Pauck summarizes this complex development in terminology.

> The Reformers customarily spoke of the minister as pastor (shepherd, in relation to certain New Testament passages, e.g., John 10:2 and 10:16; Hebrews 13:20; I Peter 2:25), but they called him most frequently "preacher" *(Prediger* or *Praedikant)*. The term "pastor" came into general use only during the eighteenth century under the

influence of Pietism, especially in Lutheranism. The German Reformers also adhered to the medieval usage and called the preacher *Pfarrer*, i.e., parson (derived from *parochia*—parish, and *parochus*—parson). The common people most generally called the ministers "preachers," but they also continued to use the terms to which they had been accustomed under Roman Catholicism, i.e., "priests," et cetera.[9]

Instead of a priest behind an altar, the striking new image provided by the Reformation was that of a preacher behind a pulpit with a Bible in hand, proclaiming the Word of God. This shift in understanding the church and ministry could not have been more shocking in the context in which it arose. All notions of priestly sacrifice in the sacrament were rejected. The idea of the religious professional as being closer to God was repudiated. The attitude that the Bible could not be shared with the laity was abandoned. Preaching replaced the sacraments as the center of Christian worship. The emphasis was on the fact that Jesus came preaching, as did the earliest apostles and missionaries, and the minister was to be foremost a herald of the gospel. Theologian Karl Barth claims that

> it is very clear that the Reformation wished to see something better substituted for the mass it abolished, and that it expected that the better thing would be—our preaching of the Word. The *verbum visible*, the objectively clarified preaching of the Word, is the only sacrament left to us. The Reformers sternly took from us everything but the Bible.[10]

It would be misleading to suggest that there had been no significant preaching until Martin Luther, John Calvin, and Ulrich Zwingli burst upon the seventeenth-century scene. Among the earliest "princes" of the pulpit were great Christian leaders such as John Chrysostom, Basil of Caesarea, Ambrose, and Augustine. "Princesses" of the pulpit also existed, but were systematically suppressed by a patriarchal power structure. Periodically in the Middle Ages preaching would have a revival, but it never gained the influence or impact that came with the reformers, for it was not until then that the fundamental theology and understanding of the church was grounded in preaching. In a sense, preaching the Word became the new sacrament. Luther declared that preaching was God speaking through the preacher. In Luther's words, "the preaching office is the office of the Holy Spirit." Though humans perform the tasks of the preaching, baptizing, and so on, "it is the Holy Spirit who preaches and teaches."[11]

The image of pastor is closely related to that of preacher. Pastor is a more inclusive term, focusing not just on one function, no matter how central that is to the life and work of the cleric in the parish. This metaphor is linked with the shepherd image that was also originally part of the idea behind the priest symbol. Due to the strong sacramental emphasis, this became somewhat obscured and emerged with new force among the reformers. Ministering, as does shepherding, sounds notes of caring, disciplining, and nurturing for the parish as a flock.

This shepherding image has continued to be a popular and pivotal metaphor in the twentieth century. Jesus Christ is imaged as the Great Shepherd, ministering to the needs of persons. A sense of self-giving, *agape* love permeates the pastor metaphor. Grounded in New Testament pictures of shepherds tending their flocks, searching for the one who is lost, and so on, it has served as an effective and appealing model for many a pastor serving his or her flock. Certain contemporary disadvantages with this image have already been noted—the idea that sheep are dumb, the lack of collegiality between shepherd and sheep, and the distance of urban persons from agrarian experiences, to name a few. These, however, negate neither the power it had in the Reformation days, nor the positive influence it still has for many persons.

The priestly image, of course, did not completely disappear. The Reformation in England was less drastic than in Europe. The sacerdotal dimension remained but was reduced from its medieval primacy. While the terminology of priest was retained, the primary responsibilities were no longer at the altar but in preaching and pastoral care. [12] The reformed image of priesthood is more that of a person in community, rather than an individualistic "holy person" model. Instead of turning one's back on the congregation, the communion celebrant faces the people across the Holy Table. This image moves away from the picture of an individual practitioner to a more corporate understanding of the Christian priesthood in the life and witness of the church.

Two other items are worthy of note in discussing the Reformation images of ministry. First, the image of an ordained Christian ministry shifted immensely with the approval of married parsonage life. What previously had been considered scandalous became idealized! Imagine the seeming contradiction, the shock, the jarring turn of events. What would compare today? Perhaps the pope's issuing an encyclical urging all Catholic priests to be married or Protestant denominations' sudden announcement they did not object to unmarried live-in lovers compares. Lest this sound too flippant, let it be noted, of course, that this decision was buttressed by a theology of marriage and family. Parsonage families actually became idealized expressions of the communal character of the faith, expected to exemplify the reformers' understanding of mutual love and service in ordinary life and interpersonal experiences.[13] Unreasonable expectations regarding the ministerial family, of course, have resulted in numerous other problems. Monogamous marriage often has proved to be at least as difficult an ideal to practice as ascetic celibacy.

The other major change for the clergy came in the area of clerical dress. In order to address the reformers' perception of the Roman Catholic garments as denoting "privilege" instead of "service," they adopted the gown of the secular scholar, the *schaube*. Zwingli was the first to wear it in 1523, with Luther following the next year, leaving behind the monk's cowl.

These new images—preacher, pastor, and reformed priesthood—all meet the test set forth earlier when writing about the reasons for seeking contemporary images. These new metaphors reached below the conscious level, emotively touching persons, inflaming their imaginations and providing new identities beyond those of simply filling offices or role expectations. As is clear from the history and consequences of the Reformation, these new images aided the clergy and the laity to gain a new sense of urgency about the church's mission and ministry. And finally, these images, undergirded by a powerful theology, helped the people and their communities of faith to find a new sense of direction and purpose.

Evangelical and Prophetic Images of Ministry

Considering the myriad of ministerial metaphors developed over the centuries in a variety of cultures and countries, one inevitably has to be selective about which ones will be highlighted. Two images, the evangelical and the prophetic, deserve special attention, however, because both have pressed to the forefront in the last century and continue to be significant images in the contemporary church.

The evangelical perspective in American Protestantism gradually supplanted the primacy of the sacramental. The "conversion of souls" both from North American and colonial powers of Europe became a powerful motif in the minds and hearts of Christians. Not only did it sweep the frontier with the circuit-riding preachers who ministered by horseback to isolated individuals and faith communities, but it also generated enthusiasm for "winning the world to Christ in the next generation." Missionary evangelists were recruited and sent forth in the spirit of the early apostles from both North America and the colonial powers of Europe. Not only did they spread Christianity, but they were also conveyers of Western civilization, both in terms of its noblest qualities (such as medicine and education) and its meaner dimensions (such as commercial exploitation and political domination).

Denominations developed for the first time in the new world of America, lay influence increased, religious competition was encouraged, and mere ritualism in religion diminished. The relationship between church and state was transformed in the American setting. The founding Christmas Conference in Baltimore of the Methodists declared that it was God's purpose for them: "To reform the continent, and to spread scriptural Holiness over these lands." It has long been debated how this should be interpreted. For some it has meant that reform will come by spreading scriptural holiness. Saving a person's soul will eventually yield social change. Thus the evangelically inclined ministers, lay and clergy, hold this as their primary responsibility. As heralds of God's kingdom, they see it as their glorious opportunity to preach salvation, call for repentance, and increase the membership of the church. J. A. James insisted that "if souls are not saved, whatever other designs are accomplished, the great purpose of the ministry is defeated." Stated even more dramatically was Heman Humphrey's advice to his son.

> I do not suppose that the exact degree of a minister's fidelity, or skill in dividing the word of truth, can be measured by the number of conversions in his parish, nor even that uncommon success in "winning souls to Christ" is a *certain* evidence of his personal piety. But I think it is an evidence that he preaches the truth.[14]

For others, this Methodist call to the preachers is a dual charge, involving social involvement and action as well as creative evangelism. Thus, the tradition of prophetic ministry has taken root in the North American soil, alongside the strongly evangelistic emphasis. The prophetic impulse on the new continent can be seen from the earliest days of the republic. A clergyman signed the

Declaration of Independence, and many Christian laity saw the revolution as their ministry of service. During the controversy over slavery, preachers of many denominations clearly were motivated by the image of the Old Testament prophet denouncing injustice and immorality.

Prophetic scriptural images clearly sustained the black people in their struggles against slavery, segregation, and racism, as witnessed by their spirituals, which uniquely combined radical messages of freedom with what seemed like safe sounding Christian words to white, slaveholders' ears. Vincent Harding captures the power these images had in breaking the bonds of both internal and external slavery. In the context of the underground railroad, he writes:

> While the guerrillas fought in Florida, quiet, anxious voices could be heard in the woods in Maryland where black people had gathered. When those voices sang, "O Canaan, sweet Canaan/I am bound for the land of Canaan," another voice pierced the darkness: "I ain't got long to stay here." Then, having given the signal, having gathered for the last prayers and broken their fears, one more group moved northward in the darkness, entering the struggle in their own best way. Others did not leave, but waited in the South with unnerving patience after singing their portentous song:
>
> > Gwine to write to Massa Jesus,
> > To send some Valiant soldier
> > To turn back Pharaoh's army, Hallelu![15]

The spirit of prophecy gave birth by 1865 to the Social Gospel movement in America, protesting against the economic exploitation of workers, leading to laws against child labor and the like. As Edward Beecher declared after the Civil War, "Now that God has smitten slavery unto death, he has opened the way for the redemption and sanctification of our whole social system."[16] Stamping out social evil embedded in political and cultural structures has proved more stubborn than first believed, but this strain of hopeful mission has not been lost among those clergy and laity who have taken the prophetic stance.

Epitomizing the prophetic model of ministry has been the black church in America. In season and out, black Christians have held to a dream of justice and mercy in keeping with the gospel. Reshaping history was the prophetic leadership of Martin Luther King, Jr., and his band of black preachers (including Jesse Jackson and Andrew Young) and laypersons (such as Rosa Parks and Coretta King), who successfully challenged the status quo of segregation in the civil rights struggle. Their witness and strategy inspired countless persons of all races and faiths to move their bodies and souls into the political fight, eventually resulting in major changes in the social and political structure of the United States. The persistence of racism, however, illustrates that the goal of "the redemption and sanctification of our whole social system" is still more in the realm of rhetoric than reality.

I spent my seminary and graduate school days in Boston during the 1960s under the tutelage of persons who either knew or taught Martin Luther King, Jr. My own pastoral involvement in a black, inner-city church during that time sensitized me to the prophetic tradition of ministry. The civil rights victories through direct action, combined with the movement to end the war in Vietnam, which mobilized large numbers of Christian clergy and laity, created a "new breed" of seminarians, clergy, and laity. Having imbibed deeply the spirit of the prophets ("let justice roll down like waters, and righteousness like an everflowing stream") and believing it both imperative and possible to mobilize congregations as "change-agents for Christ," a "new breed" generation of ministers set out, if not to redeem or sanctify the social system, at least to root out specific injustices and to join God's action in humanizing life and creating a more just society.

The image of the prophet has always been a sociologically marginal metaphor of ministry in the history of Christian communities of faith. The special circumstances of the 1960s and 1970s may have given prominence to the prophetic role, but evidence clearly indicates that most laity and clergy were not reflective of this image in their daily witness and work. Lacking personal and church support, persons often find this image has not provided sufficient sustenance during times of crisis. An evangelistic identity can often be more sustaining, since some short-term success in "converting souls" can usually be attained. But "converting society" is a long-range process, and identities built solely around this image can lead to discouragement and despair. Drop-outs from professional ministry often can be traced to unrealistic image expectations, of both the prophetic and the evangelistic type.

To admit "marginality" is simply to acknowledge that the prophet image has never been totally assimilated (and probably never will be) into the mainstream of ministerial metaphors active in the Christian churches. This is not to deny its pioneering potential on the creative edge of faith and ethics, nor to suggest that it is not truly central to understanding the meaning of the Christian mission and ministry. As will be evident in discussion of proposed contemporary images of Christian ministry later in this book, the prophetic dimension is enthusiastically endorsed and encouraged. But, even in so doing, one needs to acknowledge that only rarely do prophets like Dr. Martin Luther King, Jr., and South African Archbishop Desmond Tutu win Nobel Peace Prizes. Most of the time they suffer rejection, alienation, criticism, and sometimes imprisonment and crucifixion.

In the 1980s a merger of the evangelistic and prophetic images has occurred in some respects. Jim Wallis of the Sojourners community and Jerry Falwell with the Moral Majority have illustrated two diametrically different political platforms and social causes (the former essentially progressive and the latter reactionary) that can arise from a prophetic-evangelistic image, stance, and strategy. Clergy representatives of both perspectives, Republican Pat Robertson and Democrat Jesse Jackson, sought the presidency of the United States. The depth of support for these movements has yet to be ultimately determined, but it is probably safe to predict that no matter how powerful they may seem in the mass media or body politic, both will remain marginal minority ministries for most laity and clergy.

The Quest for Other Contemporary Images

Obviously, images of ministry intertwine and overlap. All point to the same mystery of God's grace, simply using different figures of speech and emphasizing different functions of service, to portray this gift. Even as one metaphor for ministry historically became more prominent than another, the other remains and evolves its own way.

For example, the evangelistic and prophetic modes of ministry are highly dependent on the preacher image. The centrality of preaching has been a given for both the evangelist and the prophet. Billy Graham is a gifted orator who can spellbind and persuade congregations and audiences. Few will ever match the eloquence of Martin Luther King, Jr. Until the advent of television, the spoken word was the major means of entertainment and education. Though many have predicted a decline in the value and power of preaching, considerable evidence suggests that communicators who can project well through the mass media have an even greater chance of conveying their message.

The cult of personality with the individualistic focus on the preacher can often be a serious problem. When Phillips Brooks declared "truth through personality" as the description of real preaching, he may have been speaking accurately, for it is clear that the personality of a speaker makes an enormous difference as to how a message is presented or heard. But it also creates a dangerous difficulty in that the Word of God becomes too highly identified with the character of the preacher. The doctrine—that the efficacy of a sacrament is not dependent on the character or personhood of the one who serves it—has too often not been applied in the case of the spoken Word. Long ago P. T. Forsyth warned that no one has a right to the pulpit by virtue of personality. A magnetic personality may endanger the communication of the gospel and result in the idolization of the preacher. "The Church," said Forsyth, ". . . does not live by its preachers, but by its Word."[17]

Images of ministry are never static; the search for contemporary expression always persists in every culture and era. Our time is no different. Stereotypes cluster around certain images so that new generations seek to abandon dead metaphors in hopes of finding more dynamic ways of conceiving of themselves and their service.

Commentators have suggested that there is an image vacuum in both Catholic and Protestant ministries. The quest for new images is not felt everywhere, for many find strength and satisfaction from traditional understandings of priest, preacher, pastor, prophet, shepherd, and evangelist. There has been a shift from one or two clearly defined definitions of what it is to be clergy, "depending on whether the emphasis is Catholic or Protestant—the representative of the authority of God's Church or the preacher of the Word—to a different and poorly defined role."[18]

For many, the "counselor" or "therapist" image has surpassed any of the other images as the most formative perspective about one's task in ministry. Especially for Protestants, the pastoral care and counseling movement has captured imaginations, supplied new identities, and given new purpose and meaning to ministry. Likewise, the idea of a "professional" ministry, comparable to doctors and lawyers, has spurred creative impulses and constructive thought. Raymond Cunningham's metaphor of the "Physician of the Soul" suggestively links these two images, counselor and professional, together. Clergy have discovered that they are often on the "frontlines" of mental health battles and that they can effectively help their congregations and communities by taking professional clinical pastoral education (CPE) courses, engaging in counseling, and mobilizing lay support services.

As persons have sought to bring imagistic language to describe what is happening to persons in ministry, numerous terms have emerged. For some, terms such as *counselor*, *administrator*, and *professional* have become paramount. Some have drawn analogies from the world of sports, such as player/coach, to describe their ministries as both personal involvement and encouraging participation. Persons have been urged to be *enablers* or *facilitators* or *midwives*, casting off authoritarian leadership characteristics and reaching out to assist without imposing. More colorful images, such as *clowns*, *mana-persons*, *storytellers*, and *wagon masters*, have been proposed.[19]

H. Richard Niebuhr's portrait of parish pastors as "pastoral directors" certainly fits much of the work, but hardly inspires, motivates, or sustains a person in ministry. Essentially an administrative model, it mirrors the management impulses of America in the latter half of the twentieth century. Instead of imagining the altar or the pulpit as the central location of ministry—or even the pastor's study—the architectural symbol becomes the professional office. From this spot, the cleric "directs the activities of the church . . . studies and does some of his pastoral counseling." The primary work of the "pastoral director" is "that of building or 'edifying' the church." To achieve that end, Niebuhr urged that persons gain the skill to "administer the church as a church." Even this new conception, Niebuhr noted, had its historical antecedent.

> His predecessor is to be found in the bishop or overseer of an ancient church, a man who, unlike modern bishops, was not primarily entrusted with oversight over many clergymen and local churches but was elected to oversee a single local church. As bishop of Hippo Regius, Augustine was such a pastoral director. The bishops described in the First Letter to Timothy were such men—the heads and overseers of the Household of God.[20]

This brief synopsis of the shifting historical images provides a context to search for contemporary images of ministry appropriate for the Christian church and its mission on the eve of the twenty-first century. The next chapters will move beyond certain common misunderstandings of ministry today in order to reaffirm some basic understandings that serve as a basis for examining five dialectical or paradoxical images that could motivate and sustain laity and clergy in ministry.

Chapter Three

THE DIVINE MADNESS
OF MINISTRY

*You're only human, even if you are a minister. But if you stand up in
the pulpit and say that, the first thing people in the congregation will
think of is adultery! And the second thing is "with whom and when?"*
GARRISON KEILLOR, *"A Prairie Home Companion"*

On Yom Kipper eve in 1965, Elie Wiesel, noted Jewish novelist and
humanitarian, was worshiping in a crowded synagogue in Russia.
While the cantor was chanting, Wiesel reports:

Suddenly a mad thought crossed my mind; something is about to
happen; any moment now the Rabbi will wake up, shake himself,
pound the pulpit and cry out, shout his pain, his rage, his truth. I felt
the tension building up inside me; it was becoming unbearable. But
nothing happened. . . . For him it was too late. He had suffered too
much, endured too many years. He no longer had the strength to
imagine himself free.[1]

Far from the setting of oppression felt by that rabbi, the experience
is repeated tragically every time Christian ministers are unable to
respond to the calling of "divine madness" because they no longer
have the strength to imagine themselves free.

In his play *Zalmen or the Madness of God*, Wiesel struggles with
this prophetic understanding of hearing and obeying the voice of God.
It is to speak the truth in love even when silence is the better path to
survival. It is "divine madness" to utter a word of redemptive
judgment even when career success is guaranteed by pulpit pablum
about social injustice. It is "divine madness" to act with integrity and
freedom even when the pressures of cultural and congregational
conformity seemingly ensure personal and professional benefits. It is
to forsake gospel faithfulness because genuine fear has conquered
one's courage. Zalmen, the rabbi's beadle or lay assistant, persistently

47

pleads that the rabbi must proclaim the Word of God: "One has to be mad today to believe in God and in man—one has to be mad to believe. One has to be mad to want to remain human. Be mad, Rabbi, be mad! . . . Become mad tonight and fear will shatter at your feet, harmless and wretched." But burdened with a sense of possible consequences and no longer able to imagine himself free, the rabbi responds: "Not so easy, Zalmen, not so easy. Fear and I, we have shared the same roof for a long, long time."[2]

Commenting on this drama and the dilemmas posed for Christian ministry, Gary W. Charles perceptively notes that the principled idealism of a seminarian often is lost to the compromises of congregational circumstances. Compromise itself is a noble art, but sometimes clergy and laity become chameleons unwilling to speak the maddening voice of God, though it is clear that the divine has mandates against bigotry, violence, and other forms of injustice.

Carl Sandburg once told of a chameleon who succeeded in changing its environment, until it had to cross a plaid garment. Then it died heroically trying to relate to everything at once. Church communities are plaid garments, and a leader needs to know and articulate his or her deepest convictions about the gospel of Jesus Christ. Responsiveness to holy imperatives, such as peacemaking and a commitment to human rights, can expand the scope of one's ministry as well as release one from cultural captivity. Charles concludes in his essay on Wiesel's play:

> As we participate in the drama of ministry, the Word of God calls us to listen, to speak, and to act in ways that others, and even our inner voices of caution, consider madness. The grace of divine madness is that is does not result simply from our deliberate decision-making. It comes to us more as a gift. The theological, ethical, political and pastoral issues before the church are overwhelming and will only increase in the days ahead. Undoubtedly, God will provide us, as he did the rabbi, with moments for madness. We will hear that disturbing voice crying out to us, "Be mad! Be mad!" Will we fall upwards? Or will we sit, disillusioned by our own silence?[3]

Moving Beyond Stereotyped Images

Critical to the process of accepting God's gift of ministry is to move beyond the stereotyped images that we encounter, create, accept, internalize, or perpetuate. Mention to someone that you are a member of the clergy, and you will detect from his or her expressions and body language that the person has preconceived images of who you are and what you do. Spoken in a church context, the reception is generally open and positive. Spoken at a cocktail party or a neighborhood political meeting, the response can be quite different, if not difficult. Apologies for their drinking, swearing, or whatever are not uncommon. Ask persons on Main Street what their image of the clergy is, and you can expect to hear certain stereotypical characteristics such as: perfect, holy, preachy, pollyanna, and the like. People often get visibly nervous in a pastor's presence, trying to keep themselves in check, guarding against saying anything offensive. Not necessarily mentioned, but underneath, is a special wariness about speaking of sex; after all, that is a *verboten* subject.

These misunderstandings are distorted perceptions; yet they are disturbingly persistent both within and outside Christian communities. The term *minister* is now so commonly associated with the clergy that almost everyone would be surprised if a layperson used the term for self-description, even though it is quite valid for both Protestants and Catholics. As Catholic theologian Hans Küng notes: "In the Church of Jesus Christ, who is the only high priest and mediator, all the faithful are priests and clergy."[4] But all the faithful do not see themselves as priests and clergy—far from it! Many insist on a double standard of morality to separate the laity from the clergy. What is right behavior for the clergy is not considered possible for the laity.

Caught in this web of cultural expectations and church equivocations, sometimes clergy themselves begin to accept the assigned stereotyped roles, to wear masks hiding their own human identities, and to spin theological justifications for their being treated differently from the rest of the human race. Motivated by various sociological and psychological impulses, they perpetuate the ministerial myths. Somehow they feel that by distancing themselves from people in their communities and congregations they can find status, security, and spirituality that otherwise would escape them. This path, of course, is ultimately a dead end, for such unrealistic role playing hardens the arteries of spiritual vitality, paralyzes personal development, and clogs the veins of interpersonal relationships. What is repressed is like fire in the framework of a house. It may emerge anywhere, often in more detrimental ways than if openly expressed in the first place.

The passivity of many Christian ministers, lay and clergy, ought to be a matter of concern. Many seem to expect to be told what to say and to think and how to act. It is especially dismaying to see ordained clergy acting like the character in Franz Kafka's little parable "The Watchman."

> I ran past the first watchman. Then I was horrified, ran back again and said to the watchman: "I ran through here while you were looking the other way." The watchman gazed ahead of him and said nothing. "I suppose I really oughtn't to have done it," I said. The watchman still said nothing. "Does your silence indicate permission to pass?"[5]

Persons who need outside permission for ministry are easily cowed by controversy and paralyzed by polarities of opinion. Those who spend all their time with their ears to the ground are in no position to move rapidly forward. One has to take responsibility for one's own life and ministry.

Far better than pretending to be perfect, or allowing oneself or others to create a moral gap between laity and clergy, is confronting the common stereotypes and exposing them for the fictional fallacies they are. In the words of Colbert S. Cartwright:

> Ministers are not professional holy men or women, but representatives of the people of God. They are samples of what it means to open up one's heart to Christ, and let his work be done within one's life. Ministers are examples of God's work in progress—not the finished products.[6]

Viewing ministry in the spirit that "God is not finished with me yet" will find three common misunderstandings of ministry that need to be critiqued in order for newer understandings of ministry to emerge. Most of these misconceptions pertain more directly to clergy and other religious professionals than to laity, though they do clearly have some relationship to the ministry of the laity as well.

Hired Hands

The hired hand is the first distorted image of ministry needing examination. It is a historic, but unbiblical, portrait of the clergy as paid functionaries. This mercenary metaphor suggests that the clergy basically should do what they are hired to do—namely, to serve the needs of the congregations paying the salaries. Pocketbook politics reduces the freedom of the pulpit and restrains the minister from church and community involvements that may be in harmony with scripture but outside the spirit of those who pay the bills.

50

Ministry is in danger of being reduced to a series of professional functions. As more and more churches become management minded, and even as they institute evaluation procedures and job descriptions that are ostensibly designed to be fairer, the tendency is to negotiate contracts that may or may not be open to the voice of "divine madness," which sometimes prompts the prophetic sound of the trumpet instead of the pastoral strings of the violin. As Bill C. Davis has the priest saying in his drama *Mass Appeal*, "Those priceless lunatics that come along every so often and makes the church alive."[7]

This image of "hireling clergy," of course, is not new; it has long plagued Christianity. Bishop Francis Asbury comments in his journal about a preacher named Richard Wright, who had to return to England from the United States because he was, among other things, "preaching empty stuff to please the ear, instead of change the heart." Asbury says, "Thus has he fulfilled as a hireling his day."[8] The financial and political dependency of the minister on the local congregation in the free churches has prompted some persons to conceive of clergy as simply hired help; if they do what is expected and do not spark ethical controversy, they get paid a stipulated sum; if not, they are sharply criticized or even dismissed. A more common pattern is to get a pastor who will do the functions prescribed and not "meddle" in controversial matters.

A conscientious pastor caught in this type of circumstance needs to understand clearly that, while ministry belongs to the whole people of God, it does not mean that those set aside for clergy roles are subservient to the whims and wishes of the congregation if they are contrary to the will of God.

These universal claims of the gospel, however, often result in raw conflict with financial needs. Clergy do not live in an economic vacuum and historically have necessarily been sensitive to parish provincialisms. Alienating a congregation and moving on to another church situation does not automatically ensure that either community or faith will grow in the Christian faith and spirit. This dilemma offers no easy answers; individual clergy must wrestle with the hard choices when to speak and when to remain silent, when to stay and struggle for changes and when to move on, "shaking the dust from one's feet."

One who did yield to the cultural ministry tendencies was Ernest Fremont Tittle. Pastor of First United Methodist Church in Evanston, Illinois, during World War II, he maintained and promoted his

Christian pacifist convictions despite enormous pressure. Thanks to his courage, along with laity committed to a free pulpit, that church became the symbol of a free church, in which the gospel could be preached without fear or favor. Over the years many others have had the bravery to match their convictions, and they have demonstrated how one can be a faithful shepherd without becoming a hireling of the flock. Once, when being intimidated by pious patriots who sought to muzzle him, Harry Emerson Fosdick, of Riverside Church in New York City, declared: "May I be permitted to suggest that these gentlemen have somewhat seriously misapprehended the temper of the Christian ministry of America? I am speaking for the multitudes of my brethren when I say, 'Before high God, not for sale!' "[9] Christ has paid for our freedom by the price of the cross; as ministers, we dare not reject this grace.

While these illustrations have focused on the freedom of the pulpit and social involvement, the hired employee conception affects other dimensions as well. Fear of alienating someone in the parish can mean always placing the needs of the family last. Or it can be translated into never taking the time for study, because of a perception that the people will think "I am not working." It may result in not asking for funds for continuing education, parsonage repairs, or even salary increases, lest it create any conflict or controversy in the parish. A scene from a "Peanuts" cartoon epitomizes the dilemma many clergy feel. Lucy walks by just as Linus is preparing to launch a snowball. Lucy, who relies more on naked threats than subtle suggestions, declares:

> Life is full of Choices.
> You may choose, if you so wish to throw that
>   snowball at me.
> Now, if you choose to throw that snowball at me,
>   I will pound you right into the ground.
> If you choose not to throw that snowball at me,
>   your head will be spared.

Pity the cleric who says, like Linus as he throws the snowball to the ground, "Life is full of choices, but you never get any."[10] The hired employee clergy do not understand what it means to live openly and at great risk, because they do not know what it means to live by the freedom of God's grace.

Sexless Servants

The image of sexless servants is a second stereotyped misconception of ministry. Unfortunately, potholes exist in the English language. If clergy were only men, then terms like *emasculated* and *eunuch* would fit. The meaning of the "sexless servant" metaphor is that "sex" is the great taboo of ministry, whether for male or female clergy.

Sigmund Freud may have identified sexual energy as a fundamental human drive, but the Christian church has spent two thousand years trying to suppress its expression, especially among its clergy. The effort has not lacked proponents from the pope to every Protestant parish. It is said that in the Middle Ages, Christian couples were urged to abstain from sex on Thursday in respect for the Lord's Supper, on Friday because of the crucifixion, on Saturday to honor Mary, on Sunday due to the resurrection, and on Monday for the poor souls. The byword became, "Thank God it's Tuesday!"[11] Yet the campaign for celibacy, chastity, continence, and fidelity in marriage has not met universal success. In the Roman Catholic Church, it was not until the Spanish provincial council of Elvira in A.D. 306 that continence, as distinguished from celibacy, was made obligatory. But, as noted in the last chapter, the exceptions to this norm were numerous and scandalous.

The Protestant reformers dealt with this human quandary by approving of marriage for religious professionals with the clear understanding that sex was reserved for the marital state only. Even then, clergy have often been imaged as a "third sex." As Charles Merrill Smith satirized in *How to Become a Bishop Without Being Religious*, one's "image depends in part on the inability of the congregation to imagine you engaging in sexual intercourse." If children come to the parsonage, persons "will imagine that the accouchements were accomplished through immaculate conception or parthenogenesis or artificial insemination." The most they can believe is that one was fulfilling one's social responsibility and "really didn't enjoy the procedure to this end very much."[12]

But clergy do enjoy sex and lovemaking, believing both are good gifts of God's creation. Head-in-the-sand attitudes can no longer prevail as pregnant pastors preach the Sunday sermon or celebrate the Eucharist. Clergy often are the most sensitive, caring, and loving persons one can find. *Agape*, self-giving love, cannot always be neatly quarantined from *eros* or *filial* love. The complexity of human emotions, along with the weaknesses and fallibility of human sinfulness, are the same for both lay and clergy. Urban T. Holmes contends that there is a strong erotic element in the symbol of priest and that:

> To be a priest is by necessity to share deeply the antistructural dimensions of people's lives, to face the erotic realities both in their demonic and angelic form, and to discern what makes whole and what destroys. The choice is to be an ineffective "cold fish" or to risk being consumed. We must choose this risk, but prayerfully in the grace of God.[13]

There are no simple answers or neat solutions to this human condition. Sexual indiscretions occur among persons of all theological persuasions, from the fundamentalist types to traditional institutional mainstreamers to the more liberal clergy. If church laws, easy moralisms, or punitive professional consequences were the solution, then the dilemma would have been resolved centuries ago. Few believe that total sexual freedom, permissiveness, or antinomianism (the idea that since Christians live by grace, they need not follow any moral laws) will resolve this human problem. Needed are prohibitions against sexual harassment and misuse of clergy status and authority for sexual purposes. Proposing a responsible sexual ethic, appropriate to both lay and clergy, is beyond the scope of this book, but a few more comments are in order.

Communities of faith respond differently to this predicament. Studies clearly indicate that undisciplined living among the clergy, particularly involvement in extramarital affairs or "illicit" sexual relationships, prompts criticism and diminishes the chances of ministerial effectiveness.[14] For denominations that expect their clergy to be flawless models of moral excellence, exemplars of faith and life, the penalties for sexual sins have most often been severe, usually resulting in professional excommunication. Other groups, who reject traditional stereotypes of puritanism among the clergy, do not value the "Christian example" idea so highly. Writing particularly about Anglican-Episcopal Churches, but expressing a sentiment shared by many, if not a growing majority in other churches, David E. Richards states:

> If they [clergy] fail to uphold certain social and moral standards, they may still be tolerated in ministry. Even though it might precipitate a move to another community, the lapse or "slip" may not be seen as

cause for being forced out of the ministry, nor out of the church. It is almost as though members do not wish to see their clergy as being too perfect in terms of their personal life-styles. They prefer that their clergy be open and honest about who they really are and what they are like.[15]

Another dimension worthy of consideration is cultural mores, which are often confused with Christian morals. What is deemed scandalously immoral in one generation is often accepted in another with no outcry of ethical indignation. Card playing, dancing, and movies on Sunday were once the work of the devil. Until 1936 it was both immoral and illegal for men to wear topless bathing suits in New York! Ministers who smoke or drink any type of alcoholic beverage are pariahs in some denominations, but most communities of faith do not express such shunning. In fact, George Barna and William Paul McKay, who operate a research bureau for evangelicals, report that of the Christians (presumably "born again") who have cable television, 23 percent of the television sets are wired for adult-only programming (fare such as X-rated movies and other explicit, sexually oriented material).[16] Either mores or morals among Christians change, or you have to accept Martin Marty's wry analysis: "They probably are wired only and don't watch."[17]

Not long ago, clergy who were divorced could expect severe professional penalties, perhaps even the revocation of their ordination papers. Despite clear scriptural injunctions against divorce, there is now widespread acceptance of it within almost all Protestant churches. Evangelical researchers have discovered that this is not just a phenomenon of the more liberal churches or secular society. "Born again individuals are every bit as likely as non-believers to have suffered the agony of a broken marriage." Almost no consternation was expressed when a well-known evangelist's son and his wife were divorced. One day they were together on the television screen, singing and testifying to the love of Christ. A few days later, with no explanation, the man appeared again, only this time he introduced his new partner for life and ministry.[18] Despite growing acceptance of divorced laity and clergy, this experience, inevitably one of great pain and tragedy, is made more difficult by church people who prefer to be judges of humanity than agents of healing.

Since neither church proclamation nor punishment is likely to resolve the dilemmas of human sexuality or sinfulness, the road of redemptive loving is the best track for Christians to take. In confronting these inevitable human crises, one does not have to take the lead in offering criticism or judgment—there are always enough persons who feel free to toss the first stones. Besides, the persons involved generally are burdened by enough guilt. Effective ministers, says Michael E. Cavanaugh, are "unconditionally present . . . whatever decisions people make and however far from the Kingdom their paths wander." Ministers are called to be present by those "sinners" being stoned, in order to offer assistance and the light of faith. In the process, the minister also can expect to be pelted with rocks.[19]

Loving is not to be confused with approving. Instead move beyond simply preaching forgiveness and see if the church can actually practice it. This is not a question of "cheap grace" or "costly grace," but a matter of "free grace." Beware of believing a person deserves only the grace she or he earns. Above all, be thankful the latter is not God's standard!

Superhuman Saints

The similarity of the third stereotype to the second is clear, but it has broader implications. The image of the clergy as superhuman saints or perfect persons seems so self-evidently impossible that it hardly deserves exposition; yet it is a widespread assumption or attitude in the church and community.

A standard of perfection is incompatible with all that we know about humanity from the social sciences. It also stands in direct contradiction to the Christian teaching that all persons are sinners. But the presumption still exists that the priest or pastor should be at least a little better, or "more perfect" (contradictory concepts since perfection cannot be "more" of anything), than the average layperson. Not only are clergy expected to be "exemplary" in morals, but they are also to be unswerving in faith. Many persons in the pew dislike a pastor who openly acknowledges his or her own struggles of faith and feelings amid life's ambiguities.[20]

Incredibly, this "perfect person" image has been internalized by more seminarians and clergy than one might imagine. In the scriptures "saints" were common folk committed to the Christian faith. Over the centuries, however, a narrower understanding has emerged so that "saintliness" now implies a pious purity of superhuman dimensions. Psychiatrists discover many clergy suffer from the "burden of the ideal self-image," of saintliness. Seeking to fulfill such an unrealistic self-descriptive norm can be self-destructive. "The pastor is an embodied person," says Gary L. Harbaugh, and failure to recognize this usually prompts signals of stress in one's body and life. [21]

Clergy who seek perfection are ultimately going to find sinfulness. If we do reach a higher or more "holy" level of living, we inevitably have sinful feelings of pride at our accomplishments and compare ourselves in superior fashion to others whom we may feel have not given their full energies at moral or spiritual reform. Even United Methodists, who ask all incoming clergy whether they intend to "go on to perfection," know that only God is perfect.

The negative exaggeration of the "superhuman saint" stereotype ought not disguise certain unique and positive dimensions. For clergy, the issues of character, spirituality, and moral obligation are interrelated. "It is not simply a question of piety," says James L. Waits, "or of the pious expectations others have of ministry. For the minister the integrity of life and profession is instrumental to authentic practice."[22] Stanley Hauerwas argues that "the character of those serving the ministry should be determined by the character of the office to which they have been ordained . . . there is a connection between the sacramental character of the ministry and the moral character of those who serve in the ministry."[23] Harvey Cox, reminiscing about ministers in his childhood, says that preachers were "always to some extent a stranger in a strange land." For Cox that provided an "aura of transcendence or at least of the 'otherness' the representative of God must always signify, whether one likes it or not."[24]

Urban T. Holmes, inspired by *shamans* and medicine men, speaks of clergy as needing to be "extraordinary," possessing charismatic qualities which would mark them as "liminal" persons.[25] He also suggested that the priest must be an "angel." By what a priest says, does, and is, "the cleric . . . 'catches' that awareness that lies amid and alongside the mystery from which God speaks to humanity. When the priest is effective he is this angel, this symbol enabling the coming-to-consciousness of God's vision for us all."[26]

Lest their words mislead, it should be noted that none of these theologians are suggesting, that clergy can be morally pure or infallible. They are speaking of the positive value of how others perceive clergy—perhaps even the divine madness of ministry—

that somehow transforms the cleric into a means of God's grace.

William K. McElvaney, while rejecting "superhuman saint" perspectives, says the clergy must accept a degree of ecclesiastical inconsistency and live with the reality that double standards do persist in the church between lay and clergy. The moral behavior of a layperson tends to be regarded as a *personal* matter, while ethical behavior of the clergy "is more likely to be seen as a *professional* issue related to accountability to an office or function of the church." McElvaney further contends:

> If, as ordained ministers, we seek a ministry in which personal example is not intimately related to our practice of ministry, the differential of which I've been speaking can only be a burden to us. But if we see our personal example as part of the fabric of our ministry that God can utilize, then we will learn the blessing of our dependence on the grace of God.[27]

Whether the "burden" is a gift or a curse depends on many factors, circumstances, and the individuals involved. No wand can be waved to erase this peculiar dimension of ministry. For the cleric, personal and public morality are, in reality two intertwined strands—like the double helix structure of DNA, the basis of life itself. It is an inherent tension within the church and society. Most of the time it is a "burden" that one can bear, but other times it erupts in tragic consequences.

There is a strain of the Donatist heresy for which no apparent "vaccine" has been found. The Donatists, emerging in the fourth century, believed that a priest's moral rectitude directly related to his spiritual ministrations. Freedom from sin (especially murder, apostasy, and adultery) were presumed necessary for effectiveness in ministry. The church's teaching, as formulated by Augustine and others, was that the worthiness or unworthiness of the minister did not affect the validity of the sacraments since Christ was always the true minister. Though in Christian thought the ground is level at the foot of the Cross, today there tends to be a distinction (false as it may be) between "cold sins" —such as moral blindness, insensitivity, racism, and sexism—and "warm sins"—relating to human passion and behavior. Unfortunately, it is the latter that usually bring the punishment when the former are often more destructive and dehumanizing. Quite often, the "cold-sinning" clerics remain in the ministry, while the others are driven out, though the latter often demonstrate more caring, loving, and sensitive spirits.

One of the most famous ministers of the twentieth century, Dr. Martin Luther King, Jr., was not immune to this human struggle. Opponents of his campaign for racial equality and justice tried to discredit him and his movement by using illegal wiretaps designed to expose extramarital affairs. As novelist Jeffrey Archer notes in *First Among Equals*, "It's a game of hide and seek. Very few people other than saints have nothing to *hide*, and the problem with public life, is that a lot of busybodies want to *seek*.[28] King, who repeatedly protested against saintly and "messiah" labels, was sought by none other than the Federal Bureau of Investigation, led by the legendary J. Edgar Hoover. Summarizing King's struggle with his sexual self, public responsibilities, and Christian convictions, his noted biographer, Stephen B. Oates, says that King had "a troubled soul." What he writes about King might be said of others.

> When King spoke of "the deep longing for the bread of love" in the world, he was not just talking philosophically. True, he still believed in Gandhi's Satyagraha as the salvation of the human race—as the great moral force that would bring on the brave new order he had long prophesied. Yet he also needed love personally, needed companionship, acceptance and approval.[29]

Another way of struggling through this dilemma is to seek to distinguish between "validity" and "fruitfulness." The validity of a cleric's authority does not rest with inner intention or outward sinful expressions. God becomes present through the ministry of a person, sacramental or otherwise, regardless of the status of the soul or selfhood of the cleric. As long as the person is validly ordained, so the traditional theory since Augustine has suggested, then the layperson has no need to fear. The clergy have a priestly "character," even if it is not readily self-evident. On the other hand, the concept of "fruitfulness" has also been important to the church over the centuries. If the life-style of a priest is such as to scandalize and cause those of fragile faith to "stumble" in the faith, then such a minister might be removed from duties not because of invalidity but because he or she lacks a fruitful ministry. It is not the sins *per se* that destroy one's ministry, but the unfruitful effect those sins have on one's ministry to others.

> This negative effect can vary from time to time and person to person. I find little evidence, for example, that a tenth-century French priest who kept a concubine and raised numerous children was rendered

ineffective in the average tenth-century French village. In most contemporary communities he would not last forty-eight hours. In small-town America a priest of dominantly homosexual orientation cannot function, no matter what his actual social practices. In our larger cities he can have a very effective ministry. So the fruitfulness of the priest is relative to the subjective consciousness of those to whom he ministers.[30]

On Sinning Bravely

These three distinct, but overlapping, misunderstandings of ministry—hired hands, sexless servants, and superhuman saints—are images that persist and perplex. Embedded as they are in the culture, literature, and minds of so many, they are unlikely to disappear quickly. Instead they, along with other stereotypes, are factors of ministry that must be confronted, experienced, and critiqued. Theologically, the light of God's grace must shine on Christ's ministry. Instead of being preoccupied with the weaknesses of the human flesh, the problems of temptation, and the ambiguous complications of living, it is better to underscore the understanding that God did not intend ministry as a test of one's purity, but rather as an opportunity to express divine love in human affairs. As Roman Catholic layman Mario M. Cuomo, governor of New York, says, "We are meant to live actively, intensely, totally in this world and in so doing to make it better for all whom we can touch, no matter how remotely."[31]

Clergy and laity in ministry have to live with the uncertainty of life's ambiguities, but trusting in the certain advice of Martin Luther, who counseled, "Sin bravely." Novelist Frederick Buechner counsels:

> I don't think there should be any tension between men and women's personal identity as clergy. We are called first of all to be human as Jesus was human, whatever else he was too. To be ordained doesn't mean some kind of ministerial falseface, to conform to somebody's notion of what a minister ought to be. The doctrine of the priesthood of all believers means to me not only that all human beings are called to be priests but that all priests are called to be human beings, to be themselves, and not to worry too much about traditional views of their role.[32]

Lest I be misunderstood, "sinning bravely" does not mean surrendering to sin without a struggle. It reminds us to be realistic about life's frailties, but it does not justify neglect of the call to a more holy life, befitting the gospel. The goal of sanctification by faith is not negated by remembering that all life and ministry depend on God's free grace. "Sinning bravely" does mean, in H. Richard Niebuhr's words, that "at all times human frailty and sin make the ministry whose business it is to point to the highest reality and the profoundest faith a morally perilous vocation."[33]

Forget being a perfectionist; be human. Shore up your weaknesses; build on your strengths. Trust God's grace; enjoy the divine madness of ministry! Lest one become too individualistic, or forget that one is sinning bravely (but still sinning!), seven theological criteria are provided in the next chapter to assist in analyzing one's self-understanding of Christian ministry.

Chapter Four

A THEOLOGY OF MINISTRY

*In the primitive Church there were chalices of wood and prelates of gold;
in these days the Church has golden chalices and wooden prelates!*
SAVONAROLA

Imaging Christian ministry cannot simply be a flight of the imagination without relation to a theology of ministry. Certain theological criteria, rooted in scripture, tradition, and experience, provide a normative test for the many metaphors the mind might project. Christian ministry is not just "a matter between you and me, God" but an expression of the church as a whole.

A theology of ministry is closely related, but distinguishable from what is commonly called pastoral theology. The latter focuses on the office and function of pastor, which is only one historic image of ministry. The term *pastoral theology* tends to perpetuate what Edward Farley laments as the "clerical paradigm," which makes "the tasks of ministry themselves the criteria, subject matter, and end of theological study."[1] Therefore, it is more fitting to speak of a theology of ministry that includes an understanding of the lay and the ordained.

How do we arrive at our images of ministry? What are the norms for authentic ministry in our time? Without a doubt life's experiences shape our images. How did H. Richard Niebuhr come to the pastoral director image or Henri Nouwen to the wounded healer? What prompts some persons to be quixotic prophets and others to be quietistic pastors?

We all have been influenced formatively by the people, families, events, and cultures of our own existence. The sociology of knowledge suggests that our beliefs and theories are clearly rooted in our past experience. Middle-class Americans see the world differently from seminary theologians or Third World citizens! My rural South Dakota roots, involvement in a black urban church during the civil rights movement, travels in India, experiences in Hindu and Moslem homes, administrative responsibilities, and so on all shape my perspectives and imagination differently from that of other people. Some Christians can outline a myriad of possible ministerial images without ever mentioning "prophet," while I cannot imagine a ministry without prophetic dimensions.

But experience, as valuable and determinative as it is, cannot solely be the norm for authentic Christian ministry in our time. Checking only one's own pulse is not "doing theology." As my former theological tutor, Nels F. S. Ferré, used to say, "It is not my experience but Christ's experience that is normative." Christ's experience is the revelation of God's will for me. Discerning or determining Christ's experience, however, is problematic indeed, but to aid in that search we must rely on the canons of scripture, the tradition of the church, and the logic of reason. Our own images born of experience must be tested by these criteria if we are to discover norms for authentic Christian ministry. As a theology of ministry, this chapter shares seven basic convictions I consider normative for understanding appropriate contemporary images of ministry.

When I first began to write this section, I audaciously entitled it "New Understanding of Christian Ministry." Further study and reflection, however, reminded me that little is new. What is needed is a basic statement that conveys, for our time, "renewed" understandings of Christian ministry. Appropriate contemporary images will have power and authenticity only as they are rooted in fundamental Christian teaching about the ministry of the church.

In exploring these understandings, it becomes apparent that there are, of course, differences of interpretation depending on denominational and theological orientation. However, thanks to the broad consensus of thought developed by the worldwide ecumenical movement, the distinctions are not so wide as once perceived, and certainly the disagreements are not so acrimoniously polemic in proclamation as in an earlier time. For example, the sterile past disputes as to whether word or sacrament is primary no longer interest Protestant and Catholic dialogue. It is not a question of priest or preacher, but how both can be combined for effective communication of the gospel. Avery Dulles contends that

> In ministry we are dealing with the presence of God that transcends both, encompasses both, and gives power to both. The word of God is

always somehow sacramental, for it symbolically makes God present, and the sacrament, which is the symbol of God's real presence in the assembly, never comes to pass without the word of proclamation. The official, or priestly ministry is indivisibly a ministry of word and sacrament; and because it is both of these, it can become formative of Christian community in a very special way. Thus, this wide conception of priestly ministry includes that of community building. The three traditionally recognized ministerial functions of preaching, sacramental worship, and communal leadership should all be integrated in any complete theory of priestly ministry.[2]

To lay the groundwork for exploring contemporary images of Christian ministry, it is imperative to set forth certain basic criteria, or renewed understandings, of the church, its ministry, and its mission. The eight that follow are far from exhaustive, but they are fundamental to Christian scripture, tradition, and experience.

Ministry: Gift to the Whole People of God

Ministry is the function of the church as a whole. It is God's gift, not first of all to the individual, but to the community of faith, who in turn chooses who should represent it in leadership roles. The Church is ministry. Its *raison d'être* is service to the world. There is no other reason for the church to exist.

Henry Sloane Coffin, in his Lyman Beecher Lecture, insisted that of first importance is the church's ministry that is led, not a personal ministry. "The minister is nothing apart from the church."[3] In an age of American "yuppies" (young upwardly mobile professionals), this idea of ministry as a gift of the church, not necessarily purchaseable by education or affluence, seems anachronistic indeed. Far from allowing us "to do my own thing" with a minimum of professional guidelines, this ancient church teaching stresses the covenantal ties of ministry: "We are members one of another" (Eph. 4:25). Power and authority are bestowed not on the individual, but on the congregation of Christians. What power and authority the clergy have are gifted from God to the church to the person holding the given office.

Those of us who are ordained are set apart by the church to the representative ministry—not because we are less sinful or more holy, but in order to serve different functions within the life and mission of the church in the world. To echo the words of Colin Morris: "If I am not humanely useful to the life of the world, then the laying on of hands of every bishop in Christendom will not validate my ministry. And if I manage some degree of usefulness, then the theological significance of what I do is vested solely in my action and not my status."[4]

Lest Christian ministry suffer from functional reductionism—namely minimalization to a series of tasks or functions that need to be done—a few caveats need to be added to Morris' comments. One would be to emphasize that there is a symbolic, intangible mystery to ministry that cannot be expressed in any simple functional statement. This does not require belief with Augustine in an indelible *character dominicus* imprinted in the ordinee, equivalent to a military brand *(character militiae)* or the regal imprint on a coin *(signum regale)*. Rather, it may simply be an acknowledgment that God works through the "office" of priest or pastor, despite the limitations of the person possessing or holding it. Clergy are never just private practitioners who can hang out their "shingle" for business. The "office" or role belongs to the whole church and symbolically conveys meaning beyond the actions of the personality cloaked in its garments or bearing its titles.

A second caveat would warn against trivializing the "laying on of hands" tradition of ordination. While I concur with Morris that the hands of all the bishops in Christendom will not ensure a competent and caring ministry, I do respect this ancient tradition of the church. Clergy do not become ordained by merely passing academic exams, writing learned papers, polishing their practical skills, and so forth. The process of ordination involves all of these elements, but it also questions a person's "call," the fruitfulness of one's life and ministry, the appropriateness of one's theology to one's church, and so forth. Ultimately, the decision to ordain or not to ordain is a matter for the reflective judgment of the church, not that of the individual. Since Old Testament days, hands have symbolized in a special way God's power and authority. The church borrowed this custom, making routine and ordering the ministry as well as symbolizing that those who held this office did so with the authority of Christ's church.

It is in the sacrament of baptism that Christians receive the gift of ministry. All baptized Christians are considered ministers in the church of Christ. This understanding, though widely accepted by many theologians, always seems a surprising revelation to most people. Probably, due to the widespread practice of infant baptism, few people tend to think of the sacrament as a moment of beginning ministry. Rather than over-emphasizing this dimension or rite, it may be more beneficial to follow the lead of the global ecumenical study on *Baptism, Eucharist and Ministry*, which suggests: "The Spirit calls people to faith, sanctifies them through many gifts, gives them strength to witness to the Gospel, and empowers them to serve in hope and love."[5] The call of our general ministry, be it in baptism or at other moments in the spiritual journey, is never once and for all, but a recurring cry in this broken world.

The Ministry of the Laity

We are all the *laos*, or "people of God." As noted previously, the biblical perspective emphasizes that all persons in the church have a ministry. Over the centuries this has been highlighted at times, such as in the life of the early church and during the Reformation, but at other times it has been obscured by excessive clericalism. When Paul urged churches "to lead a life worthy of the calling to which you have been called" (Eph. 4:1), he was not speaking to the officeholders but to every member of the church. Francis O. Ayres comments: "The basic, primary Biblical use of the term 'calling' is an urgent invitation to enter into a life of service to God, a life of forgiveness, meaning, purpose, and freedom. It is issued to all . . . without distinctions of any kind."[6] Martin Luther was convinced that a person of faith had all the same spiritual powers as had been previously reserved for the clergy alone. Luther declared: "Every Christian has the power the pope, bishops, priests and monks have."[7]

This doctrine of the universal priesthood of all believers has a dynamic quality, with the potential of transforming both the church and the world. Contemporary images of ministry that focus exclusively on the clergy—such as the models of professional, enabler, or pastoral director—ultimately are sterile because they cannot give birth to the fresh energies and vision needed to meet life at the edge of the twenty-first century.

This teaching is eminently social—that is, every person is a priest, a communicator of the gospel between God and other people. No hierarchy is needed as a channel of God's grace. Any person can minister to another. This does not mean that one can be a self-sufficient priest unto oneself, but rather that the fellowship of believers can minister to one another. However, it did not rule out the role of clergy, for Luther did not believe all should assume the same functions. Certain persons could be selected from the community for specialized tasks, such as preaching, teaching, and counseling. In

Luther's language: "We are all priests, insofar as we are Christians, but those whom we call priests are ministers [diener] selected from our midst to act in our name, and their priesthood is our ministry."[8]

Fresh reappropriations of this understanding of ministry generally yield new vigor and vitality in the church's mission. When the church is imaged as a boat or ark, one might envision that there are no passengers, only crew members. Instead of expecting laypersons to do primarily "church work," meaning the internal church school teaching, trustee duties, ushering, and the like, conscious efforts and programs are designed to encourage both lay and clergy in the "work of the church" in the world—bearing witness to one's faith in the marketplace, politics, and so on. Both dimensions are crucial; both expressions are truly ministries of service. Thank God for persons like John R. Mott who, as a Christian layperson active in the Y.M.C.A., lifted a vision of evangelism and ecumenism around the globe. Just days before he died, he was asked to say a few informal words at a meeting. He stood up and offered what may have been his last public utterance: "When John R. Mott is dead, remember him as an evangelist. The proclamation of Jesus Christ was his passion throughout his life."[9]

The tragedy of so much twentieth-century Christianity has been the divorce between private and public discipleship. In Nazi Germany, Christians continued to live pietistically, while outside their doors the most heinous holocaust in human history was being systematically perpetrated against Jews, persons with handicapping conditions, homosexuals, and Eastern European ethnics. The gap between worship and work, between personal morality and public policy, is dramatized by the case of the executive head of a major international corporation. He was described by persons who knew him as "an upright man, a devout Christian, a teetotaler, a tireless worker who cared little for personal gain." Yet in his professional capacity he presided over one of the biggest bribe-giving schemes ever. Nightly, he would visit his invalid wife in the rest home where she was confined, but ultimately he had to resign in disgrace from the head of one of the world's largest multi-national corporations.[10] The challenge of the church is to encourage and empower laypersons to challenge the Goliaths in their working midst, realizing the truth to Dietrich Bonhoeffer's claim that: "The sin of respectable people is running from responsibility."[11]

A Calling, Not a Career

A modern heresy is the idea that ministry is primarily a career rather than a calling. While it is true most seminary graduates spend their entire adult lives in the clergy, any time ministry becomes just another way of making a living, an occupation, or a profession, then a critical New Testament dimension is missing. What is absent is the sense of being summoned, even commanded, by God into ministry. Since the earliest disciples were "called" by Jesus to drop their work and follow him, the church has asked of its prospective leadership the nature and meaning of their call. For Paul, the decision to enter the ministry was not a choice among professions, but a response to God's summons on the Damascus road. That call motivated, sustained, and empowered Paul in his missionary travels, despite persecution, imprisonment, controversy, and setbacks. Whenever in the history of the church the ministry has become more of a career than a calling, the church's mission has stagnated, and the people have suffered.

All Christians are called into ministry; this is the essence of the doctrine of the ministry of the laity, discussed previously. As Leo Tolstoy would say: "The vocation of every man and woman is to serve other people." In terms of the priesthood of all believers, service is understood to be in conjunction with one's other responsibilities in life.

Speaking of calling into the ordained ministry, John Calvin distinguished several dimensions to the concept of call. First is the "secret call," or inner call, of God, which the church does not witness. This was a witness of the heart, ensuring that one was entering the ministry without selfish ambition or avarice or other selfish desire. Second is the "churchly call" by which the Christian community measures the outward manifestations of the "secret call" by the fruits of holy living, sound doctrine, and talents to determine whether to ordain or not. Finally, there is the "congregational call" (or for United Methodists the "episcopal appointment"), which involves the consent and approval of the people. [12]

Periodically in Christian history the misunderstanding of the meaning of the divine "call" has led the church in the direction of anti-intellectualism. Especially on the American frontier, a tendency existed to minimize the importance of theological education and to exalt the "call," as if the summons provided a person all that was needed for competent ministry. Quite often persons have preferred to stick simply with the inward call of God, rather than to engage in the discipline of study required for faithful understanding and interpretation of the scriptures, the thoughtful exposition of theology, and the in-depth appreciation of the cultural history of the church. In most of frontier America learning and piety were viewed as being antithetical, and seminary education was considered unnecessary. The "call" of God was often viewed as the only requirement for effective ministry. Opponents of theological education, such as Peter Cartwright, said that preachers trained in schools were as pale as "lettuce growing under the shade of a peach tree" and their preaching as awkward as "a gosling that had got the straddles by wading in the dew."

High on the agenda of concern has always been that "book-learning" would supplant, rather than supplement, the spiritual validity of the clergy. Evangelicals have always pressed that "those whose calling it is to convert persons to Christ should themselves be converted; they who guide believers should themselves be persons of faith—and that "for the lack of this, no talents, however brilliant or attractive, can compensate."[13]

Ordination and Authority

Integral to this understanding of ministry as the divine gift to the whole people of God—from whom some are "called" by God, not for special status but to special service for the community of faith—is the theology and authority of ordination. The process of ordination is not equivalent to professional licensing procedures. It is not an individualistic act simply of one's deciding to be ordained, gaining proper academic credentials, spending time under professional supervision, and hanging out one's shingle. Ordination is always a communitarian act, bonding persons to the church and conveying authority on behalf of the church. The church authenticates God's call and authorizes the persons called by God.

Historically the meaning of ordination has been interpreted differently over the centuries. Conflicting perspectives on ordination have developed due to contrasting theological and ecclesiastical propositions. Persons holding differing models of the church are likely to view ordination dissimilarly. Baptists might view it as the recognition of a divine call or as being commissioned or set apart by God for special service. Catholics might speak of the apostolic succession of the pastorate or of a sacramental action of God.

Presbyterians might emphasize the dimension of the congregational call. United Methodists speak of ordination as "persons within the ministry of the baptized who are called of God and set apart by the Church for the specialized ministry of Word, Sacrament, and Order."[14]

The word *ordain* stems from the Latin *ordo*, implying orderly succession. In the Christian community the origin of ordination is traced to Jesus when he commissioned the twelve apostles (Matt. 10:15, Mark 3:13-19, Luke 6:12-18) and seventy others (Luke 10:1) for the mission work of the kingdom. Whether Jesus intended to institute such a ritual might be problematic, but these scriptural passages, along with the laying of hands on Barnabas and Saul in Antioch (Acts 13:1-3), Paul's reference to bishops as having been appointed by the Holy Spirit to tend the church, and the warning to Timothy not to lay hands hastily on anyone (I Tim. 5:22), became the biblical basis for regulating the order and "orders" of the church. Whether communities of faith subscribe to the imperative of a strict "apostolic succession" or not, all churches have insisted on some form of order and have generally retained the understanding that ordination is the work of the whole church, not the individualistic wish of the religious professional.

Fundamental to the Roman Catholic perspective is that ordination is one of seven sacraments of the church. Augustine believed ordination conferred an "indelible character" on the recipient. A person experiencing ordination received something sacred, even if administered by a "heretical" bishop, since the gift came from God, not from the person whose hands conveyed the sacrament. Since the gift was permanent, a person should not be "reordained" even if for some reason the priest had relinquished the office for a period of time and then was restored into the priesthood.

The Protestant reformers accepted only two sacraments: baptism and the Lord's Supper. The focus shifted from the enacted to the proclaimed Word of God. The image of preacher gained prominence. The Reformers disputed the idea of an "indelible character." Luther argued:

> Everyone who has been baptized may claim that he already has been consecrated priest, bishop, or pope, even though it is not seemly for any particular person arbitrarily to exercise the office. Only by the consent and command of the community should any individual person

claim for himself what equally belongs to all. If it should happen that anyone abuses an office for which he has been chosen, and is dismissed for that reason, he would resume his former status. . . . Certainly a priest is no longer a priest after being unfrocked. Yet the Romanists have devised the claim to *characteres indelibilis*, and assert that a priest even if deposed, is different from a mere layman. They even hold the illusion that a priest can never be anything else than a priest, and therefore never a layman again. All these are human inventions and regulations.[15]

Though the sacral quality of ministry was denied, the Protestant emphasis on the "calling" of the Holy Spirit somewhat substituted for the dimension of sacredness or holiness implied in the sacrament. Urban T. Holmes argues that the

indelibility of priestly character is found in the internal call. . . . once the priestly image has fallen upon an individual it "haunts" him. As for the "whisky priest" in Graham Greene's *The Power and the Glory* . . . the priesthood is like the stigmata in the hands and feet of the risen Christ. They remain despite all.[16]

Luther's rhetoric aside, the clergy—Catholic or Protestant—usually find the psychological and spiritual phenomenon of setting aside their ordination and returning to the lay status an exceedingly traumatic experience. Likewise, this "haunting" dimension probably helps explain the difficulty many Christians experience in accepting clerics who return to lay ministry. Even more upsetting to many is when the return is occasioned by actions or life-styles the community of faith finds incompatible with spiritual discipline, sexual fidelity, personal integrity, and so forth.

Without question the act of ordination does convey authority. The presumption is that the recipient will exercise the power of the church in a responsible manner for the good of the whole, not for the selfish interest of the clergy. An in-depth survey of forty-seven denominations in the United States and Canada, *Ministry in America*, affirms the church's normative expectation that priests and ministers should rely on God's grace and serve others "without seeking a personal reputation for success or infallibility."[17]

The authority of ordination, however is not a passport for professional or personal freedom without due regard for the nature of the community of faith. It is not to be confused with being authoritarian, giving orders without consultation. Neither does it mean becoming enslaved as a hired hand, doing only what the community votes to permit. Rather it is more like the authority of a general overseer, supervisor, or bishop, in the sense of the early church when that office was focused on leadership of a local congregation, prior to becoming a more regional position.

The authority of ordination, however, is not the power charted on hierarchical corporation pyramids or university organization tables. In reality even those are less powerful than the outsider thinks, since shared authority often means that the leader is working within a web of conflicting expectations and circumstantial exigencies. People do not automatically follow a member of the clergy; authority and trust must be gained through loving, caring service. On the other hand, a learned clergy brings to every community of faith qualities of intellect and wisdom gained from theological education. There is authority in knowledge. Bible study is not simply a matter of exchanging opinions about what one thinks it might mean to the individual reading it at the moment. It also involves the hermeneutical task of understanding what it did mean when it was written, how it was composed, and in what context it was expressed.

Probably no guidelines can be developed to fully determine what is appropriate and inappropriate for those who hold the office of cleric. More attention, however, should be given to developing clergy codes of ethics. Christian lay professionals—for example, in medicine and psychology—have much to teach pastors in this regard. Amid the ambiguity of the local parish, it is not always easy to determine what roles or functions a pastor should handle. Since there are so many avenues of possible service, it is easy to stretch into areas that might be more appropriately and effectively handled through the ministry of the laity.

The supportive assistance of a pastor-parish committee can often helpfully mediate differences of both the pastor and the congregation. They can help establish reasonable limits. Seldom do we see ourselves as others see us. Often we are more demanding of ourselves than our congregations want. In one pastorate I taught part-time at a local college during the noon hour. When the pastor-parish committee learned I thought I had to skip my luncheon break in order to remain faithful to my pastoral duties, they were alarmed at such personal and family neglect and told me they considered such teaching an extension of their church's ministry.

A pastor's authority derives from both personal attributes and the formal office of a priest or minister. Jackson W. Carroll does not consider these mutually exclusive categories. He notes that office authority, like the administration of the sacraments, "are valid *ex opere operato*, regardless of the personal characteristics of the priest."[18] The religious tradition is protected through the office. The authority of the person—evolving from ascribed or achieved personal attributes of the minister—ensures authenticity. The *Ministry in America* study verifies the continued importance of personal qualities in ministry. The most important qualities undergirding ministry are fidelity to tasks and persons, positive approach, and flexibility of spirit. The personal qualities that most undermine the authority and effectiveness of a minister are alienating activity, professional immaturity, and a self-protecting ministry.[19]

These two dimensions of contemporary clergy authority need always to be held in tension. Evidence suggests that clergy who rely solely on authority based on personal legitimation by the community are less likely to be involved in controversial social action than are those whose authority stems more from the traditional office they hold. It also should be noted that even in communities of faith where authority derives more from the office than from personal charisma, there is usually a major emphasis on spiritual formation and socialization into the priesthood.[20] As the novelist Walker Percy reminds us, one can "get all A's and flunk life," meaning that as ministers we can brilliantly know all the right religious rituals and offer profound theological answers, yet be totally ineffective and insensitive to the complex needs and questions of persons in an ambiguous and sinful world.

Clergy who think of themselves solely as "enablers" or "facilitators" need to rethink the meaning of ordination and the authority of the clergy. The purpose of theological education is to develop a learned clergy and laity who can give leadership to the church and to the world in Christ's name. James Forbes, a black Pentecostal pastor and professor of preaching at Union Theological Seminary, points out that the black pastor seldom suffers all the pangs of guilt over authority that plague the white pastor. Forbes contends that unless the minister claims authority, the community of faith loses its sense of purpose and direction.[21]

The Servant Nature of Ministry

Inherent to the nature of Christian ministry is the understanding of servanthood, a concept that distinguishes the clergy from other professions. No matter how elevated the title or how fancy the job description, at the heart of ministry is the common touch, the washing of dirty feet, and the idea that one who would be first must be last. Amid the pomp and circumstance of life, what is valued is the cup of cold water, the crust of bread, and the compassionate spirit. Much may change, but the challenging words of the Roman Catholic Bishop of Zanzibar remain hauntingly pertinent.

> You cannot claim to worship Jesus in the tabernacle if you do not pity Jesus in the slum. Now go out into the highways and hedges, and look for Jesus in the ragged and the naked . . . in those who have lost hope, and in those who are struggling to make good. Look for Jesus in them; and when you have found him, gird yourself with his towel of fellowship and wash His feet in the person of his brethren.[22]

The biblical, theological, and historical precedents for regarding ministry from the perspective of servanthood are reinforced by findings of contemporary social science that indicate that church people expect a service orientation from theologians and that even scholarly commitments are valued primarily as a means to serving other people, rather than scholarship for its own sake.[23] The centrality of Jesus as a caring human figure in human history shapes decisively the portrait of Christian ministry throughout the ages. It is Jesus the servant, not Jesus the professional, who symbolizes the mystery of ministry.

The servanthood ideal reverses the world's values. Christian ministry is constantly caught in the struggle between the norms of Christ and the mores of culture. Christians are called into serving their neighbor without regard for the impact this will have on their social standing or career promotions. The measure of a spiritual person is not how fast he or she "climbs up" but how quick he or she "reaches out" to persons in need. Far from the "yuppie" profile, the Christian minister is measured vocationally by a cross, not by a credit card.

The gap between the ideal and reality is evident in the life of every person who seeks to live out consistently the servant shape of ministry.

To be a servant is not to be a sponge, simply absorbing the blows of a church or wiping up the catastrophes of a community. A pastor may discover that the demands of a parish are so encompassing as to crush legitimate self-interest or family concern. Maintaining a personal identity related to, but not fused with, the clerical office is imperative. Pastors who pretend they are no longer sinners, struggling with the tensions and ambiguities of life, falsify the servant role and lose touch with the sources of their own God-given vitality. Finding one's proper balance between self-giving servanthood and self-fulfilling ministry is a lifetime struggle that offers no simplistic answers.

A Covenant Ministry of Grace

The Christian church is a covenantal community, and ours is a covenant ministry of grace. Church organizations, of course, have complicated regulatory systems for systematizing and disciplining ministry. What ultimately bonds persons together in this ministry, however, are not rules and regulations but a trusting, covenantal understanding rooted in relationship to Christ and the personal conscience of each person.

Christians can never substitute the primacy of spiritual and moral attainment within their lives for the primacy of grace and faith offered as a free gift by a merciful God. The Church is not a community of the morally pure, but rather laity and clergy standing equally in need of God's grace. Relationships with one another are to be characterized by Christ's redemptive spirit, forgiving one another as God in Christ has forgiven us.

None of us operates in ministry unto ourselves. As part of Christ's church we are "members one of another"; therefore, we need to be in dialogue with other Christians, including those who share differing perspectives and convictions. We need to hear the criticisms others would make of our own stances, learning how God's spirit of truth may have imparted insight to others that we have not acknowledged.

In the twentieth century, the list of prohibited actions that clergy have been asked to pledge to avoid have included going to the theater, dancing, drinking, playing cards, and smoking. Persons who divorced usually experienced excommunication and hostility usually expressed toward criminal behavior. In recent years most denominations have relaxed many of these prohibitions, often looking back and wondering what gave the church such authority and certainty to control individual behavior. In recent years some communions have written rules that have aimed at restricting the clergy office from "self-avowed practicing homosexuals."

In a covenant ministry of grace there is inevitably tension between the individualism of persons and the discipline of clergy. The temptation of the church through the centuries has been to develop legalistic interpretations. Hopefully, the church in the future may find ways of building trust, maintaining discipline, and yet not unduly invading the privacy of persons.

At the same time, however, it must be remembered that we cannot ignore the disciplinary law of the church, even as we recognize the right for persons to object conscientiously to particular teachings. The church alone decides whom it shall set aside for the ordained ministry. Ordination is a church rite, not a civil right.

In focusing on the covenantal ministry of grace, the emphasis should not be on the rare exceptions when behavior problems arise but rather on the glory of the unity shared. By recognizing that all who minister in Christ's name are equal, not in merit or talent, but in grace and forgiveness, we affirm a unity that is deeper than any natural endowment or educational qualification. The words of Loren Eiseley might appropriately be used to describe Christian ministers: "They sang because life is sweet and sunlight beautiful. They sang under the brooding shadow of the raven. In simple truth they had forgotten the raven, for they were the singers of life, and not of death."[24] In a covenant ministry of grace we are all singers of life, not of death.

Beyond Professionalism

The frustration Reinhold Niebuhr experienced as a young pastor in Detroit often has emerged on the lips of other clergy: "Sometimes when I compare myself with these efficient doctors and nurses hustling about I feel like an ancient medicine man dumped into the twentieth century."[25] Seeking to overcome such feelings of impotence and powerlessness, a renewal of interest in the image of clergy as professionals has captured the thinking of many theological educators and pastors.

Popularized by James D. Glasse in *Profession: Minister*, this image underscores high standards of education, skill, dedication, and institutional integrity and draws similarities with the professions of medicine, law, and teaching. In contrast to the thesis of this book, which advocates exploring a wide variety of metaphors for ministry, Glasse argues that the church has too many images, which only serve to confuse persons. The dilemma for him is that "we tend to recruit ministers through one kind of image, train them in light of another kind, and then require them to practice in terms of yet another kind."[26] For Glasse the clergy professional model, derived from the management metaphor, provides a holistic lens through which to view ordained ministry in this age.

The recovery of the positive dimensions of professionalism should not be minimized. Clergy should emulate laity who exercise ministry in their vocations, such as psychologists, medical doctors, teachers, nurses, social workers, and others. In their professional lives they often demonstrate the highest standards of competency, character, and care. This does not mean, however, that it is always appropriate to adopt totally these secular standards for the church and clergy. A case in point is the controversial use of the term *pastoral counselor* for those engaged in private fee-based religious counseling outside the parameters of the faith community.[27]

Once when speaking to pastors, I discovered that my criticisms of the excesses of professionalism in the life of the church prompted greater appreciation than I had expected. Pastors interpreted my initial remarks to justify no more sermon preparation, no planned parish visitations, no systematic continuing education, no strategic steward-ship campaigns, no code of ethics, and so forth. The Spirit would provide. The discipline of professional expectations, controls, and standards had obviously not taken deep root.

Originally, the concept of profession had a broad definition, roughly equivalent to a religious calling. There is no doubt that the clergy ranked high among the learned professions. Professional work was a response to a divine summons. Over the years, however, this idea increasingly has been restricted to membership in and mastery of guilds committed to specialized knowledge and skills. Today almost every trade or occupation publicly claims to be a profession, and word inflation has rendered the term *profession* almost useless. Unfortunately, today most work is viewed as a means to one's personal advancement rather than as a contribution to the public good.

The professional model is a needed antedote to the dilettantish clerical amateurism. Too often "the call to preach" has become a lame excuse for sloth and an embarrassing dodge from ignorance. William K. McElvaney deplores the fact that we ministers can

> operate out of a grossly irresponsible individualism which is blind to the gifts and insights of our brothers and sisters in Christ. In the name of divinely given charismatic gifts we can seduce ourselves into thinking that we are above and beyond the evaluations of others in the Christian community. Deploying the transcendent as our shield, we can reject any self-exposure which asks us to hear the opinion of others, to be sensitive to the perception of others, to be open to a maturation process involving realistic notions of competent practice.[28]

The professionalization of the clergy is a radical departure from past understandings that acknowledged no rights and no boundaries for a pastor's work. The institutional church had all power, manipulating persons in God's name. But by imaging clergy in relation to other professionals, certain appropriate norms for competency, standards for excellence, means of evaluation, and levels of appropriate compensation can be envisioned. The caring church community will want to embrace for its personnel the best possible programs for recruitment, continuing education, retirement, health care, and so forth.

The limitations of the clergy professional model, however, necessitate that the church adopt it as a "base point" rather than as its "bottom line" image. The professional image is a helpful evaluative instrument, but it can never contain the full richness or the depth of the ordained ministry. Moving away from the professional model does not mean abandoning the need for professional competence and ethical standards, but it does insist that ministry can never be reduced to professional functions. Ministry is more than applying good skills to life's problems. Love and care flow from a heart steeped in empathy and tenderness. Prophetic words and actions sometimes may gently arise from a professional mind-set, but the thunder of moral outrage more often flows from a heart sensitive to the pathos of God. Martin Luther and John Calvin broke from the medieval concept that only professional work in the church was a divine calling. Every occupation became dignified as a way to serve God and humanity.

Two contemporary Christian ethicists have further illuminated this relationship. Darrell Reeck defines a contemporary professional as one who is:

(1) a broadly educated person, (2) possessing highly developed skills and knowledge, (3) working under the discipline of an ethic developed and enforced by a body of peers, and (4) commissioned to satisfy complex needs, by making judgments entailing potentially dangerous consequences.[29]

Too often clergy forge the essential link between "calling" and "profession," denying one or pretending that one can exist without the other. In James Gustafson's forceful words:

A "calling" without professionalization is bumbling, ineffective, and even dangerous. A profession without a calling, however, has no taps of moral and human rootage to keep motivation alive, to keep human sensitivities and sensibilities alert, and to nourish a proper sense of self-fulfillment. Nor does a profession without a calling easily envision the larger ends and purposes of human good that our individual efforts can serve.[30]

The professional image alone can never truly "fit" the person and role of clergy. Ministry understood as the gift of God to the whole people of God, or the divine madness of God, cannot slip neatly into a sociological category. Being a pastor or priest involves more than simply accumulating sufficient academic credits or being credentialed by the church. The personal qualities of the religious professional are intrinsic to the office. The evangelical model of ministry always stresses the personal piety and charisma of the preacher. Sacramental responsibilities add important dimensions. The priestly image of ministry is grounded in an authority not just of religious expertise, but on the perception that the cleric is a representative of God.

Moving beyond professionalism is essential for the clergy. It is not a question of performing one's responsibilities with less attention to excellence or to the welfare of others, but that of seeking to serve in ways that exceed the generally accepted norms. Measuring professional competency by standards of *agape*, self-giving love is really beyond the scope of social science. Professional job descriptions, while protecting the person employed, may in the long run be detrimental to the church's ministry and mission. In Carl E. Braaten's language, defining clergy solely in terms of what the people want done can create a "captive flunkie of the status quo."[31] Some forms of professionalism can domesticate God's priests into hired functionaries or institutional employees.

Christian Ministry as God's Mystery

Ultimately Christian ministry, both lay and clergy, must be acknowledged as God's mystery, never fully understood or disclosed. It is both a human profession and a gift of God; it is both cultural and transcendent. It is rooted in this time and place, yet belongs to no time or place. It is a divine calling to communicate through one's own life the redemptive love of Christ for all humanity.

Defining Christian ministry is like trying to nail Jell-O to a tree—it is never quite possible. A theology of ministry, however, enables a person to confront the mysterious, indefinable nature of ministry and to critique the paradoxical images of ministry set forth in the next five chapters. No single title, metaphor, or concept can ever fully illustrate or illuminate the fullness and mystery of Christ's ministry.

Chapter Five

WOUNDED HEALERS IN A COMMUNITY OF THE COMPASSIONATE

I began to think maybe our suffering could help to change, could help to heal, could help to make new life in this world. . . . Our tears may even be the power necessary to change violence into love—change human madness to human kindness. The tears may be the water of new life.

So now I offer you the tears of all Cambodian children who have suffered so much, and we join with the tears of all those who suffer yesterday and today, and we cry with you, "Please, never again. No more Cambodian genocides, no more Jewish holocausts, no more Beirut massacres, no more El Salvadors."

A CAMBODIAN REFUGEE, *Matchbox (Amnesty International)*

Being a minister is not the equivalent of the Lone Ranger riding the range, doing good, crushing evil, aiding justice, and then riding with one's associate into the sunset. Ministry is not simply individualistic acts of service, but God's gift of grace to the corporate people of God.

We act, both as laity and clergy, not because we are such fine, caring, ethical people, but because we are sinners who know, in the words of Mark Twain, that God's "forgiveness is the fragrance the violet sheds on the heel that has crushed it." We are not freelancers, but representatives called by God and confirmed by the church as ministers. Ours is not a private religious faith but the gospel of Jesus Christ as delivered to the saints. When we do good, crush evil, and aid justice, it is not our righteousness being manifested but God's grace at work through us. Our eschaton is not riding into the fading sunset with Tonto but being resurrected in the glorious sunrise with Christ.

Vision of the Church

One's image or vision of the church is indeed pivotal to one's image of ministry. History abounds with evidence to confirm this theory. If

81

one's model of the church is primarily that of a visible institution, complete with constitution, rules, rights, and powers, then one's understanding of ministry is likely to be hierarchical, managerial, and dogmatic. Vatican II criticized this image of the church as being too clerical (over-emphasizing the clergy at the expense of the laity), too juridicist (turning the gospel into a new law), and too triumphalistic (acting as if one is spiritually superior to everyone else in the world). Many Christians absorb this institutionalism mind-set, wrapping their lives in the flag of denominationalism and letting their ministry mirror more the organizational person than the carpenter of Galilee.

When in history the church has been conceived of as a "mystical communion," as in the body of Christ or the people of God, then the image of ministry has been different. The stress has been far more on the corporate, the church as a community or fellowship. Instead of emphasizing the institutional, this metaphor accents the interpersonal. Ministry is focused on personalized services aimed at enhancing interpersonal relationships in the community of faith.

If the church is imaged as primarily "sacramental," then quite a different type of ministry emerges. Avery Dulles has suggested that this model of the church became popular because "the institutional model seems to deny salvation to anyone who is not a member of the organization, whereas the communion model leaves it problematical why anyone should be required to join the institution at all."[1] By emphasizing the sacramental nature of the church, both the institutional and the interpersonal dimensions were integrated via underscoring the visible church as the channel of God's grace to people. Stress on the sacraments, however, has tended almost always to deemphasize the ministry of the laity and overstress the primacy of the priesthood.

Many Protestants have adopted an image of the church as a "herald," drawing from the metaphor of an officer of the royalty announcing a decree in the public square. Instead of a priest behind an altar, the Reformation brought to the forefront the picture of the preacher in the pulpit with an open Bible in hand, proclaiming the Word of God. Not the Eucharist, but the proclaimed Word became central. The minister as preacher or evangelist or prophet became paramount. Sometimes this image of ministry becomes more word-oriented than action-dominated. Lost in the many words can be the symbols and sacraments of grace.

How we envision the church has consequences for our understanding of the church's ministry and mission. If we primarily see the church as an institution, a mystical communion, a sacrament, or a herald, our image of ministry may be significantly different if we view it as the community of the compassionate, the servant church, a prophetic community, the rainbow church, and/or a post-denominational communion. Therefore, each paradoxical ministerial metaphor is presented in the context of an understanding of what the church is called to be as we near the third millennium of its life and mission. These images of the church are not meant to supplant but to supplement other, more traditional understandings, such as the body of Christ or the family of God. Likewise, they are not to be seen as contrasts but as visions of the church, blending together to the glory of God and the service of humanity.

The Church as the Community of the Compassionate

Central to the biblical portrait of the church is that of the community of the compassionate. Compassion is out of style in many parts of the world today; it is almost an anachronistic term in an age when the predominant attitude often seems to be: "What is in it for me?" *Bleeding heart* is a term of derision applied to any person or politician who thinks government should care for "the least of these" in society. In Catholic dogma the phrase *invincibly ignorant* sometimes has been used for those unpersuaded by faith. Many today might be called "invincibly indifferent" to the cries of their neighbors. Has the milk of human kindness turned sour?

Sometimes you wonder when you read the daily newspapers. You begin to despair when you read that the Salvation Army has been forced to suspend one of its leaders for allegedly siphoning off goods designated for the impoverished or that investigators are checking on possible mishandling of Catholic relief supplies for Ethiopia. On another page you see a report that an elementary school teacher claims that due to the fear of AIDS, she will not wipe the tears of a student. Also frightening is the fact that hundreds of soldiers-of-fortune and arms dealers gather periodically to buy dart guns, laser gunsights, semi-automatic pistols, and the like. One popular sweatshirt features a skull and the words: "Kill 'Em All—Let God Sort 'Em Out."

Additionally, there has only been a casual response of concern by many to the astronomical budget deficits caused by escalating military budgets in the United States. These now threaten to jeopardize nearly every program to aid the poor, the hungry, the homeless, and others less fortunate. They may prevent the nation from ever again mounting major social legislation. Has the United States decided to settle for living with a permanently poor underclass, as it pays eight million dollars per hour of interest on the deficit? Has compassion in this culture become a sneer word?

No, *compassion* has not become a dirty word! Rambo is not the new creation! Jesus the Christ is the new creation, and his call in Galilee continues to echo some two thousand years later: "Be compassionate as your Father is compassionate (Luke 6:36 NEB). God is compassion. God enters into the suffering of creation. People resist pity, for it suggests condescending charity, with those on the top sharing the crumbs from under their tables. But people rightly welcome compassion, for it means to suffer with other people, to enter into places of pain, and to share in our common weaknesses, fears, confusions, and anguish.

The divine compassion is made most manifest in the incarnation of God in Jesus Christ—God with us in our broken humanity. It was not just tender-heartedness or polite kindness, but rather the witness of a God who bore the mark of sorrow. Far from avoiding pain at any price, Jesus ran the risk of associating with the wrong crowd, consorting with tax collectors, harlots, and other pariahs of his time. His associations with outcasts—having table fellowship and sharing friendship with the least respectable in his society—were enacted parables.[2] Jesus was compassion incarnate, reaching out to heal the pain of others, telling parables of compassion—such as that of the good Samaritan and the shepherd looking for the lost sheep—and ultimately offering forgiveness to those who nailed him to a cross. We can look to Jesus to understand what Albert Schweitzer meant when he said "the purpose of human life is to serve and to show compassion and the will to help others."

Every example of extreme personal selfishness can be more than matched by persons epitomizing care and compassion. Who can forget the incredible generosity of Christians worldwide, raising millions for African famine relief? Who wasn't touched by the spontaneous caring for persons trapped in the Mexican earthquake? And why shouldn't Christians celebrate the church's in-season and out-of-season caring through church bread lines, overseas relief, and support of health, education, and welfare institutions and programs? The government may be becoming colder and more callous to human need, but there is still hope that the church will not forget the central dimension of compassion that motivated the life and work of Jesus. That must be our vision of the community of faith, our image of the church for our day, our witness for Christ amid the culture of our time. Our contemporary image of ministry must reflect the ideal presbyter envisioned by Polycarp in his Letter to the Philippians (c. 135).

> The presbyters must be tenderhearted, merciful toward all, turning back [the sheep] who have gone astray, visiting the sick, not neglecting widow or orphan or poor man, abstaining from all anger . . . being far from all love of money, not hastily believing [anything] against any one, not stern in judgment, knowing that we are all debtors because of sin.[3]

Reflective of this historic image in contemporary times is Mother Teresa, who refutes the Rambo logic of our time. For her all life is sacred and cannot be reduced to statistics or life-boat ethics, which suggest that some must die so that others may live. She once appeared on a Canadian talk show with a brilliant Nobel prize-winning biologist who was speculating on future DNA break-throughs and the possibility of everlasting biological life. Having listened quietly to the scientist, she was pressed to make a remark. Her unexpected remark was simply, "I believe in love and compassion." Startled by its seeming irrelevancy, the biologist later admitted that it was as close as he had ever come to a spiritual conversion. Mother Teresa refused to enter into a realm alien to her own vision and concerns as a Christian servant. In doing so, she unexpectedly brought the biologist into her spiritual realm of love and compassion.[4]

Compassion is the core of a new spirituality that can transform both the church and the world. In Matthew Fox's words:

> God's compassion points the way to humanity's compassion as a spirituality which becomes the art of walking in God's way. This way takes over at a deep, more than conscious level. It becomes an entire attitude toward life, a consciousness or spirituality.[5]

Too often spirituality is defined in Hellenistic terms as contemplation or withdrawal, rather than understanding spirituality in Judeo-Christian terms as compassion or empathy. Jesus, as the Jewish prophets before him, demonstrated that *compassion* is a verb—a deed of love and justice—a way of life.

Christians are called, not just to be isolated individuals with caring inclinations, but to be the church, the community of the compassionate in the world. The compassionate life is a life together. Compassion is best cultivated not as an individual character trait or special talent, but as a way of life nurtured by other compassionate people within an empathetic ethos. There are always exceptions, but generally compassionate persons, unsupported by the fellowship of others who care, can easily "burn out," feel isolated, unsupported, tired, and dispirited.

"Ministry," says Mary Pellauer, "occurs when the skin of the soul is rubbed raw."[6] Breaking the silence of a previous divorce, a pastor preached to the congregation about the struggles of that personal experience. That night a woman from the church was beaten by her husband. When a psychologist visited her, the woman said that she was going to see the pastor the next day because she felt she would find understanding. By revealing personal wounds, the pastor had created an opportunity to be a healer.

Christians are not more compassionate because they are more sensitive or more ethical people. Quite to the contrary, Christians are called to lives of compassion out of a sense of gratitude for the compassion God has for us in Christ. "We love, because [God] first loved us" (I John 4:19). Because we know ourselves as selfish sinners, forgiven by God, we can enter into the suffering of others, exercising a ministry of compassion. Our prayer could be that of Thomas à Kempis from his *Imitation of Christ*.

> Endeavor to be patient in bearing with the defects and infirmities of others, of what sort soever they be; for that thyself has many failings which must be borne with by others. If thou canst not make thyself such a one as thou wouldest, how canst thou expect to have others in all things to thy liking.[7]

On Being Wounded Healers

In this vision of the church, agents of brokenness are transformed into angels of healing. A most compelling concept of what it means to be a minister in a world hungering and hurting for spiritual care is that suggested by Henri J. M. Nouwen: Christians are called to be wounded healers, transforming personal life struggles and scars into sources and spirit of healing. "The minister," notes Nouwen, is called to recognize the sufferings of his time in his own heart and make that recognition the starting point of his service. Whether he tries to enter into a dislocated world, relate to a convulsive generation, or speak to a dying man, his service will not be perceived as authentic unless it comes from a heart wounded by the suffering about which he speaks. [8]

Suffering turned inward, unexamined and unshared, can breed loneliness, despair, and cynicism. Norman Cousins suggests another possibility. During his own hospitalization he and fellow patients discussed matters of sickness and pain that they could not bear to share even with their doctors. Cousins claims that "the psychology of the seriously ill put barriers between us and those who had the skill and the grace to minister to us."[9] Theologian Dorothee Soelle suggests in her book *Suffering* that only those who themselves have suffered can fully recognize and respond to those who around them suffer. [10]

The image of a wounded healer suggests at least three implications for persons in Christian ministry, whether clergy or lay. *To be a wounded healer, one must, first of all, affirm and accept one's own life story.* Along with the happiness of life come heartaches; with triumphs and success come temptations and scars. All of us limp through life, crippled by certain weaknesses and handicapped by various tragedies. Though we may earnestly desire to "go on to perfection" in accordance with John Wesley's dictum, the probabilities are far greater that we will continue to struggle and stumble as sinners.

Historically, many of the images of the ministry that have dominated the church's thinking have underscored a separation between clergy and laity rather than a partnership of ministry. The priestly portrait accented the difference between lay and clergy by requiring celibacy of the latter. The Reformation pastor model sought to overcome the distance between lay and clergy by encouraging the latter to marry, but in the process it often idealized family life in the parsonage beyond the realm of reality. Stereotypes of clergy as sexless servants or superhuman saints were encouraged by many images of ministry that suggested that the clergy had to be spotless models for the rest of humanity.

James D. Glasse noted that a medical doctor with a broken leg could with proper assistance set the broken leg of another person. Such action would probably rate a headline extolling the doctor's professionalism. Likewise, Glasse suggests that a pastor as a professional must "continue functioning as a priest even when he confronts difficulties in his own life of prayer." Like the doctor, the clergy would like it better if they did not experience brokenness, but that in itself is not sufficient reason to abandon ministry.[11] Authentic ministry emerges amid suffering and ambiguity. People look to leaders to speak out of their own human predicament, not to those who shout from the sidelines of life. People want pastors who neither deny nor trivialize the struggles of living. They seek out persons who have known pain, tragedy, and brokenness but who have moved beyond bitterness, despair, and hopelessness.

The wounded healer image of ministry suggests that persons begin with their humanity, not wearing their wounds as badges, but realizing that they suffer from the same predicaments of life as those whom they seek to serve. Ernest Hemingway was right; life does break us all. Some break at the point of marriage or of health or of business or of spirit. But Hemingway was also correct when he observed that many are strong in the broken places.[12] Because of their financial struggles, they may have more empathy; because of their marital or sexual difficulties, they may have more understanding; because of their disabilities, they may climb greater mountains. It is not a matter of being proud of one's weaknesses but of accepting the good news that God can make a mosaic out of the shattered stones of our lives.

F. Scott Fitzgerald is one of the most admired American authors of the 1920s. But by 1936, at the age of thirty-nine, he experienced what we today would call a midlife crisis. His career was on the skids; he was neglected both by critics and by the public. Financially, he was bankrupt. His wife had been fighting mental illness for years; he was engaged in a losing struggle with alcoholism. In a series of memorable articles in *Esquire*, he described himself as one for whom the salt of life had lost its savor. He told of how it felt to experience life "breaking down" and to feel oneself "cracking up," and to realize that one had been "mortgaging" oneself "physically and spiritually up to the hilt." Poignantly and pathetically, he describes his destitution, saying that "in a real dark night of the soul, it is always three o'clock in the morning, day after day."[13]

Fitzgerald was up against the wall. He, like Jeremiah, could find "no balm in Gilead," no healing physician for his soul (Jer. 8:22). It was "always three o'clock in the morning, day after day." Crushed, he let cynicism ensnarl him, and he chose to

cease any attempts to be a person—to be kind, just, or generous. . . .
In thirty-nine years, an observant eye has learned to detect where the

milk is watered and the sugar is sanded, the rhinestone passed for diamond and the stucco for stone. There was to be no more giving of myself—all giving was to be outlawed henceforth under a new name, and that name was Waste.[14]

And waste it was, for the wounds of life destroyed him. Suffering makes some strong but others callous, bitter, insensitive, and defeated. In contrast, the wounded healer accepts life's struggles and suffering, "making friends with pain,"[15] and draws from the well of life's triumphs and tragedies the healing waters that flow from the divine spring within each of us.

In contrast to the Fitzgeralds of life are those who are able to affirm with Paul that God's grace makes us strong in our weaknesses (see II Cor. 12:9-10). Persons affiliated with Alcoholics Anonymous have long demonstrated how their weakness has become their strength in helping other persons cope with this disease. One church has a group for former prisoners, led by an ex-convict who found Christ. The same church has a group for persons struggling with drug abuse, headed by a person who was addicted to cocaine. They have turned their greatest shortcomings into authentic forms of Christian ministry. When America's former First Lady, Betty Ford, spoke candidly about her own struggle with alcohol and drug abuse, some thought she would do irreparable damage to her reputation. Instead she is greatly admired. Television personality Barbara Walters reports: "This first lady turned her own personal wounds into weapons to be used against cancer, drug abuse and arthritis. By letting her guard down completely, Mrs. Ford has helped thousands. She's warm, refreshing, and, in public and private, very human."[16]

Each person knows painful dilemmas of life and death. When all is going great, it is easy to think we have no need of others. Martin Luther is portrayed in John Osborne's *Luther* as saying, "It's hard to accept you're anyone's son, and you're not the father of yourself."[17] Biblical talk about how "we are members one of another" seems like dinosaur thinking, until suddenly and inevitably we are swept from success to defeat or celebration to sorrow. During the earthquakes that shake our existence, we often are forced to take a new look through the kaleidoscopes by which we view life. At such times we may realize how much we need a supportive community of the compassionate.

Ideally, this is Christ's community, the church. Unfortunately, sometimes this very body has been the least compassionate. At times some may have been made to feel like lepers, as if God's creation were not good. Others have felt themselves shunned by silent stares or stunned by forked tongues. Novelist Richard Wright said that he found strife wherever he found religion in his life. Individuals or groups were always trying to rule others in the name of God. Wright observed that "the naked will to power seemed always to walk in the wake of a hymn.[18] A few may have felt cast out because they didn't measure up to someone's expectations. Those who have experienced divorce know how many poison arrows can be shot and how deep can be the daggers. As someone has said, "The Church is the only army that shoots its wounded soldiers."

On the other hand, Henri Nouwen assures us that a Christian community can be a "healing community not because wounds are cured and pains are alleviated, but because wounds and pains become openings or occasions for a new vision."[19] By affirming and accepting ourselves, we can begin to give our lives for others, "to cry with those who cry, laugh with those who laugh, and to make one's own painful and joyful experiences available as sources of clarification and understanding."[20] The paradox of ministry may be that our very weaknesses can be the source of our strengths, and our hurts can be the hope for the healing of others.

Too often the story of the church has been rejection of those who have "fallen" in the eyes of the community. But there are also redemptive stories to be told. Illustrative is one congregation that suffered through the experience of learning that one of its lay leaders had been convicted of embezzlement and sentenced to prison some miles away. The congregation systematically arranged for weekly visits and offered other forms of assistance to the family. Instead of condemnation, they offered compassion, reaching out to suffer with the person and family involved. When time came for the release, the ex-convict was met at the gate with loving embraces by the entire governing board of the local church. The gospel was reenacted: "The Son of man came eating and drinking, and they say, 'Behold, a glutton and a drunkard, a friend of tax collectors and sinners!' " (Matt. 11:19).

The healing, redemptive nature of the wounded healer also can be manifested through the ministry of the laity in other occupations and professions. The motto of one law school is "Lawyers Can Be Healers." In that spirit, former Supreme Court Chief Justice Warren

Burger addressed the American Bar Association and urged lawyers to focus more on mediation, negotiation, and arbitration rather than always emphasizing litigation. Other possible wounded healers might be:

* The businessperson who does not view every possible shoplifter as a hardened criminal.
* The nurse who walks a grieving family all the way to its car after a loved one has died in a strange hospital.
* A spouse who gives an unfaithful partner another opportunity.

Grace, for the wounded healer, is not an abstract theological doctrine, but the very blood of life. We know what it means to be alienated and then forgiven. Grace, for the wounded healer, is not simply the amazing words of a gospel song, but the very breath of life. With Jeremiah, we have known griefs "beyond healing" but have found in Christ the great Physician. As Paul Tillich reminds us:

> Grace strikes us when we are in great pain and restlessness. . . . It strikes us when we feel that our separation is deeper than usual. . . . Sometimes at that moment a wave of light breaks into our darkness, and it is as though a voice were saying "You are accepted. . . . Do not seek for anything; do not perform anything; do not intend anything. *Simply accept the fact that you are accepted!*" If that happens to us, we experience grace.[21]

Yes, the wounded healer, first of all, must affirm and accept his or her own autobiography, knowing that by grace our story has already been accepted by God. But remember—even the risen Christ had scars!

Second, by learning to accept who we are—the broken people Christ came to save—as wounded healers we can empathize with those who suffer. The wounded healer's motto ought to be "Treat kindly all persons you meet, for they are having a hard time." Effective ministry means to enter into the lament of the prophet Jeremiah, "for the wound . . . of my people is my heart wounded," and to "weep day and night for the slain of the daughter of my people" (Jer. 8:22 and 9:1).

My first parish assignment after seminary was in a rural and barren part of South Dakota, a small church fifteen miles from even the smallest town. It was called Ideal Presbyterian Church, though its name didn't match its reality. My mission was primarily to promote healing for this small congregation of fewer than seventy members, which had just been split in two by a theological controversy over the meaning of the virgin birth. They were a hurting people, neighbor divided against neighbor, family members alienated from one another, because they didn't subscribe to the same dogmas.

Traveling from farm home to farm home, I learned not only their agony about this crisis of faith but also their personal anguish about marital conflicts, mental depressions, and unresolved grief after tragic deaths. Instead of an idyllic rural village far from the frantic pace of urban life, I discovered it was "three o'clock in the morning, day after day" for these people, and they needed the loving care of a pastor and the reassuring, redeeming, reconciling word of the gospel. A recent seminary graduate, reflecting on life in the parish, reports that is "three o'clock in the morning" for that church's parishioners as well.

> My church is a suburban church in a new, growing community. To drive through and see the wealth, the boats going to the lake on Sunday, etc., you'd think that what these people need most is a word of judgment—and sometimes they do. But for all their success, there is unbelievable hurt. The mid-life slump, divorce, mixed-up kids, inability to control credit-card buying, lack of time, etc. are all very real, and I feel . . . that theology must have a healing word for them.[22]

Our model for a ministry of identification with those who suffer is, of course, Jesus. Leaping from scripture is story after story of how he reached out and brought a healing touch to those in pain. But his style of ministry—if not his life-style—was impolitic and irritating to the good, righteous folk of his day. Jesus had a propensity for hanging around the wrong crowd, of consorting with the most controversial and questionable people in the community.

Despite vocal critics, Jesus was not deterred from entertaining, for example, tax collectors and prostitutes, the scum of his society. Philosophically, he believed ostracism was wrong and that strategically it was foolish. As Martin Luther King, Jr., once said: "Whom you would change, you must first love."[23] Treating persons as pariahs offers neither care or cure. Thus when asked why he ate with tax collectors and sinners, Jesus responded: "Those who are well have no need of a physician, but those who are sick. Go and learn what this means. . . . For I came not to call the righteous, but sinners" (Matt. 9:12-13). And then, as if things were not already controversial enough, imagine the reaction when Jesus said," Truly, I say to you, tax collectors and the harlots go into the kingdom of God before you" (Matt. 21:31).

A healing ministry should not be equated with inevitable restoration of health. Healing may even include death. Illustrative is the experience of the head nurse who became a friend to an elderly woman in a convalescent center. Having outlived her family, the patient had become dependent on a suction machine. Every day or so, her lungs would fill up with fluid, and the staff would hook tubes into her body while she lay helpless. Reduced to an object of intervention, she protested to the head nurse that she no longer wanted to be so treated. Her life was complete, and she was prepared to die.

One day the nurse happened to be alone when the congestion developed in the patient. When the nurse started to move toward the machine, the patient urgently signaled "no" with one hand and with the other hand pulled the nurse toward her. At that critical point, the nurse decided to forego customary treatment for a more profound type of healing. The two reminisced together, holding hands, while the older woman finished life on her own, supported by the care and tears of the other. Being reconciled to the inevitable or the unavoidable is a form of healing. All Christian healing is not restoration of health; it, rather, can be the healthy acceptance of the way things are.

Wounded healers are ministers who reach out to the broken people Jesus came to save. They seek out those who suffer. They stand by a hospital bed. They sit in a waiting room. They walk into a court chamber. They kneel in a prison cell. They march in a picket line. They embrace the hurting without regard to race or station or nationality or gender or sexual orientation. By so identifying with the brokenness of humanity, the wounded healer experiences what Albert Schweitzer called the fellowship "of those who bear the mark of pain."

But above all, wounded healers understand that healing and health and wholeness come not simply because of our life experiences or by our empathy toward those who suffer, but from the One to whom we witness: Jesus Christ. Our faith and ministry must ever point to the suffering servant described so movingly by Isaiah.

> Surely he has borne our griefs
> and carried our sorrows;
> yet we esteemed him stricken,
> smitten by God, and afflicted.
> But he was wounded for our
> transgressions,

> he was bruised for our iniquities;
> upon him was the chastisement that
>   made us whole,
> and with his stripes we are healed.
> (Isaiah 53:4-5)

Proclamation by word and deed of God's saving love for humankind calls us to a public ministry in a global village. John Wesley's old slogan, "The world is my parish," has taken on a new meaning in an era when the madness of the arms race and thermonuclear annihilation threaten the very survival of the human species.

It is three o'clock in the morning, day after day. We stand at the precipice of our own Armageddon with the doomsday clock of nuclear annihilation ticking away. If we fail to control the nuclear arms race, all the values we hold dear, all the dreams we envision, all the goods we cherish will mean nothing, for the United States, says Jonathan Schell, will simply be "a republic of insects and grass."[24]

Though we have not faced the horrendous consequences of nuclear war, yet we are already wounded. Speak to any child; children will share with you their deepest fears. Broadway's Annie may sing that tomorrow is only a day away, but our children and youth are far less certain.

Many of us are haunted by visions of death and destruction. Over the years I have periodically experienced recurring thoughts or daydreams of catastrophes—the house exploding, a building collapsing, a sudden flash. I have said nothing to anyone, lest someone have a psychological explanation too painful for me to face. Imagine, then, my surprise when I picked up an issue of *The Christian Century* and read Walter Wink's report that more and more people have shared with him "dreams of conflagrations, explosions, firestorms." He contends that "we are internalizing the genuine threat at last—but not in a way that leads to action." Instead he contends:

> People are paralyzed. The issue is too vast, the government too unresponsive and paranoid, the public too powerless. We believe that nothing can save us that is possible. And so we quietly make ready to die together. We are stricken by a state of advanced nuclear paralysis.[25]

But the prospects are not quite so bleak; even since Wink wrote these words a tremendous grass roots movement has begun to stir around the world. And at the forefront must be the churches, led by wounded healers who seek to bring health and wholeness to the body politic and the international realm. Such a public ministry in a global village can be the very "balm of Gilead" that the prophet Jeremiah could not find among his people.

Perhaps the most appropriate paradigm for the priesthood of all believers emerges from the powerful, liberating hope of the black people of America. In the Christ of Calvary, the black slaves discovered healing for their hurts and hope from their bondage. As J. Garfield Owens has noted:

> No people were better prepared to speak of Christ's making the wounded whole than those humble and lowly slaves. For they knew what it meant to be wounded in body, mind, and soul. They knew the deep hurt and sorrow of separation from their dearest ones, mother and children. They knew what it meant to be beaten and driven like dumb cattle. They knew what it meant to be stripped of all human dignity, to be alienated and depersonalized. Yet they could proclaim in an uncanny way that they had found in Christ a balm that made whole even such wounded.[26]

Out of their experience and faith in God's healing presence have come lyrics that continue to speak to all who are beaten, broken, and battered by life today. All of us pulsate to the cry of the captives as they sang:

> Sometimes I feel discouraged
> And think my work's in vain,
> But then the Holy Spirit
> Revives my soul again.

As we begin or reaffirm our ministry, the triumphant testimony of the shackled slaves reassures us in our vocation wherever we are.

> If you cannot preach like Peter,
> If you cannot pray like Paul,
> You can tell the love of Jesus,
> And say he died for all.

Yes, this is the joyful good news of Christian ministry—the Word and the Sacrament we have to share.

> There is a balm in Gilead,
> To make the wounded whole;

There is a balm in Gilead,
To heal the sin-sick soul.

Wounded healers in a community of the compassionate witness beyond the brokenness of life to renewing wholeness possible in Jesus Christ.

Chapter Six

SERVANT LEADERS IN A SERVANT CHURCH

At the end of the days of truly great leaders, the people will say about them, "We did it ourselves."

LAO-TZU, Sixth Century B.C.

In Hermann Hesse's novel *Journey to the East* a group of people are portrayed on a mythical pilgrimage. The key character is Leo, who has been invited to be the group's servant, doing menial chores as they travel. Additionally, he sustains them with his spirit and his songs. The journey is highly successful until one day Leo disappears. Chaos ensues, and eventually the adventure collapses. Without Leo, the servant, the group cannot survive. Too late, they discover that the person whom they had known and treated as a servant had actually been the titular head of the organization that had sponsored their trip. In truth their servant had been their leader.

In 1955 a black woman by the name of Rosa Parks had finished her day's work as a maid. With feet and back aching, she boarded a Montgomery, Alabama, bus. She flopped down in one of the first row seats. Soon the driver ordered her to the back of the bus, as the front was reserved for white riders. But she said no. Her "here I sit" declaration sparked a civil rights revolution, eventually ending the reign of segregation and terror in America. Eventually even whites came to understand that in truth their servant had been their leader.

When the cardinals of the Roman Catholic church gathered in Rome for the election of a new pope in 1958, the mood was that this was a time for transition, a quiet pause in the life of the world-wide church. When the white smoke puff arose from the Sistine Chapel, it signaled the selection of an elderly caretaker servant of the church, Angelo Riuseppe Roncalli, whose lifetime was expected to be short and whose papacy was anticipated to be undistinguished. This was right in one regard: Pope John XXIII was a humble servant. But he also proved to be a revolutionary leader, convening Vatican II, throwing open the windows of ecumenism, and calling the church to servanthood in the modern world. Roman Catholicism now knows that in truth its servant had been its leader.

The three vignettes drawn from contemporary literature and history underscore anew a fundamental teaching of the gospel as taught repeatedly by Jesus: "Whoever wants to be great must be your servant, and whoever wants to be first must be the willing slave of all—like the Son of Man; he did not come to be served, but to serve, and to give up his life as a ransom for many" (Matt. 20:26-28 NEB).

Theologian Paul Tillich suggested that symbols cannot be created or destroyed by deliberate human effort. They are born or die within a mysterious process beyond our control and possibly our comprehension. Whether a symbol catches on or becomes compelling within a religious community depends on whether the psychological conditions are ripe.[1] In contemporary times the conditions appear to be somewhat supportive of the servant-leader symbol of ministry. Allergic to authoritarian leadership styles and positive toward participatory democracies, both church and society seem inclined to agree with John Naisbitt, in *Megatrends* that "the new leader is a facilitator, not an order giver."[2]

Robert Greenleaf, in his book *Servant Leadership*, suggests that today "the great leader is seen as servant first." He thinks this is the new moral guide for our time, that this is an anti-authoritarian age. People do not readily accept authority in other persons. In other eras, just to be selected as teacher or appointed as pastor brought immediate respect and trust. Now Greenleaf says: "The only authority deserving one's allegiance is that authority which if freely and knowingly granted by the led to the leader in response to, and in proportion to, the clearly evident servant stature of the leader." Those who are granted the permission and power to lead are those who prove to be servants first.[3]

The metaphor of servant leaders, however, ought not to be confused with the popular pressure toward making ministers "enablers" or "equippers" or "conflict managers." Drawn from humanistic psychology and the small group movement, this facilitating function also has a biblical base ("some to be . . . pastors and teachers, to equip God's people for work in his service" [Eph. 4:12 NEB]). Reducing ministerial leadership solely to this function, however, may in the long run be detrimental to a person's self-esteem and counterproductive in the life of the church. As Neill Q. Hamilton notes:

> The effect of facilitator, enabler, and conflict manager as master roles tends to be a bland and temporary peace at the expense of any unifying and energizing vision. The roles of enabler and conflict manager discourage any prophetic input from the minister. An enabler serves others' vision; a conflict manager does not complicate the scene with one more contending point of view. Actually these master roles are more appropriate to the therapeutic community from which they came.[4]

These models may provide peace and unity in the church, but the calling of ministers as leaders is to project a vision, to offer directions, and to exercise authority as well as to participate as partners in congregational life. From the Orthodox tradition of Christianity, another perspective helps clarify this distinction.

> In the liturgical texts . . . the priest is not a leader in the usual sense of the word. He is neither dictator, nor charismatic, nor visionary, nor perfect personal example. His role is a derived one, dependent for all to see on a higher (reality). Even as an enabler, he admits freely that he himself must be enabled.
>
> Yet in spite of all these negations, the priest is a leader. But his leadership is clearly not of the kind which the world describes as such. . . . It is only in that paradoxical relationship of the priest at the altar that we can find the unique quality of the leadership of the priest of the liturgy. . . . His leadership consists of showing his people how to say to God with their whole lives: "The things that are thine do we offer to You according to all things and for all things."[5]

While the conditions may be right for a new image, this does not mean that we are naturally inclined to be servant leaders. The idea of servanthood as the pathway to power, greatness, and leadership is as paradoxical and absurd to us today as it was to the people in biblical times. First-century emperors ruled by force, not by the favor of populations they conquered and controlled. The axioms of that Palestinian society were strikingly similar to the motifs of modernity: "look out for Number One," "dress for success," and "nice guys finish last." Greatness for the world, George A. Buttrick once noted, is like a pyramid, with the greatest at the top and others scrambling to reach higher levels with fewer equals and more subordinates. "But," said Buttrick, "Christ's idea of greatness is like an inverted pyramid: the nearer to the peak, the greater the burden, and the more people are carried in love."[6]

The Servant Church of a Servant God

Throughout much of Christian history the image of the church has been that of an institution expecting to be served rather than that of a serving institution. Church structures—be they great European cathedrals or modest white buildings—have often been viewed as ends in themselves. People and money poured in, but little flowed out to the surrounding neighborhoods to the world at large. When the church is viewed as the dispenser of sacraments essential to salvation or the power broker setting the standards for mores and morals in the community, ministry has often become captive to clergy domination, and authoritarian styles have imprisoned relationships between people. When the church is envisioned in terms of prestige and social status, then we are likely to discover ourselves saying our "leading church member" is the bank president or corporation executive, rather than the person who quietly volunteers to collect, repair, and distribute clothing to the needy or struggles to aid and protect abused children and spouses.

Part of the great revolution evoked by Pope John XXIII was a new self-understanding within Roman Catholicism of being a servant church. The Pastoral Constitution on the Church in the Modern World, issued by Vatican II, explicitly teaches that just as Christ came into the world not to be served but to serve, so also the Church in carrying on the mission of Christ must seek to serve the world by fostering the brotherhood and sisterhood of all.

The Servant Songs of Isaiah could be ascribed to the Church as well as to Christ. Implicit within the gospel of Jesus Christ is a vision of the faith community as a servant church, under obligation to serve human needs in this world. The servant church is not deemed as an end in itself, but as a means to God's kingdom. In Dietrich Bonhoeffer's *Letters and Papers from Prison*, he implores that "the Church is the Church only when it exists for others."[7] It is the institutional incarnation of Jesus washing the feet of disciples or the good Samaritan taking risks to care for the stranger.

In exploring what it means to be a servant church, four distinctive dimensions should be noted. *First is the understanding of God as servant.* Contrary to almost any other portrait of God, the Christian affirms a servant God. This radical departure from ordinary human thought is rooted in the scriptures. Reversing the tendency to picture God as all powerful and remote from human experience, Paul in Philippians declares: "Christ Jesus, who, though he was in the form of God, did not count equality with God a thing to be grasped, but emptied himself, taking the form of a servant, being born in the likeness of [humans]" (Phil. 2:5-6).

This servant image of God compels us to rethink our own responses. How awesome it is to imagine that the Almighty could care enough to enter humbly into this universe for the sake of saving humanity. Jürgen Moltmann notes that "the religious and humanist world which surrounded Christianity from the very first despised the cross, because this dehumanized Christ represented a contradiction to all ideas of God."[8] On the basis of his own example, Jesus repeatedly urged his disciples to be servants to one another (Mark 10:44; John 13:44). Thus early Christians understood themselves as "servants of God" (I Peter 2:16) and "servants of Christ" (I Cor. 7:22; Eph. 6:6). The servant church of a servant God especially understands "service" as the root meaning of the word *ministry*. Since ministry is the gift of God to the corporate community of faith, it is always a shared vocation.

Second, Christians understand that God is present in servanthood. Far from being a Deist God, uninterested and uninvolved in human affairs, Christians image a God often present in incognito ways. The parable of the last judgment visualizes how God is present in the hungry, homeless, imprisoned, and so on. By identifying with "one of the least of these, my brothers or sisters," we are in solidarity with God.

This motif of God present in servanthood can be an impelling motivation for mission. In an act of hospitality to a stranger, we chance the opportunity to meet Christ. In accepting the yoke of obedient service, we may discover the freedom of knowing God's will. As Paul D. Hanson notes, this vision of God present in servanthood can give us

> the grace and power to acknowledge the depth of human bondage and the dearth of loving servants and yet enter the fray with courage and energy, knowing that where a human servant acknowledges her or his solidarity with a human in need through an act of loving service, God is present, and God's realm is coming.[9]

Lest we become too romantic, a story told by Jim Wallis bears repeating. He told of a major march on Washington, D. C., for social justice on a very hot, humid August day. The crowds were far greater than had been anticipated, exhausting by far the facilities for food and drink. One older man, dirty and ragged, obviously was desperate for something to quench his thirst. Thus a kindly Christian woman, remembering "the least of these" and how in helping a stranger one may be hosting an "angel unawares," decided to give the person her only cold drink. Handing the thirsty man a cup of the cool beverage, she was astonished when the man spit it all out and sputtered: "Yuck, why didn't you tell me it was *Diet* Coke!"[10] One does not always meet God in the strangers one encounters!

Third, a servant church understands that Christian servanthood is defined by the Cross. Too often communities of faith forget the centrality of the Cross, offering a pablum of happiness without sacrifice, joy without suffering, and peace without conflict. In contrast, James H. Cone declares that:

> The servanthood of the church is defined by the cross of Jesus and nowhere else. . . . To be a servant of Jesus means more than meeting together every Sunday for worship and other liturgical gatherings. It means more than serving as an officer or even a pastor of a church. Servanthood includes a political component that thrusts a local congregation in society where it must take sides with the poor.[11]

The Cross reminds us that suffering is endemic to servanthood. The Suffering Servant image in the New Testament is not a mirage apart from reality. Jesus warned his disciples of the consequence of being followers (John 15:20), and they personally experienced its truth (cf. I Cor. 11:23-33). Believers, as well as unbelievers, may find it scandalous that both Jesus and his followers inevitably suffer for God's sake. Those who choose to be faithful servant leaders are likely to be "crucified" in any sociogeographical setting.

When one reads that a Southern Baptist volunteer is suing his denomination for five million dollars because, he claims, denominational officials did not warn him that mission service could be hazardous to his safety, one wonders what has happened to Christian teaching about suffering servanthood.[12] Such an incident, reflecting the litigious nature of contemporary Christians, stands in stark contrast to the great servant leaders of Christian history. Illustrative is Ignatius Loyola, founder of the Jesuits, who started with six persons, including Simon Rodriquez d'Arevedo. Of a class of people noted for cleanliness, they were aware of the dangers they risked in Christ's name. Leprosy was the AIDS (Acquired Immune Deficiency Syndrome) of their day. Imaging themselves as soldiers of Christ, their battlefields were the hospitals. Ludwig Marcuse records that

> Rodriquez shared his bed with a leper who had been denied admittance at the hospital. The empty gesture scarcely benefited the leper, but the student won a moral victory over himself. Francisco had to massage a man whose back was running with open sores. The young nobleman was filled with dread and nausea but he was well-repaid, spiritually. He smeared his hands with the infection, then touched his lips. He passed the night in horror, convinced leprosy had already reached his throat. It was an experience that paved the way to a wonderful, lifelong assurance. He lost his repugnance to foul diseases; he had passed another stage on the road to freedom. [13]

These three dimensions of the servant church underscore the imperative that the servant church has not room for a pampered priesthood. The towel and the basin, not pomp and power, are the symbols of redemptive ministry. The Cross, accepting suffering as the heart of God, not the computer, rejecting pain because it cannot be quantified and controlled, is the symbol of the servant leader. Both clergy and lay ministers can discover, in the words of Martin Luther King, Jr.,

> Everybody can be great. Because anybody can serve. You don't have to have a college degree to serve. You don't have to make your subject and your verb agree to serve. You don't have to know about Plato and Aristotle to serve. . . .You don't have to know the second theory of thermo-dynamics in physics to serve. You only need a heart full of grace. A soul generated by love. [14]

Preparation for daily service prompts us to pray: "O Lord, help us to be masters of ourselves that we might become the servants of others."

The Dangers of Being a Servant Leader

The servant leader paradigm of ministry is not without dangers or difficulties for persons in ministry. Four in particular need to be noted.

First, in adopting the servant leader image of ministry it is critically important that a person not simply resolve the paradox by stressing either the servant or the leadership dimension to the exclusion of the other. A hyphen perhaps should be added between the words *servant* and *leader (servant-leader)* to remind us that we need to live and work in tension or balance with these two images.

A cautionary word at this point needs to be added for women in ministry. The biblical understanding of servant was closely identified with slavery. In the Old Testament, the Hebrew word *ebed* is customarily translated as "slave" in English. Likewise the Greek term *doulos* has the literal English meaning of "slave." To apply such terms to Christ and the ministry of the church was to reverse dramatically the world's values and to coin a surprising new metaphor for early Christians. Traditionally within the Church women have been allocated the most servile positions. Service within the community of the faithful often has been limited to church school teaching, hosting bazaars, women's groups, and so on, while the men have served as trustees, led the liturgy, and been ordained. The danger today is that women may adopt the servant leader model of ministry and live only on the service side of the equation. Women need not surrender their caring, nurturing qualities, but they do need to assert their vision and values in leadership ways.

A second closely related danger for both women and men is for ministers to settle for too little power. Power itself is a neutral term. Too often it is associated in negative terms, such as using power to control or manipulate another person. But service of any kind requires a degree of power if one is to accomplish anything of value. For example, the office of pastor has power. Just being identified as a member of the cloth often will open hospital doors, homes, and offices that are otherwise closed to other persons and professionals. A judicious use of that power provides opportunities for service in the name of mercy and justice that can be provided by no one else.

By accenting the powerless servant image to the exclusion of the leader metaphor, people eventually discover that their own self-worth suffers and the church struggles for vision and vitality. Many contemporary churches are hurt more by pastoral default than by pastoral domination. The creative wholeness and self-fulfillment that comes from leading when one has the capacity for leadership is often lost when individuals adopt only a *laissez-faire* enabling or laid-back facilitating function.

No necessary service is beneath the dignity of a Christian minister (after all, the "slave" or "table waiter" notion is the biblical basis of the symbol). For example, ordained clergy may do custodial tasks, but the normative covenant expectations of the church should be that these persons devote themselves to other forms of human service in the church and in the world.

A *third difficulty clergy experience is the crossfire of mixed signals as to the type of people and the styles of leadership the church wants.* Surveys suggest that churches often want both "humble, self-effacing clergy" and "vigorous leadership." The *Ministry in America* study revealed that the most highly rated characteristic, "service in humility," meant that church people expected clergy to rely on God's grace and serve others without concern for personal success or infallibility. The servant leader metaphor for ministry sets forth this ideal, though it recognizes the incredible difficulty of achieving it. In David E. Richards' words:

> The care of souls is one thing. Making a parish a howling success is another. The perpetual dilemma is how to combine the sensitivities of a gentle, loving, thoughtful, theologically reflective, deeply spiritual pastor (which the church would like to have) with the attributes of an excellent organizer, a person who is skilled in group development and management, and a person who is competent to provide aggressive leadership (which the church actually calls for). [15]

Fourth, the danger of a cultural or chameleon ministry must be recognized as a possible servant leader interpretation. The servant leader may become so comfortable with the status quo or so enthralled with the avant garde that the gospel or kingdom of God become synonymous with contemporary causes or culture.

Historically in the United States clergy have often fallen into this trap. Southern white clergy were long identified with slavery and segregation. The majority of Protestant clergy in the North from 1861 to 1876 supported the optimistic morality of the Gilded Age while overlooking the immorality of the "robber barons." Protestant Christianity later identified "demon rum" as the devil and the temperance movement with the gospel. During World War I the overwhelming percentage of clergy adopted the "crusader" model, blessing the war without question. In the decades that have followed this same characteristic has emerged, as clergy have blindly served their nation or their cause, forgetting the critical distancing dimension of genuine leadership within the church.

Voices of prophetic servant leadership have always questioned wars, challenged oppression, and condemned cultural mores and morality, but they have tended to be marginal and not mainstream within the life of the church and society. Now with the proclamation of the birthday of Martin Luther King, Jr., as a national holiday, we easily forget that those white clergy who marched with him were usually ostracized in their own parishes and communities and that the black clergy were typically characterized as subversives or even communists by the FBI and others in power.

In every age the pressure is to be "Reverend Chameleon," changing colors to correspond with the wishes of the culture instead of the will of Christ. Since most congregations are like plaid jackets, the danger of constantly attempting to blend in with the kaleidoscope of color inevitably results in succumbing to stress or subservience, causing burnouts and drop-outs in church leadership. A clearer sense of what it means to be a servant leader in a servant church of a servant God is needed.

Identifying Marks of Servant Leaders

What then are the identifying marks of servant leaders in contemporary times? In noting four of these traits, I have also sought in the next few pages to suggest some practical implications of ministry that flow from this theoretical metaphor.

First of all, servant leaders understand ministry as basically not a status but a service to humanity. We are not elevated to status offices in the church, such as pastor or district superintendent or seminary president or bishop. We are called to these specialized positions to expend ourselves for others. Following the imagery adopted by Gregory the Great, the Christian's role is to be *servus servorum dei*—the servant of the servants of God.

The contemporary Christian minister must be a "lover." Studies of small churches suggest that what the people want in a pastor is not primarily an efficient leader or a great preacher or an innovative programmer. What they want is a "lover" who establishes authentic relationships based on genuine care and commitment. That kind of "lover" becomes a real leader not only in the church but also in the community. Dom Helder Camara, one of the genuine servant leaders of our time, introduced himself to the people of Recife, Brazil, this way:

Who am I? . . . A human being who regards himself as a brother in weakness and sin to all men, of all races and creeds in the world. . . . A bishop of the Catholic Church who comes, in the imitation of Christ, not to be served but to serve. . . . Let no one be alarmed to see me in the company of men who are supposedly compromising or dangerous, men in power or in the opposition, reformists or anti-reformists, revolutionaries or anti-revolutionaries, men of good faith or bad. . . . My door and my heart will be open to all, absolutely to all. Christ died for all.[16]

Because servant leaders are free from status worries, they can be bridge builders between peoples and between God and humanity. The Latin word for "priest" is *pontifex*, literally meaning "bridge builder." The bridge building servant leader can reach across community chasms, seeking to be a reconciling force among groups in conflict. A. James Armstrong, in his inaugural speech as president of the National Council of Churches called the church to this "pontifex" function. He cited an ancient Welsh phrase on the coat of arms of a British Parliament member: *"Bid ben bid bout."* ("He who would be a leader must be a bridge.")

Theologian Langdon Gilkey contends that the starting point for pastors who want to be effective servants of their congregations and the world is to be spiritual leaders. The cure and nurturing of souls and the development of personal experiences of the religious and of God, must be a prime commitment of the servant leader.

The servant pastor must not only be preacher, counselor, and ethical adviser (as well as organizer and money-raiser), but also, above all, "spiritual leader," one who can lead his or her community from the beginning of the spiritual life through its many stages to some form of fruition.[17]

One way of being a spiritual leader and building bridges is through worship. The famous British Archbishop William Temple suggested in a broadcast over BBC, just before his untimely death in 1944, that "the world will be saved from political chaos and collapse by one thing only: that is worship."[18] The ethical dimension of worship is clear by his definition: "To worship is to quicken the conscience by the holiness of God, to feed the mind with the truth of God, to purge the imagination by the beauty of God, to open the heart to the love of God, to devote the will to the purpose of God."[19] When servant leaders stimulate that style of worship, a bridge is built between peoples and between God and humanity.

The term *leitourgia*, or "liturgy," literally means the "service" or "work" of "the people." Laypersons and clergy can together be involved in creating liturgies that draw persons closer to God and "quicken the conscience" to the needs of the world. Depending on the circumstance, this may mean revitalizing traditional services of worship or reappropriating ancient truths in contemporary and creative ways. Servant leaders understand the power of classic Roman Catholic masses or John Wesley's New Year's Covenant service. They also may design new liturgies based on the suicide of a teenager, the plight of refugees seeking sanctuary, or the quest to end the nuclear arms race.

William H. Willimon appropriately cautions against a utilitarian approach to worship. *"Leitourgia,"* he notes, "must be celebrated for its own sake, not simply as a means of rallying the faithful for *diakonia.* Worship must not be one more 'resource' in our pastoral bag of tricks for getting people to be more just or more loving or more anything else."[20] Worship, however, does build bridges between the human and the divine and shapes both individual character and a community's vision of what God intends.

At the heart of Christian life and worship are the sacraments. To the clergy the church has given the authority for administering these sacraments. Historically, this power has been abused whenever clergy have sought status at the expense of the laity. Servant leaders approach this privileged responsibility with a sense of humble service, being used as channels of God's grace. In celebrating baptism and the Eucharist, the minister is the servant leader, offering Christ's gifts to the people. Perhaps during those sacramental moments, more than at any other time, does the minister as servant leader personally experience and publicly epitomize the understanding that ministry is not status seeking but service to humanity.

Second, servant leaders recognize that authority is fundamentally not ascribed by position but derived from service. Power is not given automatically by election or appointment; it is more often gained by loving service. Catholic theologian Edward Schillebeeckx even suggests that the grounds for apostolicity is not the continuity of laying on of hands, but rather faithful service in the apostolic community. Ministry, for him, is not a status but a service to the community. He argues that "suffering solidarity with the poor and insignificant is an essential mark of the apostolicity of the ministry."[21]

Even in the rough and tumble world of partisan politics, there are those who understand power as servanthood. President Jimmy Carter once remarked that he should not be viewed as "First Boss" but as "First Servant." Senator Mark O. Hatfield of Oregon says the Christian in politics "is called to be a servant-leader. Self-preservation is no longer the key motive of all political activities; rather, it becomes the service of human need, and prophetic faithfulness to a vision of God's will being done 'on earth as it is in heaven.' "[22]

Likewise in the business and corporate spheres there is an awareness that treating employees as partners, not as automatons or capital expenditures, is not only more humane but also the way to greater productivity and profits. Thomas J. Peters and Robert H. Waterman, Jr., discovered *In Search of Excellence* that America's best-run companies are people-oriented. Because of this, companies like Hewlett Packard, IBM, and 3-M have been "truly unusual in their ability to achieve extraordinary results through ordinary people."[23]

By looking at the contemporary worlds of politics and business, we are reminded that leadership is not assigned by status but acquired by servanthood. There is really nothing radically new about this discovery. We can trace it back to the Gospel of Mark when Jesus found his disciples quarreling as they were traveling to Capernaum. When he asked why they were arguing, he learned that they were disputing about who among them was the greatest. In essence, they were fighting for position—who was to be senior apostle and who was to be associate minister. Upset, Jesus counseled the twelve, saying "If anyone wants to be first, he must make himself last of all and servant of all" (Mark 9:35 NEB).

Contemporary clergy probably do less pastoral calling in homes and places of work than ever before in the history of the church. The mere suggestion that one ought to do such visitation will prompt from colleagues an endless list of reasons why it is impossible in their community or how it is a problematic use of one's time. Interestingly enough, politicians and college fund-raisers do not accept these reasons, finding home and business visits very productive.

Fortunately, the first pastor with whom I worked did not know those arguments. So every day, in the heat of summer, we pounded the streets, climbed the hills of Deadwood, South Dakota, and knocked on the doors of present and potential members. In a large city parish (3,000 members) I went from business to business daily, being received with unexpected joy and appreciation. People want their pastors to visit them; pastors need to know their people if they are to sense the rhythms of anguish and activity in their communities.

Sermon preparation using a lectionary is important, but understanding the life of the people is imperative. Sitting back in one's professional office waiting for "clients" to come in is not the style of the good shepherd or the servant leader. Authority may be ascribed to the physician or to the psychologist by reason of education and credentials, but for the pastor, authority is derived more from personal service, which evolves from making oneself available and vulnerable to the hurts and needs of people.

Lest I be misunderstood, I am not arguing for a manipulative use of service as a means for Christians to gain power. One does not serve the needs of others simply as a means to achieve influence. Service has its own intrinsic Christian worth. As Martin E. Marty writes:

> A minister does not make a pastoral call to the ill in order that when the person comes to health he or she can be supportive of some program or other. A good minister is too busy to think about such side benefits. He does not help nurture families only so that they can help integrate a community. A person does what the situation demands.[24]

But without a doubt, the servant leader inevitably gains in stature and authority within the community because of faithful and responsible Christian service.

The authority of a Christian minister is not undermined, but confirmed by servanthood. When a minister, lay or clergy, is oriented to a life of service, pointing toward a Christ who came into the world to serve, whatever power is derived from such relationships has a legitimacy distinctly different from that derived from self-serving actions designed solely for self-promotion. Servant leaders do not function as freewheeling, autonomous professionals but realize that their mediated authority flows from the community they serve. Ministry is penultimate; the gospel is centered in Jesus Christ, not in the person of the pastor. In Paul's words: "This is how one should regard us, as servants of Christ and stewards of the mysteries of God" (I Cor. 4:1).

Third, servant leaders are empathetic to the human condition, understanding all life to be ambiguous and truth often paradoxical. The servant leader approaches people not in the spirit of condemnation or rejection, but in the spirit of love and hope. The servant leader loves the sinner, not the sin. The servant leader accepts the person, but sometimes refuses to accept the person's level of effort or performance as not quite good enough.

Robert Greenleaf has properly noted that "an educator may be rejected by students and must not object to this. But one may never, under any circumstance, regardless of what they do, reject a single student."[25] As a college and seminary president, I believe the same holds true for administrators. Regardless of the personal provocation, a Christian educator should not reject a single faculty member. Because I have been disappointed by someone or even know that person's dislike for me, I am not permitted to let petty prejudice blur my respect for that person and that person's potential. Likewise, a pastor, no matter how irritating the parishioner, has no right to reject or ignore that person. In the imagistic language of Jesus, the good shepherd keeps searching to find the lost sheep, ever seeking reconciliation and new relationships with the alienated.

To be a Christian requires that one have a tolerance for imperfection. The enigma of human nature, Greenleaf has noted, is that even the typically imperfect person can be

> capable of great dedication and heroism *if* wisely led. Many otherwise able people are disqualified to lead because they cannot work with and through the half-people who are all there are. The secret of institution building is to be able to weld a team of such people by lifting them up to grow taller than they would otherwise be.[26]

An empathetic perspective on the brokenness of the human condition is indispensable for effective pastoral care and counseling. People will not seek out a rigid moralist to share their most wretching pains and perplexities. They will reach out to servant leaders who have a shepherding perspective and offer the gifts of healing, sustaining, guiding, and reconciling pastoral care.[27] The servant leader identifies with the brokenness and pain, offering comfort in times of crisis and counsel to those in distress.

Within the church we are painfully aware of our flaws and our failures. Pastors are human beings, not perfect people incapable of mistakes and misjudgments. Every church is more a congregation of sinners standing in need of forgiveness than it is a community of saints stretching for perfection. Many persons leave the church because they have a rigid view of what the church ought to be. They cannot adjust to the reality they experience. Communities of faith often do not live up to the biblical vision.

Ambiguity always characterizes a local congregation. Those who seek to serve it cannot be intolerant of imperfection. Quite to the contrary, the servant leader has to have a tolerance for warts and all, empathizing with the brokenness of the human condition and the inadequacies of all social systems, including that of the church. The ground at the foot of the cross is level. The pastor stands with his or her parishioners with the same need for forgiveness and grace.

The way of the Cross has always been a cruel contradiction, a scandal the world cannot understand. But for the Christian it always has been the way of redemptive love. Somehow it moves us from simply accepting statements or conditions that are logically at variance and assists us in discovering truth in the paradoxes of life, which appear on the surface to be contradictory but in reality hold a deeper truth. The Cross reminds us that we cannot simply accept the ambiguities, but must live through the contradictions of life, understanding that God's sacrifice in Christ was not "cheap grace" but "costly grace," given to us freely and without condition. In the words of Jesus: "If any man would come after me, let him deny himself and take up his cross and follow me" (Matt. 16:24).

Being a pathfinder, not simply a problem solver, is the fourth identifying mark of a servant leader. Pathfinders are problem solvers, able to sort through confusing issues, organize responses, and resolve differences. But pathfinders are more than mundane problem solvers. They have a vision of what the future should look like, how persons need to be motivated, organizations changed, and what values need to triumph.

Robert Frost, in his poem "The Road Not Taken," wrote:

> Two roads diverged in a wood, and I—
> I took the one less traveled by,
> And that has made all the difference.

Taking the less traveled path, the pathfinding servant leader moves beyond transactional forms of leadership to offer transforming leadership. James McGregor Burns notes that both types show respect for the mutual needs of leaders and followers alike. The transactional type usually focuses on an immediate need or goal, such as meeting the needs of the hungry and the homeless by some stopgap action. Transforming leadership would seek to reposition the agency or institution so that long-range needs are met, such as the creation of new jobs or low-cost housing.

"The result of transforming leadership," says Burns, "is a relationship of mutual stimulation and elevation that converts followers into leaders and may convert leaders into moral agents." Moral leadership, for Burns, is the highest form of transforming leadership. His description corresponds closely to that envisioned in the image of the servant leader. This moral leadership, he suggests "emerges from, and always returns to, the fundamental wants and needs, aspirations, and values of the followers," so that the moral leader acts to "serve ultimately in some way to help release human potentials now locked in ungratified needs and crushed expectations."[28]

The need for pathfinding leadership in church and society can hardly be overstressed. Robert F. Kennedy once said that "only those who dare to fail greatly can ever achieve greatly." Too many clergy are caught up in the mechanics of ministry—going about the routines of administration, preaching, calling in the hospital, etc., having lost the mystery of ministry—the transforming vision of God's grace. Churchly mediocrity not Christian ministry has become the norm. They neither fail greatly nor achieve greatly. Likewise too many laity have forgotten the relationship of their daily work to God's greater calling for peace and justice in this world. William Butler Yeats' grim comment on the modern world, in his poem "The Second Coming," bears repeating:

> The best lack all conviction, while the worst
> Are full of passionate intensity.

Pathfinders are not just facilitating conflict managers, but persons of passionate Christian commitment with a gift for inspiring others to work together toward achieving those commitments.

Each pathfinder is unique. Harry Chapin, for example, was a popular folksinger and was deeply committed to finding solutions to world hunger. His life was cut short by a tragic car accident in 1981, but his efforts were the inspiration that have led many other entertainers to get involved in aid for Ethiopia and to help the homeless in America. His own brother, Tom Chapin, has continued Harry's efforts to fight world hunger. When asked if he was filling his brother's shoes, Tom Chapin's quick response was that the last thing Harry would want is for somebody to fill his shoes. "What he'd want is that we fill our own shoes a little fuller."

Servant leaders set an example. Ministry proceeds out of the integrity of personhood. Lee Iacocca says that he took one dollar a year salary when he was rescuing Chrysler from bankruptcy. He did this not because he wanted to be a martyr, but so that when he sat across the table from the union president, he could look him in the eye and say: " 'Here's what I want from you guys as your share,' and he couldn't come back to me and ask: 'You SOB, what sacrifice have *you* made?' "[29] Likewise, people look to Christian ministers to set an example. They want leadership to reflect in their personal and professional lives significant signs of faith and spiritual renewal. People are offended by self-indulgent and self-serving ministers who have forgotten the servant shape of ministry. The values of leaders are more often caught than taught. Servant leaders who want to inspire others to capture their vision must incarnate their faith and ethics. Joseph C. Hough, Jr., and John B. Cobb, Jr., contend that

> the members of the churches expect their leaders to be deeply affected by and formed in the memory of Jesus Christ so that they, to some degree, embody their vision for the church and act out their own commitment to its ministry with comprehensive integrity. In a word, church members expect their leaders not only to be skilled practitioners but leaders with a Christian vision.
> . . . The greatest need of the churches is for pathfinders.[30]

The Legacy of a Servant Leader

When world-famous business tycoon Aristotle Onassis died, *Time* magazine ended his obituary on a harsh note. "He left little legacy—no monuments, no great acts of achievement other than a succession of business deals. All that remains is the memory of a vital, tough, self-made millionaire who clearly believed that living well was the best revenge."[31]

Though he left a fortune estimated at more than half a billion dollars, *Time* contended he left no legacy. Commenting on this devastating epitaph, columnist James P. Shannon, wrote: "To leave no estate is not shameful. To leave no legacy is tragic. Recall the awful words of Christ after the suicide of Judas Iscariot: 'It were better for him if he had not been born.' "[32]

In contrast to Onassis is the little-known story of Claudie Peyton, who defied medical advice and went to Africa as a missionary, becoming a legend in her own lifetime within Zambia. Experiencing a call from God to enter the mission field, she completed her education at the age of thirty-two, only to be denied missionary duty in

Zambia after a rigorous medical examination. The unanimous and considered opinion of the physicians was that she could not live for more that a year in Africa's climate. Two years later she headed to Zambia, where she remained for fifty-four years, returning to the United States only once. She founded an orphanage and personally adopted eighteen children. She epitomized John Wesley's admonition that a minister should be "ready to do anything, to lose anything, to suffer anything, rather than one should perish for whom Christ died."[33] Just before her death, Zambian President Kenneth Kuanda awarded Claudie Peyton the Zambian Medal of Honor in special ceremonies in Lusaka, Zambia's capital. The chief of the Tonga tribe buried her in the missionary compound. She left no estate, but what a legacy of love she bequeathed in Christ's name!

To paraphrase the kind of question Jesus asked at the end of the story of the good Samaritan (Luke 10:29-37), it might be asked: "Who do you think proved to be a servant leader?" And when we respond, "The one who showed mercy," we might just hear Jesus say anew to us, "Go and do likewise."

Chapter Seven

POLITICAL MYSTICS IN A PROPHETIC COMMUNITY

The bird with the thorn in its breast, it follows an immutable law: it is driven by it knows not what to impale itself, and die singing. At the very instant the thorn enters there is no awareness in it of the dying to come; it simply sings and sings until there is not the life left to utter another note. But we, when we put the thorns in our breasts, we know. We understand. And still we do it. Still we do it.

COLLEEN McCULLOUGH, *The Thorn Birds*

Most acts of ministry are quietly performed far from the press of public attention and the pressures of public policy. Occasionally, however, a Christian cleric is thrust into the spotlight of television cameras and the headlines of the world's journals. In recent years, Archbishop Desmond Tutu of South Africa has found himself in the heated vortex of political struggles and international tensions. Claiming no political ambitions of his own, Nobel Peace Prize winner Tutu has simply sought to proclaim the gospel and to oppose apartheid. Reflecting on his own role amid the turmoil, Tutu remarked, "I am the marginal man between two forces, and possibly I will be crushed. But that is where God has placed me, and I have accepted the vocation."[1]

Being a marginal person, caught between conflicting, controversial forces, has been the dilemma of prophets since biblical days. Seeking to be a channel of communication between the divine and the human has meant that the prophet has often run the risk of being misunderstood, resented, and crushed. The Cross symbolizes for the Christian layperson or clergy the ultimate risk involved in accepting the prophetic vocation.

In popular theology and church life the notion has arisen that being a prophet is synonymous with being a social activist, a life-style inimical to the spiritual life. Politics and mysticism are perceived either as polar concepts, antithetical to each other, or as

116

characteristics highly unlikely to be experienced side by side. Yet, Matthew Fox contends, people "want their spirituality to synthesize their personal and political lives and not prolong the schizophrenia that has so dominated spirituality in the West since Augustine and Pseudo-Denis."[2]

Likewise, the pastor-shepherd-of-souls role has been sharply differentiated from the task of the prophet. This misconception, says James D. Smart, would not have been understood by any of the biblical prophets, including Jesus. For them the "soul" was not a detached spiritual entity but the total self of a person. The shepherd's task was to care for all of the sheep; the prophet's responsibility is for the total life, personal and social, of humanity.[3]

The image of a political mystic as a contemporary expression of Christian ministry is indeed paradoxical or dialectical in the minds of many persons. It seems impossible to be engaged in both embracing inner spiritual disciplines and outer political developments. Christian ministers especially can appreciate the lament of E. B. White: "When I arise in the morning, I am torn by the twin desires to reform the world and to enjoy the world. This makes it hard to plan the day."

Yet that is the challenge of the Christian in ministry, uniting in person and practice a commitment to both meditation and action. Mysticism, broadly defined, points to the experience of personal communion or direct knowledge of God. It is popularly associated with the lonely individualistic quest of the monk or the nun, renouncing the world and abandoning social responsibilities. To the contrary, the interrelationship of mystical and social vision has been well-demonstrated through the ages. Mohandas Gandhi, Dag Hammarkskjöld, Abraham Heschel, Dorothy Day, Georgia Harkness, Martin Luther King, Jr., Albert Schweitzer, Howard Thurman, and Thomas Merton, to name but a few, fused mysticism and politics, creating what Martin E. Marty calls a "constant symbiosis between mysticism and politics."[4] Each of these persons has incarnated the truth to which Pascal pointed when he declared that a person does not show "greatness by being at one extremity, but rather by touching both at once."

The Political Mystic Metaphor

This movement from schizophrenia to symbiosis in our spiritual and political lives is most fully represented by the contemporary ministerial metaphor of the political mystic. *Politics*—understood as the total complex of human relations in society, not just those relating to public policy—is a broadly descriptive term. Combined with the image of an other-worldly mystic, a jarring incongruity in this metaphor forces us to look afresh at the meaning of ministry.

Typically in modern times we have pondered the "chicken or egg" question: Does mysticism lead to politics, or does the world set the church's agenda? Are we driven by Bible study into the world, or does life in the world push us to search the scriptures? The early twentieth-century French Catholic spiritual and political leader, Charles Peguy, argued that "everything begins in mysticism and ends in politics."[5] My suspicion is that no one normative response can be provided to these queries, for it depends on the personality, background, experience, and life stage of the individual in relation to the cultural circumstances and political movements of the time.

What is critical is not which comes first, but that the two dimensions not be polarized but held in tension. It is possible to be so involved in protesting social injustice that one misses celebrating God's gifts in the present life. The interior life of the spirit must be married to the institutionalized life of action. Christians who are committed to social transformation need not be joyless ascetics, but can be both life-celebrators and world-changers, affirming joy amid suffering even while searching for a humane and hopeful future.

The divorce of mysticism from politics can be the cause of many of the frustrations, pains, and disappointments of Christian ministries. In the best of all possible worlds, ministers are appreciated and rewarded if they share their lives generously with others, sacrifice themselves in reconciling efforts, and courageously risk their beings and positions out of genuine love. Unfortunately, too often thanks are left unexpressed; the very person you tried to help seeks to undermine your ministry; progress in your career appears stymied due to no fault of your own; and victories in social causes are beyond one's grasp. Ministers can feel emptiness, exhaustion, fatigue, and frustration. Cynicism casts its shadow across one's spiritual path.

Ultimately, ministry must be justified by faith, not by works. Our calling is to love people, to preserve the earth, and to share the good news of the gospel. Few of us will ever actually see "success" in our world-changing efforts or be publicly hailed for our lifelong commitments. What will sustain us in obedience and faithfulness will be the sense that God loves us, forgives us, and empowers us to face each new day's challenges. Politics without mysticism can be superficial altruism devoid of the energy of faith. Mysticism without politics can be spiritual narcissism barren of any fruits for our neighbors. By uniting the two, so long divided, the political mystic can walk with less fear among the explosive mine fields of life, ministering to torn and tattered victims while struggling for justice and peace.

This paradoxical image of the political mystic stands in rich contrast to the sterility of the professional model of ministry. The reductionistic tendency of the latter is to portray ministry as little more than the sum total of one's roles, function, knowledge, or skills. In James Glasse's language, ministry is "paying the rent"—that is, appropriately discharging the congregation's expectations and then doing what one pleases ("march for peace, fly an airplane . . . paint pictures, pursue advanced education, play a lot of golf, work for the denomination—almost anything").[6] A caricature of the clergy as professionals is that they can faithfully fulfill their duties in a forty-hour week and then be free to pursue another avocation. Ministry becomes more a career than a calling, more a vocation of works than of faith.

The political mystic metaphor resists reductionism. The Christian minister is a spiritual person, rooted in the ambiguities of action. The mystery of God's ministry is that an individual can be a channel for God's grace in this world. Urban T. Holmes spoke of the need for clergy to be sacramental persons, "mystagogues" who "lead people into the mystery that surrounds our life . . . deepening humanity's understanding of itself by word and action, by the nature of the priest's presence."[7]

The Christian minister is also a political person, grounded in a transcendent vision. Wallace M. Alston, Jr., imagines God as a "politician," using the politics of the church to do the divine will and work. The political action of the minister is a high and holy calling: "The constituency-building, association-nurturing task of a minister who is called to participate in God's renovating activity in the world."[8] The political mystic finds the transcendent in the commonplace, the profane in the holy.

Heresy of Separating Prayer and Politics

Scripture and theology do not support the heresy of separating prayer and politics. God is known through both contemplation and compassion. God can be experienced not only through meditation and the sacraments, but also through acts of justice and mercy. Latin American theologian Gustavo Guitierrez asserts:

> Mystical language is not contrary to prophetic language. We need both to talk about God. Prophetic language speaks about our commitment to others, of a Christian love which is universal but also shows preference to the poor. Mystical language speaks about God and is essential because without sensitivity to the grace of God, it is impossible to understand the exigency to be committed to the poor.[9]

God is often incognito, hidden in the poor. Persons in the first century did not expect God to be revealed in a little baby born of lowly status, nor did they suspect that God was "hidden in the despised man Christ," to use the language of Martin Luther. It seemed incredible that God should become public in Jesus, taking on human form and functions. Yet this is precisely what the Christmas story is all about: "The Word became flesh and dwelt among us, full of grace and truth," but in the words of the black spiritual: "We didn't know who you was."

An evangelical writer, Waldron Scott, says that this may come as "a surprise to those of us who think that experiential knowledge of God comes solely through quiet meditation and prayer."[10] He cites approvingly Jose Miranda's insight that " 'to know Yaweh' is thus all the more clear, almost like a technical term: to have compassion for the needy and to do justice for them."[11] Experiencing the Divine is not a platonic, abstract, intellectual exercise. Jeremiah, for example, asked the reprobate King Hallum:

> Did not your father eat and drink
> and do justice and righteousness?
> Then it was well with him.
> He judged the cause of the poor and
> needy;
> then it was well.
> Is not this to know me?
> says the Lord.
>
> (Jeremiah 22:15-16)

Jesus might even be viewed as a political mystic. The Gospel portrait of Jesus does not paint a schizoid at war with his spiritual impulses and prophetic instincts. Before he began his public ministry, he confronted dramatic temptation in the wilderness. Jesus was tempted to be something he was not—to forsake his intended mission as God's servant to become a wonder-worker, an economic messiah, or even a political mercenary. The temptation was to interpret his messiahship in terms of power, strength, and conquest, rather than to be God's political mystic. His temptation experience was a struggle for authenticity, for purpose, and for the foundations of his faith and existence. He rejected the demonic impulse to minister to human economic and political needs to the exclusion of his spiritual mission. In Jesus, contends Henri J. M. Nouwen, the mystical and the revolutionary ways were not opposites, "but two sides of the same human mode of experiential transcendence."[12]

The mystic in meditative reflection inevitably becomes a social critic, recognizing how the goodness of God's creation and intention has been distorted. In contemplating the stewardship of nature, one is startled by humanity's lemming-like suicidal drive to damage the earth's biosphere. The "greenhouse effect" of global warming means that we have polluted our own nests to the point of destroying in a few decades the earth's temperature system that evolved over a period of more than 4.5 billion years. When thinking of God's image of the lion and the lamb peacefully resting together, one is jolted by nations arming themselves against other nations to the tune of more than 800 billion dollars a year. The sublime beauty of the Sermon on the Mount contrasts to the Stone Age mentality of nuclear weapon stockpiling. The Star of Bethlehem seems to fade in the scenario of SDI. German theologian Jürgen Moltmann offers what could be a credo for the political mystic when he writes:

> That is why faith, wherever it develops into hope, causes not rest but unrest, not patience but impatience. It does not calm the unquiet heart, but is itself this unquiet heart. . . . Those who hope in Christ can no longer put up with reality as it is, but begin to suffer under it, to contradict it. Peace with God means conflict with the world, for the goad of the promised future stabs inexorably into the flesh of every unfulfilled present.[13]

Likewise, the most noble and other-centered politician inevitably unveils in his or her own actions, personal ambitions, and manipulative qualities worthy of confession and repentance. Reinhold Niebuhr often pointed to the haughty Pharisee and the humble publican who prayed in the shadows, "God, be merciful to me a sinner." But Niebuhr added an afterthought: How long would it be before the publican recognized his own humility, took pride in it, and thanked God he was not like other human beings?

The image of a political mystic is of one who unmasks the illusory qualities of both the critic and the human societal structure being criticized. Jesus understood both the potential and the limitations of human beings. Ripping off façades, Jesus upset the status quo. He did not enable the Israelites to become better adjusted and less neurotic in relation to the Roman dictatorial rule. In Susan Brooks Thistlethwaite's terminology, "Jesus was clearly not a pastoral counselor, but one in the prophetic line who denounced injustice and oppression on behalf of the poor."[14]

The Church as a Prophetic Community

The prophetic figure often is pictured as an isolated, thundering, sometimes eccentric character bent on denouncing sin and injustice. Out of step with the drumbeat of society, cartoon images project a scraggly hermit or a love-beaded hippie, waving a "repent-the-end-is-soon" sign or distributing age of Aquarius flowers. Many seminarians, having sniffed through the pages of Amos and Micah, have imagined themselves standing in cathedral pulpits denouncing corporate "fat cats" and government "power brokers."

This image is not without some justification; the path of the prophet in the Judeo-Christian tradition often has meant a lonely loincloth-and-locust existence. The voice of God or the will of the majority sometimes has been echoed first in a raving ecstatic minority of one. But the biblical tradition is far more complex than this stereotype. Various types of prophets have played parts in the development of the faith. Sometimes they have been referred to as diviners, seers, or visionaries. An integral part of Israel's public life, the prophets related both to government activity and to religious life. Far from being anti-establishment, some were court prophets, engaged by the powers that be. Certain ones have reinforced cultural and legal authorities, while others have been agents of radical transformation. Not all have been freewheeling entrepreneurs. Prophetic guilds have flourished on occasion.

The image of the political mystic reappropriates understandings of these various prophetic types and recovers this emphasis on the prophetic community. While not denying the value of the exceptional eccentric operating in an individualistic fashion, the focus is on the community sharing a prophetic vision and function. Prophets function within the traditions and theology of the people, using the language and history of the faith as a context for interpretation.

Except in the case of the Old Testament court prophets, prophecy was seldom a full-time occupation. To be a prophet was a calling, not a career. Amos prophesied only occasionally, usually engaging himself in a secular occupation. Jeremiah and Ezekiel were basically priests. Only later in the New Testament community did prophecy become the province of a specialized office in the church. This institutional professionalizing process, with the consequent dilemma of false prophets, may have contributed to the demise of the prophetic dimension in much of Christian history. Both the Hebrew and the Christian faith communities recognized the necessity of being arbiters of genuine prophecy. While many might claim to have a direct message from God, the responsibility rested with the community of faith to determine its authenticity and legitimacy. Without some degree of social support, isolates were branded false prophets or lunatics, bereft of influence and authority.[15]

Christian ministers are not individual practitioners but representatives of the community of faith. Ministers who understand themselves as political mystics do not hang up their shingles in the public policy marketplaces without regard for God's ecclesia. The responsibility of the political mystic is not just to live out vicariously the prophetic role in society for others, but to lead and to nurture a prophetic community for church members.

The church as a prophetic community is imperative for the political mystic. The danger of the mystical approach to religion is its tendency to make radical and absolute the individualist's experience, undercutting social discipline and responsibility to the community. As Robert N. Bellah and his colleagues have pointed out in *Habits of the Heart*, mysticism may be the most common religious expression today. People say, "I'm not religious, but I'm very spiritual."

> The cultural revolution of the 1960s was in part an upwelling of mystical religious feeling and the issues to which it made us sensitive—ecology, peace, opposition to nuclear weapons, internationalism, feminism—are still very high on our agenda. Yet the particular distortions to which the mystical type is prone are also more than evident: its inner volatility and incoherence, its extreme weakness in social and political organization, and above all, its particular form of

compromise with the world—namely, its closeness to the therapeutic model in its pursuit of self-centered experiences and its difficulty with social loyalty and commitment.[16]

The idea of a prophetic community, or public church, committed to the common good, is a needed corrective to the excessive individualism of religious prophets and mystics.[17]

It is at this point that the church is often its weakest. Congregations usually are resistant to becoming prophetically engaged in public policy questions. Peace education remains a neophyte in most local churches. Hunger task forces, laboring for neighborhood pantries and soup kitchens—incredibly good as they are—fail if they refuse to address the structural societal problems and priorities that prompt poverty and malnutrition. In white-dominated denominations in the United States, the fear of mixing politics and religion is paralyzing, as faith community after faith community retreats into the "private" realms of self-actualization and family. Doing so separates the church from the voice of God, for as Parker J. Palmer notes "public life is an arena of spiritual experience, a setting in which God speaks to us and forms our hearts with words we cannot hear in the private realm."[18]

In contrast are the "base communities" of Latin America, where Christians are restructuring the church into prophetic communities struggling against oppression and fighting for liberation. It was the prophetic black church that served as the foundation for the civil rights movement in the United States. The historic "peace" churches around the globe have been a constant prophetic community witness over the centuries.

Political mystics drink deeply from these community wells. When Desmond Tutu spoke at the World Methodist Conference in Nairobi, Kenya, he began by reciting a long list of colleagues in the faith who had suffered and been imprisoned in the struggle against apartheid. He asked his fellow white and black South African Methodist Christians to stand with him during the applause. With the advent of a national holiday in his honor, intellectual histories, and popular biographies paint pictures of Martin Luther King, Jr., as a charismatic prophet motivated primarily by Gandhian philosophy, Boston personalism or political realism. Often overlooked is the source for the spring waters of his strength and inspiration: the black church as a prophetic community.

Dennis J. Geaney, a Roman Catholic priest in Chicago, believes the parish is the ideal place to initiate a peace and justice movement.

Designed not only to renew the local church community, neighborhood, and city, the prophetic parish, as Geaney envisions it, affects national and international levels of church and government. His dream of a prophetic parish is not cast in terms of the New Right or the Old Left of American politics, but rather

> offers comfort to those who accept challenge. It binds the wounds of those who suffer for justice's sake. The self-improvement parish whose narcissistic goals are to make everyone feel happy is not the parish that proposes happiness by reaching out to the poor, the grieving, the peacemakers, the people who lay down their lives for justice's sake. The prophetic parish is the parish that writes the beatitudes into its charter and uses them as the measure of its fidelity to the demands of Jesus.[19]

Increasingly, major denominations are recognizing the need for the church to be a prophetic community. Speaking on every conceivable controversial issue, however, does not equate with being a prophetic community. For many years church organizations, bureaucracies, conferences, and the like have engaged in "resolutionary Christianity"—that is writing resolution after resolution on an endless stream of topics. This style of political involvement has had minimal public policy effect, since it is evident to all concerned that the issues addressed have only been superficially examined, and constituency support is nearly non-existent. Likewise it has had virtually zero impact on the church community itself, since, with the exception of a brief debate, the issues have been forgotten as people headed down the hallway or grabbed the next airplane. The community of faith often has not struggled over time with these questions in prayer, in study groups, in sermons, or in reflective statements of theology and ethics.

In recent years, an encouraging new model has been emerging. Pioneered by the Roman Catholic bishops in the United States in the areas of the arms race and the economy, the United Methodist episcopal leaders adopted a similar strategy in preparing their document *In Defense of Creation: the Nuclear Crisis and a Just Peace*. Instead of whipping off another resolution, the church leaders developed their statements after extensive research, public hearings, "expert" testimony from opposing perspectives, and internal debate. Strategically mass media attention was focused on the processes and pronouncements. In the case of the United Methodists, the documents were read by each bishop at every annual conference, study guides were distributed to each pastor, and each congregation and seminary was urged to reflect and respond. Adopting, in essence, the political mystic stance, the United Methodist bishops contend that "peace-making is ultimately a spiritual issue," and they urge Christians to exercise a "political ministry" defined as "the positive exercise of their God-given power in the political arena."[20]

In the context of the church as a prophetic community, the Christian layperson or cleric who adopts a political mystic self-understanding can function not as an individual in isolation but as a member of a movement grounded in the purposes of God and in solidarity with others committed to peace and justice. Networks of persons who see humanity at risk and the earth in peril are discovering ways they can make a difference in public policy.

Political mystics populate Christian parishes everywhere. Harvard psychiatrist Robert Coles speaks of "strangely exalted lives—persons who may be uneducated and poor and yet be morally decisive."[21] Beyond the celebrities—like Archbishop Tutu, Mother Teresa, or Dr. William Sloane Coffin, Jr.—are ordinary persons who live out extraordinary commitments. Two such laypersons are Molly Rush, a Pittsburgh homemaker and grandmother, and Tom Seymour, a middle-aged former employee of Rockwell International of Columbus, Ohio. Molly invited possible imprisonment when she participated in an action designed to damage nuclear warheads at a General Electric plant. For her, prayer and organizing against the weapons was not enough. "We must directly confront the nuclear arms race with our bodies." Tom Seymour left his job after twenty-three years when he learned he was working on a military system designed for a first strike. He determined that his conscience demanded he resign and work for peace rather than death even though he was responsible for supporting his wife and seven children.[22]

What might happen if this understanding of Christian discipleship were encouraged and nurtured? Teilhard de Chardin once suggested that "Some day after mastering the winds, the waves, the tides and gravity, we shall harness for God the energies of love. And then, for the second time in the history of the world," said de Chardin, humanity "will have discovered fire." The pentecostal fire of political mystics in prophetic communities might inflame imaginations and provide new identities for Christian ministers, as well as spark a new sense of urgency for serving humanity and preserving the globe.

No Hitchhiking on Another's Spiritual Journey

In Peter Ustinov's drama *Beethoven's Tenth*, a resurrected Beethoven evaluates a young composer, Pascal Fauldgate. Beethoven tells the musician that there is nothing wrong with his technique. The problem is that "you have nothing to say, and you say it quite well." Likewise, it doesn't matter how eloquent the sermon is if the preacher has nothing to share. Ministry is not just a matter of gifts and graces; it also has to do with faith and the fruits of faith. The questions John Wesley asked his preachers in 1746 still need to be raised:

> Have they gifts, as well as grace, for the work? Have they a clear, sound understanding; a right judgment in the things of God; a just conception of salvation by faith? Do they speak justly, readily, clearly?
>
> Have they fruit? Have any been truly convinced of sin and converted to God, and are believers edified by their preaching?

The political mystic understands that one cannot live on borrowed faith alone. No one can hitchhike on another's spiritual journey. We can have companions along the way, but ultimately each minister must live and die by his or her own faith experience. The intimate association with the Divine is a self-transcending, all encompassing moment of mystery never quite analyzable or communicatable. Touched by God's grace, we are never quite the same, even when the absence of God seems stronger than the divine presence.

The contemplation of God is good in and of itself. One need not commend a life of devotion for utilitarian reasons. Contemplative prayer, however, is practical; it is divine therapy for the human condition. The testimony of the mystics is that the contemplative vision of God leads to "metanoia," a conversion of the heart. Such a conversion, argues William Johnston, must expand the social vision. Johnston calls for conversions to poverty, to peace, and to justice, giving up self-made security, living the way of compassion, and trusting in God. [23]

The immediacy of the mystic's experience of God has a sustaining power among the struggles and defeats of pastoral and prophetic action. It is no wonder that the great social and political activists of the Christian faith have always been women and men who have cultivated the spiritual arts. Prayer and politics were inseparable. Often these political mystics have known the intimacy of suffering.

127

Having wrestled, like Jacob, they emerge with a limp and speak the language of Job.

> I know that thou canst do all
>   things,
>   and that no purpose of thine can
>   be thwarted.
> "Who is this that hides counsel
>   without knowledge?"
> Therefore I have uttered what I did
>   not understand,
>   things too wonderful for me, which
>   I did not know.
>
> (Job 42:2-3)

Martin E. Marty has observed "that the religious person and community cannot dip into the endowment and live off the interest and the principal of a spiritual capital in which they did not invest.[24] One, can, however, benefit significantly from devotional disciplines and reading the great mystics. Becoming soul friends with the spiritual masters can provide needed illumination along ministry's way. My own mentor, Walter G. Muelder, wrote in his Boston University *festschrift* that mystics of the East and West

> have helped me in self-examination, in sorting out motives, in ecumenical understanding, in handling personal attacks, in radical dissent from established institutions, in awareness of the spiritual continuity in the Christian tradition, in distinguishing genuine from superficial piety, and in developing the trust which lies at the heart of faith . . . for the life of devotion is both serenity and struggle.[25]

Bridging the gap between the human and the divine, the finite and the infinite, the now and the "wholly other" is an uncertain and unending quest. The moments most of us feel close to God are relatively few, and the times we would claim to have had religious experiences are relatively far between. The most famous political mystics of the church have acknowledged that they, too, have known what Saint John the Divine called "the dark night of the soul" and what contemporary psychologists might call "burnout." The struggle for spiritual wholeness has always been a time of wrestling with the limitation of one's own inner self and what we understand to be the perfection and expectation of God.

God, for the political mystic, is not to be found only in private or community prayer, but by plunging into the agonies and anguish, the quagmires and quicksands of life. In Sean O'Casey's autobiography, *Rose and Crown*, there is a delightful Irish argument about God. When the question is pushed whether God is a Catholic or a Protestant, the answer is neither. Instead, O'Casey responds, God

> may be but *a shout in the street.* . . . When God is a shout in the street, the shout is never a creed. . . . It might be a shout of people for bread, as in the French Revolution; or for the world's ownership, as in the Russian Revolution; or it might just be a drunken man in the night on a deserted street, shouting out Verdi's *O'Leonora*, unsteadily meandering his way homewards.[26]

In the past, too much talk about spirituality has stressed life-denial rather than life-affirmation. "Repression, not expression; guilt, not pleasure; heaven, not this life; sentimentality, not justice; mortification, not developing of talents," says Matthew Fox, have been "the earmarks of Western spirituality."[27] Prayer has been understood more in terms of withdrawal from life than engagement with life. Often, in search of the spiritual, we have turned private and inward or locked ourselves within the church walls, only to discover that others have found God in the vitality and voices of the street.

Dorothy Day is said to have seen Christ in everyone. She found Christ in bowery derelicts, in Nazis, in Communists, and in cardinals who admired Senator Joseph McCarthy. She loved everyone who detested everyone else. She refused to fit anyone's philosophy or political mold and thereby discovered spirituality in the secular and the divine in the mundane. Yes, for the political mystic God is a shout in the streets—the shouts of joy and of sorrow, the shouts of hope and of pain, the shouts of our neighbor and of the stranger, the shouts of the mighty and the meek—the shouts of the loud and "the least of these my brethren."

Freedom for Ministry

Prophetic mystics live with an inner freedom, accepting God's gift of ministry and rejecting congregational and cultural captivities. The prophetic mystic's first-hand religious experience, cultivated by the disciplines of prayer, Bible study, and meditation, provides a depth of religious assurance and trust that does not depend on external success or visible achievements. The liberty of living life and ministering in ·

obedient response to God's grace frees one from ordinary fears, such as lack of social approval, censure from one's superiors, imprisonment, suffering, and death. "This is why the most dangerous creation of any society," wrote James Baldwin in *The Fire Next Time,* is a person "who has nothing to lose."[28]

The political mystic's freedom is not bought at the price of individualism without supportive relationships. Tragically many clergy, who themselves are incredibly empathetic and understanding of others, do not feel free to express their vulnerabilities to others. Self-protectiveness, fear of admitting weaknesses and wariness of confidences being broken, inhibit a pastor's growth in grace. Fortunate is the person who has a spouse or friends who offer unconditional acceptance and persist in letting him or her know they love her or him.

Political mystics cultivate such relationships, depend on them, and seek to be spiritual friends for colleagues. Many have formalized relationships with others who become their spiritual directors. Those on the frontlines of social action find value in retreats at camps and monasteries. Cynicism and despair, prompted by the ugliness of urban decay, human exploitation, and cruel suffering, can depress the activist. Times away from scenes of activism are needed for absorption in the arts or nature or recreation, so that visions of God's beauty, holiness, and playfulness are not forgotten. Such disciplined patterns provide sustenance and strength to continue ministry's battles even when one's faith seems shallow and one's results appear meager.[29]

The Cross symbolizes the price God in Christ paid for our freedom. Ministers need to nail their personal fears and ecclesiastical egos to the tree and accept God's free grace. The powers of death cannot manipulate or control the political mystic. Christ's resurrection has removed the sting of death and set the Christian minister free.

Practically Speaking

Practically speaking, what are some implications if one adopts the political mystic metaphor as one's own? Ideas have consequences; images have impacts. "At the end of every act," said Henri Bergson, "dangles a worldview." How we think of ourselves in ministry makes a major difference in how we respond to life.

Take, for instance, the Reverend Will B. Dunn of Doug Marlette's

Kudzu cartoon strip. "It's a dirty job, but somebody has to do it," says Dunn as he yields to a revelation received while having tea with the Tadworths in their hot tub and begins a ministry to the "fabulously well-to-do." In this specialized ministry in Bypass, North Carolina, Dunn pursues a ministry to the wealthy and culturally advantaged, quite in contrast to what might be expected of a political mystic committed to a ministry of peace and justice.

A profile of practical implications for ministry would include at least five elements. *First, political mystics take spiritual formation seriously.* They are disciplined participants in matters of faith and ethics. Prayer and politics are at the center of their lives. They devote time and energy not only in their personal pursuit of these matters, but also in the creation and cultivation administratively of ways other persons can deepen their spiritual lives and widen their social conscience. In Fred Craddock's words, "How does one become qualified to talk of forgiveness, of penitence, of the death of Christ—read a good book on the subject? It is by obedience and sacrifice. Appropriation of the gospel is the minimum condition for approaching pulpit or podium."[30]

Prayer life is not considered peripheral to the practice of ministry. People respect ministers who keep informed about the critical issues facing humanity, offer their own witness and service, *and* who also identify with the troubled of this world through intercessory prayer. How refreshing it would be for laypersons to call the church office only to be informed that the pastor was in prayer and would call back later!

Second, political mystics do not accept sharp dichotomies between material and spiritual problems. The interrelated matrixes of life make simple distinctions impossible. For example, human hunger is not just a material or a spiritual issue. As the Russian Christian thinker Berdyaev once said: "If I am hungry it is a material problem; but if another is hungry, it is a spiritual problem."[31] At night when the hungry and homeless in America curl up on the doorway steps of urban churches, the political mystic recognizes a theological challenge to the basic precept of loving one's neighbor. It also sets the mission agenda for the community of faith that is more inclusive and action-oriented than just sending dollars to missionaries in Third World nations, as critical and necessary as these gifts are.

Lest there be any misunderstanding, adopting a political mystic language does not mean that one's time is likely to rotate exclusively between prayer and picket lines. Probably 85 percent of the time will be spent in preparing sermons, pastoral counseling, answering letters, organizing committees, teaching classes, writing newsletters, calling on prospective members, and the like. But these functions will be done differently, with a new perspective and purpose, if done from convictions of the political mystic. Battles for peace and justice may either begin abroad and then become resident on one's doorstep or be initiated by the prophetic community at home and then expand nationally and internationally.

Third, political mystics travel light with the world's goods and honors. Unlike the Reverend Bill B. Dunns of this world, the Sermon on the Mount rather than *The Wall Street Journal* sets their financial and political agenda. On rare occasions the Nobel Peace Prize is bestowed or an honorary degree is awarded to a political mystic, but for most their ministry goes unheralded and unrewarded. Vocational decisions and locations of service are dictated not by convenience, but by a commitment to respond to God's will and human need.

Recently I visited the Snowmass Monastery near Aspen, Colorado. With my Protestant prejudices, I long have looked skeptically at the monastic life. Vows of celibacy, poverty, and obedience seem questionable virtues. Yet in the presence of this small group of political mystics, I gained fresh insight into what faithfulness means. While I can hardly bring myself to advocate that the masses flock to the monasteries, I have been surprised by how often I found reassurance in my busy work week, knowing that there are those who travel light with the world's goods and honors—that there are people right now devoting hours in intercessory prayer for peace and justice—that at this moment Christian laypersons and clergy are contemplating God so as to expand their social vision and deepen their resolve for fighting the tough political battles.

Fourth, political mystics believe that dreaming is a practical art. Idealism and realism are not polarities but a continuum; dreams can become one's destiny. Asked whether he, despite his impatience at progress, is optimistic about the future of blacks in South Africa, Archbishop Tutu replies: "Oh, yes. As a Christian, I'm a prisoner of hope."

George Bernard Shaw once noted that most people who are failures claim that they are victims of circumstances. Those who succeed in this world are those who search out the right circumstances. And if they can't find them, Shaw said, they make their own. Political mystics believe in the revolutionary reshaping of situations, not being mired as victims in the status quo. Illustrative was the call to prayer in South Africa on June 16, 1985. Prayer made global news when Allan A. Boesak spoke against the evil of apartheid and pleaded:

> If the rulers will not hear the cries of the people, if they will not change, if they continue to prevent justice, let us pray them out of existence. God will hear our cry. . . . We do not believe in the power of violence, but we do believe in the power of prayer.[32]

When persons become cynics about the possibilities for human or social change, they limit the potentiality for conversion or transformation. Psychologist Sheldon B. Kopp noted that when he was a young idealist on the staff of what he described as a "state warehouse" for the mentally ill, he

> spent hours talking to hopelessly unresponsive, forgotten, catatonic men and women until eventually, in some, a spark of life returned to long-empty eyes. Only after age and experience made me more "realistic" did I achieve professional sanity, so that I was no longer able to be of any help to those poor captive souls.[33]

God forbid such professionalism among Christian ministers!

And, finally, the political mystics persist and protest not simply in order to change the world but to ensure that the world does not change them. It would be hopelessly naive to believe that all our Christian dreams for this world will come true in our time. The persistence of sin and evil are too overwhelming. The intransigent powers appear too dominant and fixed. Progress is never inevitable in this world, even for those of us who believe God is working in history to make human life more human. The genius of the political mystics, however, is that they never despair of the possibilities for human and societal transformation. Because they persist and protest, they preserve their own Christian integrity and lay the foundation for a more just and peaceful tomorrow.

A story from the Jewish mystics tells of one of the just men who came to Sodom, committed to saving the inhabitants from sin and punishment. Daily he wandered the streets and markets, preaching against greed and theft and falsehood and indifference. Initially the people listened and smiled patiently. Eventually they quit listening; he no longer amused them. People kept on killing, and the wise kept silent, as if there were no just man in their midst.

On one occasion, a child, moved by compassion for this strange preacher, approached him and asked: "Poor stranger. You shout, you expend yourself body and soul; don't you see that it is hopeless?"

"Yes, I see," replied the just man.

"Then why do you go on?"

"I'll tell you why. In the beginning I thought I could change humanity. Today, I know I cannot. If I still shout today, if I still scream, it is to prevent humanity from ultimately changing me."

The political mystics of the world—the Archbishop Tutus, Mother Teresas, Martin Luther Kings, Molly Rushes, Tom Seymours, and thousands of nameless others—are the just persons of our time, the voices of God in the streets and churches, shouting not only to change humanity but also to keep humanity from changing them.

Chapter Eight

ENSLAVED
LIBERATORS OF
THE RAINBOW CHURCH

*If you are neutral in a situation of injustice, you have chosen the side of
the oppressor. If an elephant has his foot on the tail of the mouse, and
you say you are neutral, the mouse will not appreciate your neutrality.*
DESMOND TUTU

Thomas Merton was a person of many contradictions. A monk
committed to silence and solitude, he wrote more than sixty books and
became an international religious figure. He withdrew from the active
life in the world to the peaceful hills of Kentucky; yet, he became a
patron saint of many social activists because of his profound and
penetrating insights into racism and militarism. A Roman Catholic
Trappist monk, he became recognized as a universal religious figure,
steeped in Taoism and Zen, claimed by some to be an incarnate
Buddha.

Living these contradictions, Merton discovered the grace of God.
Like us, he was pulled between opposing poles and conflicting
impulses.

> I have had to accept the fact that my life is almost totally paradoxical. I
> have also had to learn gradually to get along without apologizing for the
> fact, even to myself . . . I have become convinced that the very
> contradictions in my life are in some ways signs of God's mercy to me; if
> only because someone so complicated and so prone to confusion and
> self-defeat could hardly survive for long without special mercy.[1]

Christians from all walks of life can draw strength and hope and
courage from Merton's words, praying that our contradictions
somehow are signs of God's mercy. Life is ambiguous; most of us
know that surely we are neither what we ought to be nor even what we
want to be. We are frequently perplexed as was Paul: "I do not
understand my own actions. For I do not do what I want, but I do the

very thing I hate. . . . For I do not do the good I want, but the evil I do not want is what I do" (Rom. 7:15, 19).

On Being Enslaved

Occasionally people seek to stop the world and withdraw to a seminary, anticipating purity and perfection. Disappointment awaits. They are likely to find a president living in the suburbs preaching about social action, faculty teaching liberation theology but living in comfort, and others espousing the values of love and compassion while quarreling with colleagues. The tone of a local congregation never quite matches the theory of what a church ideally should be. Reportedly a clash over how the money awarded with the Nobel Peace Prize should be distributed undermined the effectiveness of the joint Protestant-Catholic peace movement in Northern Ireland. At every step the contradictions of life claim us, and the paradoxes of faith plague us.

As Christian ministers, we experience not only the web of personal contradictions but also the social dimensions of sin. Illustrative, says theologian Delwin Brown of The Iliff School of Theology, are the world's economic systems. In the United States 60 percent of all productive assets are controlled by two hundred corporations, owned by less than 5 percent of the population. Visitors from another planet undoubtedly would conclude that our national and global systems need fundamental and immediate change. Not only external forces but also elements within us permit these systems to control us.

First World Christians are enmeshed in structures that often keep others poor. Despite the difficulty such a situation poses for effecting change, Brown says that is not the deeper problem. Rather it is how our "thoughts, feelings, and actions" are controlled by these economic principalities and powers. Speaking theologically, he asserts:

> In a factual sense, we are the enemies of freedom, and enemies of the God of freedom. We wish that we had never settled into these comfortable structures of inhumanity, although they grew up out of our own wills, but now that we are here we do not move beyond them to new forms of social and economic organization where freedom and justice are more nearly one. St. Augustine said that we willingly enter the bondage wherein we unwillingly find ourselves. It is also true that

> we *willingly remain* in the bondage wherein we unwillingly find
> ourselves. We wish we were not here, but we choose to stay.[2]

Restructuring the earth's economic systems is beyond the scope of this book and my competence. Too many of our economic "fixes" actually deepen the chasm between the rich and the poor. Supply-side economics has been described as "feeding the horse so the sparrows can eat." Other approaches can be hopelessly utopian. No economic ideology dare be baptized as Christian. No absolute transformation of material nature or human nature is possible. The ministry of enslaved liberation does not require a panacea for all of life's problems but a willingness constantly to wrestle with these problems in the light of Christian imperatives of love, justice, equality, and freedom. Enslaved liberators accept Ernst Troeltsch's classic words: "Faith is the source of energy in the struggle of life, but life still remains a battle which is continually renewed upon ever new fronts. For every threatening abyss which is closed, another yawning gulf appears."[3]

In the bondage of life's assigned and self-chosen contradictions, we know with Thomas Merton that we "could hardly survive for long without special mercy"—the grace of an infinitely loving God, who offers forgiveness even when we feel unforgivable and strength even when we seem too weak to seek transformation for our lives and our world.

Central to Christian ministry is how we wrestle with the contradictions of life. Parker J. Palmer suggests that sometimes "the contrast between God and world is so great that we abandon the spiritual quest," accepting the shadows of our life, because we can't stand to bring light into our darkness. "For others," says Palmer, "the tension is resolved by disowning the dark world and trying to live in a bright but private realm. We hold the world at a distance and seek out situations which satisfy our need to stay 'pure.' " But neither of these approaches is satisfactory for "we remove ourselves from the great dramas of life where God and world interact, where contradiction abounds."[4] The demonic danger to Christian ministers, both lay and clergy, is a privatized spirituality, lacking moral outrage at social sin.

For Christian ministry the way of the Cross has always been a cruel contradiction, but it also has been the way of redemptive love. Somehow it moves us from simply espousing or accepting statements or conditions that are logically at variance and moves us to discover paradoxes in life that appear on the surface to be contradictory but in reality hold a deeper truth. The Cross reminds us that we cannot simply accept sin and ambiguity, but must live through the contradictions of life. The Cross reinforces our understanding that God's sacrifice in Christ was an act of incredible grace, given to us freely and without condition. The challenge of the Cross in ministry is undeniable. In the words of Jesus:

> If any man would come after me, let him deny himself and take up his cross and follow me. For whoever would save his life will lose it, and whoever loses his life for my sake will find it. For what will it profit a man if he gains the whole world and forfeits his life? (Matthew 16:24-26)

Biblical Base of Enslaved Liberator Image

Living with these contradictions is fundamental to Christian ministers who understand themselves as enslaved liberators. As followers of the Great Liberator, Jesus the Christ, Christians recognize that simultaneously we are enslaved to personal and social sin. Salvation does not exempt one from being a sinner; one is still enmeshed in the complications and ambiguities of life. What one does experience is the power of grace for forgiveness and fortitude to begin each day anew.

For the enslaved liberator the paradigm story of Christian scriptures is the episode in the synagogue of Nazareth (Luke 4:16-30). Just as Hebrews would lift up the Exodus story of Moses as being their paradigm of liberation, Third World Christians repeatedly point to this incident. For the Christian it becomes a normative mandate for ministry.

> The Spirit of the Lord is upon me,
> because he has anointed me to
>   preach good news to the poor.
> He has sent me to proclaim release
>   to the captives
> and recovering of sight to the blind
> to set at liberty those who are
>   oppressed,
> to proclaim the acceptable year of
>   the Lord.

Jesus, the bondage-breaker, becomes a model for every Christian who seeks to break free from personal prisons and cultural captivity.

The tendency is to domesticate Jesus and to make trivial his teachings. Those of affluence spiritualize references to the poor, the imprisoned, and the oppressed. Lost in the translation is "the acceptable year of the Lord," which really refers to "the Jubilee year" of Leviticus 25:1-24. Not pious rhetoric but a radical proclamation, Jesus' vision of a Jubilee year points to a time when social inequities created over the years will be wiped off, slavery will be abolished, and people will begin anew on the basis of a new social and economic equality. John Howard Yoder, writing on *The Politics of Jesus*, says that "the acceptable year of the Lord" was understood to be "a visible socio-political, economic restructuring of relations among the people of God, achieved by his intervention in the person of Jesus as the one Anointed and endued with the Spirit."[5]

Is it any wonder that this hometown boy should say "no prophet is acceptable in his own country" and end up having to flee because the people were filled with wrath and intended to throw him off a cliff? Would the world's bankers and politicians respond any differently today if an enslaved liberator were to announce a Jubilee Year for Third and Fourth World nations?

Those who adopt the image of the enslaved liberator have learned to read the scriptures from the perspective of the oppressed. By starting the hermeneutical task from the underside of history, new meanings can be discerned, which are easily overlooked if one reads from the stance of the establishment. Passages that seem just poetic to the reader who is conditioned by repetition actually have political implications of a revolutionary nature.

Take, for instance, the Song of Mary (Luke 1:45-55), which we usually call "the Magnificat." Robert McAfee Brown notes how selectively we listen and how efficiently we filter out the social dimensions of her announcement of Jesus' forthcoming birth. Christmas pageants typically portray the gentleness and harmony of the babe in the manger. Discordant notes, like a political perspective within a prayer, are overlooked.[6] Easily recalled are Mary's words, saying how her "soul magnifies the Lord" and her "spirit rejoices in God my Savior." Forgotten are her prophetic words about how God "scattered the proud . . . put down the mighty . . . exalted those of low degree . . . filled the hungry . . . and the rich has sent empty away."

Costa Rican biblical scholar Elsa Tamaz, in the *Bible of the Oppressed*, says that Mary's song does not speak "of individuals undergoing moral change but of the restructuring of the order in which there are rich and poor, mighty and lowly."[7] Latin American theologian Gustavo Gutierrez concludes from this passage that "the future of history belongs to the poor and exploited. True liberation will be the work of the oppressed themselves; in them the Lord saves history."[8]

Biblical interpretation done by the enslaved liberator tends to jar Christians more accustomed to European classic translations or North American middle-class renditions. Passage after passage takes on new power when viewed through a liberation lens. Good news, however, always means bad news to someone! Those of us entangled in the comforts of military-industrial complexes, using 40 percent of the world's resources while composing only 6 percent of the globe's population, squirm when scripture is read through Third World eyes.

Some of the most provocative biblical interpretations arise out of Nicaragua. Peasant Christians insist that *Savior* and *salvation* are better translated as "Liberator" and "liberation." Mary is viewed as being "subversive" to the social order. *Liberation* is defined as being "from sin, that is, from selfishness, from injustice, from misery, from ignorance—from everything that's oppressive." The "slaughter of the innocent" (Matt. 2:12-23) is being reenacted with the military activities of the United States in Latin America. The women at the Cross, especially Mary, are called revolutionaries.[9] In Ernesto Cardenal's thinking:

> She was a "revolutionary" and a "communist" before Jesus was born. Those ideas she had received from the prophets of the Bible. And those ideas Jesus sucked in with her milk. She shaped him, she influenced him, she contributed greatly to his being what he was and to his meeting the end that he did.[10]

Whether we concur or not in every translation is unimportant; what is essential is to realize how our own social/political roots may be distorting our understanding of God's Word today. By looking afresh at the old stories the Christian senses a new leading of the Spirit and a new empowerment for ministry. Thinking of Jesus as Liberator and the message of salvation as liberation introduces a powerful new element of evangelism and mission into the practical life of the church.

The People of the Rainbow

The "royal consciousness" of contemporary culture—the economics of affluence, the politics of oppression, and the religion of immanence and static triumphalism—were outlined by Walter Brueggemann in *The Prophetic Imagination*. Brueggemann calls Christian ministers to create an "alternative consciousness." The challenge is to stand within the culture but not be of it, to counter with a politics of justice and an economics of equality and a religion of God's freedom. This is not simply a matter of addressing specific social issues, but imagining and proclaiming a vision of a reconstructed society informed by Christian values. Borrowing his language, one might envision the task of the enslaved liberator being "to nurture, nourish, and evoke a consciousness and perception alternative to the consciousness and perception of the dominant culture around us."[11]

This task, however, is never an individualistic effort but emerges from a tradition and is sustained by a community. Jesus the Liberator did not blossom in splendid social or historical isolation. His roots were deep in the Hebrew tradition, as evidenced in the Nazareth synagogue when he quoted from the book of the prophet Isaiah. His reappropriation of his heritage in his reinterpretation of this passage is a model of both how to criticize the dominant establishment consciousness and to energize "persons and communities by its promise of another time and situation toward which the community of faith may move."[12] Surrounding himself with a motley assembly of disciples, Jesus created a new community for nurturing, nourishing, and evoking an alternative consciousness. "It is a measure of our enculturation," says Brueggemann, "that the various acts of ministry (for example, counseling, administration, even liturgy) have taken on lives and functions of their own rather than being seen as elements of the one prophetic ministry of formation and reformation of alternative community."[13]

This new liberating community might be called People of the Rainbow. Unlike previous associations this new community moves beyond the closed tribalism of the past to a technicolor openness to the future. Rather than simply embracing other legitimate metaphors for this new community, such as the Church of the Poor or the People's Church, the People of the Rainbow is deliberately chosen to emphasize the plurality of peoples, economic situations, theologies, and ministries involved. This new community, Delwin Brown writes:

> broke open traditional restrictions of sex, class, piety, and even family. "Who are my mother and my brothers? . . . Whoever does the will of God is my brother, and sister, and mother" (Mark 3:33, 35). Into this

community coming to be free were gathered "not only tax collectors and sinners" (Matt. 8:11; 11:19), but also liberation fighters (Zealots), daylaborers (fishermen), women (a social outclass), foreigners (Samaritans), the poor and diseased.[14]

A more pessimistic perspective might reject an image of bright colors. The condition of the human race does not justify such joy. Besides the racist problem of identifying some colors with goodness and others with evil, a community of enslaved liberators insist on seeing hope amid ambiguity. The multicolored splendor of God's love is manifest in joy embedded in pain, wisdom experienced in suffering, faith extended in doubt, and hope exposed in hardship. The People of the Rainbow become a living sacrament of history.

In the Judeo-Christian tradition, the rainbow is not only a fact of nature but also a symbol of faith. The rainbow appears twice in the Bible, first to Noah and then again in John's vision of God. After the catastrophic flood, a rainbow appeared to Noah as evidence of God's new promise: "And God said, 'This is the sign of the covenant which I make. . . . I set my bow in the cloud' " (Gen. 9:12-13). In the book of Revelation, around the throne of God is depicted "a rainbow that looked like an emerald" (Rev. 4:3). Commenting on this biblical imagery, German theologian Helmut Thielicke wrote that "No matter what happens, no matter how meaningless and stupid the things that oppress us, and despite every human view, our way leads from the rainbow of grace at the *beginning* to the rainbow of triumph at the *end*."[15]

This covenant relationship of God with humanity is at the imagistic heart of the People of the Rainbow. The rainbow symbolizes an everlasting and unconditional divine promise. This covenant of grace is of the essence of our Christian understanding. Life is not a dead-end street; the door of death is not marked "No Exit." No matter how deep the flood of troubles we experience in this life—be it severe illness, estrangement, divorce, abuse, death, or whatever—Christians live with the promise that God cares about each of us and that we will be sustained by a love that will not let us go.

The covenantal character of ministry binds us to God and bonds us to other ministers among the People of the Rainbow. Qualitatively different from a contractual one, a covenantal relationship does not require complete satisfaction of the interests of both parties. In the death and resurrection of Jesus, God has confirmed the covenant, despite the drastic contradictions of our lives. The Church is a covenantal community, and ours is a covenant ministry of grace. The primacy of spiritual and moral attainment can never replace the primacy of grace and faith offered as a free gift by a merciful God. Far from being a community of the morally pure, the People of the Rainbow know that they desperately need divine grace.

The kaleidoscopic colors of a rainbow are possible because of the refraction and reflection of the sun's rays as they pass through the prism created by a raindrop. The prism breaks up the sunlight into colors of the spectrum and sends colored light back to our eyes. Thus, for the Christian, the rainbow reminds us of a prism of pluralities that comprise life in its fullest. Christ's sunlight beaming on the human community creates the People of the Rainbow. A community of faith composed exclusively of persons of the same sex, nationality, race, class, or whatever is not the new rainbow community envisioned by Jesus. In Leonard I. Sweet's vision:

> A rainbow church embraces the entire climate of the human experience—whether the prevailing weather pattern of each soul is sunny and bright or damp and dreary. In this church, Christians are not afraid to believe or doubt or to believe and doubt simultaneously. Members are nurtured while they experience the vast sensorium of human emotions—from stumbling in the light to dancing in the dark, from cries of "how long. . . ?" to shouts of "Hallelujah!"[16]

The People of the Rainbow metaphor for the church also symbolizes the special responsibility people of faith have for preserving creation. The Bible uses the flood as a form of uncreation to express God's judgment on sinners and the salvation of the remnant on Noah's ark. The striking similarity of the Flood image and our own contemporary situation cannot be overstated. When we catalog the threats to human existence, it does seem that, as in biblical times, the creation is in reverse. The "good news" is that God decided not to destroy completely the earth. God entered into a covenant with humanity, ensuring that God would never again destroy all living creatures on the earth.

What frightens an enslaved liberator is not that God will now destroy the earth, but that humanity will annihilate every living being. As black Christians long ago taught us to sing:

> God gave Noah
> The Rainbow Sign:
> No more water—
> The fire next time!
> (James Baldwin, *The Fire Next Time*)

That fire, we have reason to fear, will be a global thermonuclear holocaust, or a warming of the earth's atmosphere that will radically change the climate of the earth. The People of the Rainbow are called to be God's people of *shalom*. Enslaved liberators reject the "royal consciousness" of our time and seek to substitute alternative visions because, in the words of Arthur Waskow:

> The first "species preservation act" is not the one passed by the United States Congress in 1977; it is the command of God to Noah. . . . Today we know there is no Ark large and varied enough to preserve all of the species that live upon the earth—except Earth itself. No fallout shelter, no hollowed-out command post under the Rocky Mountains, no cave filled with microfilmed corporate records can carry out *that* task. So the story pushes us in the direction of accepting conscious responsibility to preserve the Earth as a whole.[17]

Implications for Evangelism and Mission

In considering the various metaphors for ministry, it cannot be overstressed that one image is not being set over against another. These contemporary models do not seek to supplant the more traditional understandings of pastor, prophet, evangelist, and so forth. Rather, they supplement or complement these perspectives. One cannot be a wounded healer on Monday, a servant leader on Tuesday, a political mystic on Wednesday, an enslaved liberator on Thursday, and so on throughout the week. Rather, the collage of images is meant to offer a fuller portrait of what Christian ministry means on the eve of the twenty-first century.

The images chosen do not pretend to be exclusive of one another. Often overlapping implications can be drawn for practical ministry. The paradigm of the enslaved liberator certainly has consequences for one's preaching, pastoral counseling, community service commitments, and the like. Certain distinctive dimensions for evangelism and mission, however, can be distinguished and their meaning explicated.

First, enslaved liberators among the People of the Rainbow emphasize the evangelistic challenges of Christian ministry. Often forgotten in discussions of Latin American liberation theology is the central role of evangelism in their life and thought. Bringing the message of salvation or liberation to individuals and communities ensnared in the grips of personal and social sin is not an option but an obligation. Anders Nygren, as Bishop of Lund, once defined what he considered essential in the minister's calling. We are not primarily instructors and guardians of pure doctrine. We are not religious virtuosos imparting God-consciousness. We are not propagandists of particular world views and ideologies. Nor are we even primarily spiritual guides utilizing sound psychological and therapeutic insights. No, says Nygren, *"We are heralds*—that and nothing more. The Gospel which we have received from God constitutes our whole being as ministers."[18]

What has given evangelism a bad name is a kind of triumphalism masquerading as compassion; a "numbers game," resembling more a "body count" than a shepherd searching for lost sheep. Evangelism to many now conjures up the manipulative image of a "saw-dust trail," rather than walking with the suffering majority of the world.

Life experiences affect how we view the evangelistic task. When I was about six years old, my small-town church in Kimball, South Dakota, contracted its summer Bible school program out to a team of fundamentalist teachers from Chicago. Probably no one in the church had volunteered to teach. I can still remember vividly the day our instructor asked all of us first-graders: "How many of you are saved?" Only my cousin and I raised our hands. When queried again, and pushed as to whether we were "certain," we stayed firm in our conviction of salvation, even when all of our friends knelt down and were "saved" on the spot, thanks to the visiting evangelists.

This incident haunted me during my childhood years, causing me to wonder whether I should have kneeled just to be safe. Why had my cousin and I been so stubborn? Eventually I came to understand that I had been blessed with a loving home and that my parents had, by example and precept, given me what might be called a "developmental" sense of salvation. The love of God had been communicated to me by a family and by a community of faith that did not treat words as if they were magical incantations but by actions that gave me a sense of identity and assurance.

To this day I remain skeptical of many so-called evangelists and the tricks of their trade. My belief in the saving, liberating power of Jesus Christ and the good news of the gospel does not equate with "born again" dogmatists or the "electronic evangelists" who often dilute the milk of the faith and skim the cream to pay for their adventures. But I am deeply committed to an authentic evangelism that seeks to proclaim and live out the gospel in ways that can positively and creatively meet the urgent needs for personal Christian development, church growth, and human justice.

Personal experience alone should not dictate one's understanding of the evangelistic mandate. In the New Testament, to evangelize literally means "to proclaim the good news" of Jesus Christ and the kingdom of God. A winsome and passionate sense of evangelism must permeate the ministry of the enslaved liberator. More than thirty-five years ago the great Sri Lankan Christian D. T. Niles, suggested that "evangelism . . . is one beggar telling another beggar where to get food."[19] Evangelism, understood in this manner, is a response of love to the neighbor, a caring concern to share the riches of life, a humble assertion of help. It is neither a "hell-and-damnation" threat nor an imperialistic action motivated by a sense of spiritual superiority. Rather it is an invitation for others to move away from the malnutrition of the soul and to feast on the life-giving nourishment of the gospel of Jesus Christ.

The biblical mandate for evangelical witnessing must be incarnate in the life and ministry of the enslaved liberator. The Word was made flesh in Jesus the Christ. It is not simply a matter of verbalization—of proclaiming the good news—it is also a matter of one's life's becoming the gospel. Gandhi often remarked that the idea of Christianity was appealing; it was what he failed to see in the lives of Christians that prompted him to remain a Hindu. The individual witness remains central. Illustrative is the cartoon picturing two teenagers talking. One says: "When I was twelve years old, I was almost converted by a church movie, but the projector broke down." Persons are brought to new relationships with Christ not by a technology of innovation but by a theology of incarnation.

Jose Miguez Bonino tells of meeting an old woman in Montevideo, Uruguay, where Emilio Castro, General Secretary of the World Council of Churches, had been pastor fifteen years earlier. She approached Bonino somewhat mysteriously and asked: "You meet Emilio Castro sometimes?"

"Yes, of course," Bonino replied, "I'll be seeing him in a few weeks."

"Please, greet him for me. You know, he was *my* pastor, he introduced me to Jesus." Noting Castro's distinguished career in Latin America, his courageous and controversial struggles for justice, and his leadership of the global ecumenical movement, Jose Miguez Bonino concludes his tribute by saying: "But when speaking about Emilio, not a few will first of all say: 'He was my pastor; he introduced me to Jesus.' "[20]

The enslaved liberator among the People of the Rainbow understands evangelism as offering the gospel of liberation for the whole person and the whole of the created order. Expanding membership is imperative, but the "homogenization" principle of church growth, which creates congregations on the basis of race, class, and other social criteria, is anathema to a diverse rainbow church.

After decades of rejecting the "social gospel," evangelicals have participated in a great "reversal," now rejecting as false and unbiblical the vertical/horizontal dichotomy that separated the "spiritual" and "social involvement" concerns. An evangelical statement, the Lausanne Covenant, declares:

> The message of salvation implies also a message of judgment upon every form of alienation, oppression and discrimination, and we should not be afraid to denounce evil and injustice wherever they exist. When people receive Christ they are born again into his kingdom and must seek not only to exhibit but also to spread its righteousness in the midst of an unrighteous world.[21]

On the other end of the theological spectrum, Christians of a more liberal persuasion are recovering a renewed sense of personal evangelism. Rather than being "fishers" of men and women, many have become only "keepers of the aquarium."[22] Serious leaks have resulted in continued membership drains, stimulating serious reexamination of what is happening in local congregations. The United Methodists, for example, were shocked to discover recently that 16,000, or 42 percent, of all their congregations reported they had no constituency lists, not even a set of names scribbled on the back of an envelope. Some 25,000 of the 38,000 congregations conducted no new member or confirmation classes. One-third of all the United Methodist churches did not baptize a single person in a given year. The gap could not have been more appalling between actual evangelistic practices and the gospel mandate to "Go therefore and make disciples of all nations, baptizing them . . . teaching them to observe all that I have commanded you" (Matt. 28:19-20).

The preacher stepping into the Casper, Wyoming, United

Methodist church always sees a gold-plated sign: "Sir, We Would See Jesus." Now that the church has been served by a woman pastor, the language is outdated, but the imperative has not lost its power. Enslaved liberators know that the people expect that ministry will not just be pious platitudes or even thoughtful theologies, but will point to the light in the darkness of life: Jesus the Christ.

Second, enslaved liberators among the People of the Rainbow affirm a missional understanding of God's preferential option for the poor. The epigram of Emil Brunner is the slogan of the People of the Rainbow: "A Church exists by mission as a fire exists by burning." This inseparability of faith and action is fundamental to the Christian life. The People of the Rainbow exist to give themselves away in loving service. With Dietrich Bonhoeffer, they live a worldly spirituality,

> taking life in one's stride, with all its duties and problems, its successes and failures, its experiences and helplessness. It is in such a life that we throw ourselves utterly in the arms of God and participate in his sufferings in the world and watch with Christ in Gethsemane.[23]

With God's grace, this mandate for mission, coupled with a passion for evangelism, empowers the Christian to cast off the chains of slavery and to participate in God's liberating activity in the world. Central to that mission is an understanding that the ministry of Jesus was oriented to the needs of the poor and oppressed. The biblical bias is toward the poor, a prejudice rejected by the rich of this world. Emilio Castro has helped the ecumenical church to understand, in Johannes Verkuyl's words,

> that the biblical message of salvation speaks not only of the complex of human *sin* and God's *grace* but also of that of human *misery* and God's *mercy*. Those who are discriminated against, the oppressed, the hungry, the naked, the "sinned-against," the victims of unjust structures are the special objects of God's attention and have a special place in God's heart; for that reason the poor should also have a special place in our attention and hearts.[24]

To join in God's activity in this world is to identify with the sufferings of the poor and oppressed. Harvard psychiatrist Robert Coles, commenting on his extensive interviews with the poor, especially children, in the United States says: "I don't want to sound melodramatic, but I think that Jesus still lives among the poor of this world; if he lives any place he lives among sharecroppers and tenant farmers and the black people of this country. [25]

Liberation theology and ethics do not begin in abstract theories, dogmatic theologies, or even infallible books. They begin with a commitment to the suffering, struggling poor of this world who refuse to accept passively the misery imposed on them. The *Global 2000 Report* noted that "Today, some 800 million people live in conditions of absolute poverty, their lives dominated by hunger, ill health, and the absence of hope. By 2000 . . . their number could grow to more than one billion." [26] *The New York Times* estimated that there were thirty-five million poor in America (meaning a family of four with income less than $10,178 per year). [27] These are not just staggering statistics, they are sacred human beings made in the image of God.

The pornography of poverty experienced by the majority of the human family makes one wonder if we should not translate John 3:16 to read: "For God so loved the poor, that he gave his only Son." God in creative love gave the globe an abundance, but human schemes of distribution and destruction have thwarted God's purposes. "There is enough for everyone's need, but not for everyone's greed," said Mahatma Gandhi. By insisting that the poor are the starting point for Christian mission, enslaved liberators concur it is intolerable that:

> two thirds of the human family should go to bed
> hungry every night,
> 15,000 people should starve to death every day,
> 20 percent of the human family should control 80
> percent of the world's resources,
> human dignity should be denied to most of the
> human family even if they get enough to eat. [28]

This "preferential option for the poor," as the Latin Americans call it, summons enslaved liberators not to idealize poverty but to enter into solidarity with the poor to protest its dehumanization. Post-liberation Christians in the People's Republic of China caution against idealizing poverty. Chinese Bishop K. H. Ting, speaking after the excesses of the Cultural Revolution, declares that we should

> hesitate to think that the poor, just because they are poor, are necessarily the bearers of truth and that the mandate of history is necessarily in the hands of the poor in their struggle against the rich. To be poor is miserable. The poor deserve justice. But poverty is no virtue, unless voluntary, and does not always bring with it wisdom. To make a

messiah of the poor just because they are poor and to pit the poor against the rich . . . is neither Marxist nor Christian.[29]

Unlike the historic institutional church, the People of the Rainbow do not naturally side with the rich and console the poor with promises of heaven. Yet, the mission is not to exclude the non-poor. As the poor of this world are liberated, the enslaved rich will also be free from being oppressors. New relationships of equality and justice will be possible. The church for centuries has always begun with a preference for the non-poor, resulting in an alienation with the masses.[30] Using Bernard Dumas' imagery, Joseph C. Hough, Jr., and John B. Cobb, declare that:

> In this way not only will the church be the hope for the poor, but the poor are the givers of hope for the church. As Dumas has put it, the two faces of Christ, the poor and the church, cannot remain alienated and expect to be whole. It is only when they are together, fully with each other and for each other, that the faces of Christ are united and the body of Christ really becomes one.[31]

Ministry as an Embattled Vocation

Ministry is an embattled vocation throughout the world. Faithful obedience and witness to Jesus Christ in the midst of oppressive political and social structures have resulted in a new generation of Christian martyrs. Unknown is how many Christians languish today in prison because of their evangelistic passion or their mission mandate. Torture has grown more sophisticated and more painful since the days of the lions in the arena. Like the babe in Bethlehem, enslaved liberators often are viewed as threats to established cultural and political totalitarians, and they are forced to flee contemporary Herods and become refugees in exile.

In countries like the United States and Canada, ministry is also an embattled vocation. Though not as drastic as imprisonment or assassination, the pain and anguish of those on the frontlines of Christian ministry are no less real. The price of prophecy remains high in most communities and congregations. Pastoral faithfulness can exact a tremendous toll. If you let it, the church will kill you! The personal and family stresses and strains in every parish are incredibly high. The casualties in terms of burnout, divorce, alcoholism, lost ministries, and even suicide cannot be measured. Perhaps this is why an opinion poll taken by the National Law Journal revealed that the clergy command the most respect in our society, but it also is the vocation the least number would recommend for their sons and daughters to enter.[32]

Much ministry occurs during the interruptions of life. The kingdom of God advances on a broken front. A disciplined, planned ministry is essential, but often it is in the unexpected, surprising or crisis moments of life that the metaphor of the enslaved liberator provides motivation and meaning, vision and vitality.

During the days I had set aside to write this chapter, I was twice interrupted by experiences that moved me away from theory to practice. First, a call came from a pastor who asked to see me. Assigned to a struggling parish, in the past year he has not always been paid even the minimal salary promised. Unbelievable pressures have included a divorce, foreclosure, and bankruptcy. He had felt incredibly separated from supportive relationships during this crisis period of ministry. His temptation for alcohol did not surprise me. After we visited, and he ministered to me with his caring love of Christ and the church, he asked me to help him by removing two large bottles of whiskey that a parishioner had given him. Beside the trunk of his car, I could hear Jesus teaching us to pray: "Lead us not into temptation, but deliver us from evil."

The second incident occurred when a late night telephone call informed me that a former visiting professor of theology and ethics at The Iliff School of Theology, Jorge Pantelis, had been imprisoned without charges in his home country of Bolivia. He had been identified with the church of the poor. The government was angered by clergy who were helping the families of thousands of miners who had been laid off when the government closed their mines.

Our seminary community was mobilized to exercise a political ministry, asking Amnesty International's intervention through their global urgent action network of concerned people, and persuading congressional leaders to make inquiries with the State Department and with the Bolivian government. More than two hundred Bolivian church, labor, and political leaders, representing the incredibly impoverished of that nation, were sent off to "concentration camps" in remote areas of the country. Miraculously, three days later Dr. Pantelis was released. What actually happened may never be known, but in the judgment of the United Methodist Bishop of Bolivia, this was "the direct result of pressure from the United States and the prayers of the people."

Exercising the ministry of an enslaved liberator is seldom so dramatic, but experiencing ministry as an embattled vocation is a daily routine. By appropriating the theology and implications of this metaphor, the Christian may be strengthened and sustained in the understanding that even though enmeshed in sin and evil structures in this world, one need not be of this world, but can seek to join in God's liberating ministry for all humankind.

Chapter Nine

PRACTICAL THEOLOGIANS IN A POST-DENOMINATIONAL CHURCH

When dogma collides with experience, when the people are those you love, you see with different eyes.
CAROL LYNN PEARSON, *Good-bye, I Love You*

A popular story distinguishes between practical theologians and systematic theologians. Systematic theologians are characterized as distant theoreticians who talk about God and make endless distinctions understandable only to the angels. On the other hand, practical theologians walk humbly with their God, practicing what they preach and effectively relating the gospel to people in their concrete situations of life.

Of course, such a stereotypical distinction is a distortion. In relation to God's activity in the church and in the world, seminary theology professors are not necessarily aloof nor are Christian practitioners inevitably attuned. The widespread perception of the disjuncture between theory and practice, particularly in theological education, however, lends credibility to this characterization. Too often, theology has been understood by both laypersons and clergy as an abstract discipline reserved for academics rather than as a reflective exercise open to all within the community of faith.

Rediscovering the Practical Theologian Image

It might legitimately be argued that the practical theologian image of ministry is neither contemporary nor paradoxical, in contrast to the other metaphors proposed in this book. Medieval theologians debated the question of whether theology was primarily practical or theoretical. Martin Luther declared that all true theology was eminently practical. Friedrich Schleiermacher, early in the nineteenth century, was the first to constitute practical theology as an academic discipline in a theological faculty. He believed that the fragmented parts of theology can be made an integral whole when all the parts are interrelated by virtue of a central organizing principle, namely, that of providing church leadership.

Despite this history the image of the practical theologian has only recently been rediscovered. A number of major volumes have been published, defining and explicating practical theology.[1] A new association of practical theologians has been formed. Increasingly conferences have been held to explore this theme. Renewed interest in this model of ministry has emerged in the theological schools. Liberation theologians in particular have made critical reflection on *praxis*, or "action," central to their thought.

The decline, if not the disappearance, of this metaphor for ministry was prompted by the false dichotomy between "pure" and "practical" theology, fostered in large part by seminaries that fashioned curriculums that separated the classical disciplines (Bible, theology, history, and ethics) from the applied disciplines (preaching, counseling, education, and administration). Theology itself came to be understood as just another discipline of academic study rather than the unifying foundation of clergy and lay education. The captivity of the churches and the seminaries to what Edward Farley calls the "clerical paradigm" or "clericalization of theology" has limited the image of the practical theologian to the professional responsibilities and tasks of the clergy alone.[2]

The new thrust is envisioning practical theology in a more comprehensive fashion, not excluding the traditional applied disciplines but incorporating them within the broader contexts of church and world. Ethics and the social sciences are intimately involved. Preoccupation with technique is balanced by critical reflection on what one is doing in the light of God's activity in human history. Instead of reducing practical theology to simple pastoral theology, or of focusing almost exclusively on the internal life of the church, the emphasis is on the life of the church in the world.

Reflective of contemporary interest in practical theology is the cultural phenomenon of bumper stickers. A rich resource has emerged in the bumper sticker theology of Christians on the highways—how much more practical can theology become than when it is reduced to a slogan and stuck on one's prized possession? A whole lexicon of theological topics is addressed, from divine power ("God made Notre Dame #1") to Christology ("If you love

Jesus, tithe. Any fool can honk.") to God's grace ("Christ died for our sins. Let's not disappoint him."). Social action themes are especially prominent, such as "You can't love your children with nuclear arms."

Beyond bumper sticker theology, and in a more serious vein, I find insight into contemporary practical theology by John Deschner's suggestion that "practical theology is not simply systematic theology applied!" For him "practical theology arises in dialogue with practitioners"—persons who are at the center of "praxis" or "action" in the church and world; Christian congregations who are seeking to live out the gospel in communities of worship, fellowship, and service.[3] Thus practical theology is public theology. In a pluralistic society, Don Browning argues, the practical theologian will

> enter an open and honest conversation with the secular educator, the secular mental health worker, the Marxist revolutionary, the local Jewish mayor, the feminist member of the municipal council, and the fundamentalist senator with his huge popular following.[4]

Practical theology is not just a set of applied disciplines but rather the attempt to relate theology, church, and world together in ways that seek to overcome the unfortunate chasms between theory and practice, thought and life, classic theological disciplines and applied fields of study, and the seminary and the local church. It addresses not only the congregational practices (worship, preaching, teaching, and so on), but also cultural practices that have ethical and religious implications (public policy questions, professional standards, societal prejudices, and so on).[5]

Practical Christian Thinkers and Reflective Practitioners

Joseph C. Hough, Jr., and John B. Cobb, Jr., have advocated that the church of the future require practical theologians as its ministers. This metaphor combines two images: the practical Christian thinker and the reflective practitioner. Stressing the need for ministers to be visionary pathfinders or problem solvers, Hough and Cobb insist that thinking be oriented to practice and guided by a deep sense of Christian identity. Issues such as global survival and human sexuality need to be addressed by persons who think from the perspective of what it means to be a Christian. The reflective practitioner not only thinks but also acts in accordance with what he or she thinks. Lest visions be only illusions, it is imperative that ideas be implemented, not simply as applied theory but through reflective practice that enables one to "recognize the theory implicit in the practice, to develop it in the light of the practice, and to improve the practice in relation to the improved theory."[6] Persons reflect both *in* practice and *about* practice.

The model for all Christian ministry is Jesus Christ. Jesus himself might be described as a practical theologian, uniquely integrating the dimensions of both a practical thinker and a reflective practitioner. Deeply versed in the Hebrew scriptures and traditions, he focused on praxis, responding to the common situations of life that he faced.

To the mob that was about to stone a prostitute, he reflected that those without sin should cast the first stone. To critics who asked who was the neighbor they should love, he told the scandalous story of the good Samaritan. Some might question how practical the ideas of the Sermon on the Mount were (or are), but certainly they represent creative and critical reflections on practical problems such as human grief, prayer, war and peace, and adultery. Repeatedly he declared, "You have heard that it was said of old," and then cited the established religious teaching. But surprising for his audience, he was prone to say, "But I say to you," thus introducing a new understanding or perspective more appropriate to this context of ministry.

Every follower of Jesus Christ, lay or clergy, is called to be a practical theologian. The obligation is to think, to inquire, to explore, and to ask critical questions. Theologizing is an integral part of being a believer. Tragically, many Christians seem to leave their brains outside the sanctuary and show little interest in relating their faith to their daily activities and political opinions. Some religious practitioners appear to have given leave of their senses. Spirituality has at times been confused with irrationality. As the wall poster reminds us: "Jesus came to take away our sins, not our minds."

The rediscovery of the practical theologian model is a summons for Christians to recover their intellectual capacities in ministry. Pietism has tended to reign supreme in Protestantism since the eighteenth century, a characteristic so tragic that Alfred N. Whitehead was prompted to write that "it was a notable event in the history of ideas when the clergy of the western races began to waver in their appeal to constructive reason."[7] By combining Christian identity with intellect, Hough and Cobb do not forsake the positive dimensions of pietism, but they do lay the basis for both a learned clergy and a learned laity.

Both are imperative if the church is to confront effectively the challenges of faith in the twenty-first century.

Theory and practice are united in the image of the practical theologian. Theology does not exist for its own sake; practice is not unrelated to theology. Christian statements of faith and ethics are not disembodied concepts, but reflect a God who was incarnate in Jesus the Christ. Theology must be tested by practice and practice modified by theology. As Paul Tillich argued:

> A theological system is supposed to satisfy two basic needs: the statement of the truth of the Christian message and the interpretation of this truth for every new generation. Theology moves back and forth between two poles, the eternal truth of its foundation and the temporal situation in which the eternal truth must be received.[8]

The persistent criticism of much theological education is that it trains persons *for* the work rather than *in* the work. Practical theologians do not succumb to such a simplistic criticism. Instead *in* each contextual situation they bring their existential knowledge of God along with the wisdom they have learned *for* the work in their studies of the Bible, church history, ethics, and so on. Drawing also upon academic understandings of the arts and sciences, they seek to analyze *in* each ministry context and frame their response accordingly. Reflective judgments regarding appropriate Christian action flow out of the creative interaction and decision making of each unique moment of ministry.

Rooted in a Post-Denominational Church

The ministry of the practical theologian cannot be understood apart from participation in the life of the church in the world. Conceivably the systematic or historical theologian might function only in academia, treating the community of faith primarily from the standpoint of either sociological distance or scholarly disinterest. But practical theologians are rooted in the praxis or action of the church and reflect upon that praxis in the light of the normative standards of the faith.

Obviously participants are related to distinct, concrete historical congregational realities. This includes a denominational affiliation, since that is the predominant pattern of global church life. Even the most ecumenically minded still operate from a denominational foundation. The World Council of Churches, for example, is not a supra-church, but an association primarily of denominational-type churches of Protestant and Orthodox persuasion.

Emerging from contemporary Christian life in the People's Republic of China, however, is a fascinating new phenomenon that provides an exciting, and possibly normative, new possibility for Protestants: a post-denominational church. The new post-denominational church corresponds closely to the four basic pictures of the churches portrayed in the New Testament. Paul Minear has described these images as the people of God, the new creation, the fellowship of faith, and the body of Christ.[9] No biblical analogy quite matches the denominational, bureaucratic model characteristic of most of the globe's churches.

In 1949 when the Communists came to power, the Chinese church was cut off from the historical "foreign" denominations that had developed there due to missionary efforts. In order to survive, it was necessary for the Chinese to discover new ways of church organization. When the missionaries were expelled, Protestants numbered about 700,000.

In response, the practical theologians of China, led by Bishop K. H. Ting have evolved over the past forty years a pattern of post-denominational church life, which holds together a broad diversity of Christians who formerly included Presbyterians, Seventh Day Adventists, Methodists, Anglicans, evangelical "Little Flock" members, and so on. During the Cultural Revolution, churches were transformed into factories, pastors were forced to do manual labor on farms and in factories, Nanjing Theological Seminary was converted into the headquarters of the Nanjing Red Guards (who destroyed 90 percent of its library). Bibles and hymnals were destroyed, and Christian witness and worship were restricted to homes or often just individual hearts.

Despite long periods of oppression and persecution, the Chinese church has not only survived, but it actually has thrived as well. Resurrection again has triumphed over Crucifixion! An authentic liturgical and hymnodical revival has been experienced. A hymnal has been published with 25 percent of the songs being of new Chinese origin. A new press has been built to publish Bibles. Ten seminaries are now operating with capacity enrollments. Lay theological education is flourishing. People of all ages, but particularly the young, are being drawn to Christ. Protestant membership in the late 1980s is conservatively estimated between three and four million persons. Some missiologists predict that Chinese church growth will escalate rapidly in the next century to the point that the Chinese church will have a predominant impact on Western Christianity.

In 1987, during a visit to the churches and theological schools of China, I was deeply impressed by the vitality of the spirit as manifested in the evangelistic witness and growth of the churches as well as the ingenuity of its leaders as they struggle to minister in a secular and atheistic society. When one experiences the Chinese church today, one senses that it must be similar to life in the apostolic church; it is like revisiting the New Testament church. It seeks to be a united church, but it has not yet totally agreed upon common theological doctrines, orders of ministry, structures of mission, and the like. Understanding itself as a post-denominational community of faith, it seeks to transcend the narrow denominational histories that were imported to China. In an extraordinary ecclesial experiment, it is seeking to hold together in genuine ecumenical respect Christians who historically and theologically have been light-years apart.

Reverend Ms. Wang Shengcai, pastor of the Zhengshou Christian Church, tells of the trauma she experienced when learning that her former Anglican church building, due to road construction, had to be demolished and a new one constructed. She discovered that she had a real emotional attachment to it and the vestiges of denominationalism associated with the structure. She came to realize, however, that the demolition actually was a way of tearing down "walls between people." Yet she was overcome by emotion when it happened, prompting her to write that:

> It was God's will not just to tear down a material building, but the tearing down of the intangible hold of denominationalism within me. God wants to build a new church without any of the former denominationalism. I made a promise to God that I would tear down these sentiments, and never again emphasize this to be a "former" Anglican church. Thinking of the love of God, I wept with tears of gratitude.[10]

Practical theologians recognize within themselves "the intangible hold of denominationalism" even as they witness to a church that transcends such bias. No matter how much we love our denominational homes, none of us dare to be triumphalists about our persuasion, for we realize its own limited and sinful structures. In

H. Richard Niebuhr's famous indictment, denominations represent "the moral failure of Christianity." His argument was that "unless the ethics of brotherhood can gain the victory over this divisiveness within the body of Christ it is useless to expect it to be victorious in the world."[11] The church in China appears to have been most victorious as it has overcome its denominational divisiveness.

Elsewhere in the world there are also signs of this victory. The "base communities" begun in the 1960s in Latin America have broken through bureaucratic structures and are operating on the grass roots level with persons, most of whom are quite poor. Organized from the bottom upward, the laity serve as the basis of the church. Structures are minimal; leadership tends to be collective. Generally, numbering from twenty to fifty people, they gather for fellowship, support, and problem solving, as they celebrate their life in Jesus Christ. Though overwhelmingly Catholic in background, Protestants also are known to participate. They challenge the established parish church and tend to support popular movements in the political order.[12]

The church of the future will center more on people and less on brick and mortar. A church of wounded healers and practical theologians will emphasize both healing and learning, helping people to care and to think. Quaker theologian D. Elton Trueblood suggests that future church buildings will have "more the appearance of an Academy than that of a temple." Illustrative for him is the "Stephen Ministry," a multi-denominational program that prepares laypersons to develop their own gifts for bringing Christ's healing love to others. Watching this new movement at a national meeting, Trueblood said he felt he "was having a preview of the Church of Tomorrow." He wrote:

> All seemed to feel that they were living and working in the post-denominational age and they knew exactly where they wished to place the emphasis in their lives. They were conscious of serious human needs of many kinds and they knew that each of us is surrounded by persons who are hurting in one way or another. . . . Each one present saw himself or herself as a minister, learning all the time *how* to minister. The idea of "minister" as a *verb* had taken deep hold on each one I met.[13]

Since practical theologians stress the idea of *minister* as verb and focus their primary attention on action and thought, it is important to emphasize certain implications of this image as it affects the life of the post-denominational church in the world. As emphasized earlier, practical theology does not equate with pastoral theology. Sometimes in the past, practical theology, unfortunately, has been nearly reduced to simply a matter of clergy tasks or, worse yet, techniques. This, however, does not negate the fact that pastoral theology is an integral part of practical theology, and certain professional roles do need to be underscored. Before looking at those roles, however, it is imperative to examine both the emergence of "orthopraxis" and the "hermeneutics of suspicion."

Beyond Orthodoxy to Orthopraxy

Practical theologians emphasize orthopraxy more than orthodoxy. Doctrine arises more from discipleship than from deductive processes. "God-walk rather than God-talk" is the way Frederick Herzog characterizes this new way of forming and teaching Christian doctrine. It is not that orthodoxy (correct beliefs) is unimportant, but that the priority is placed on orthopraxy (correct action). Unlike medieval doctrinal teaching that climaxed in ecumenical councils (often with significant political participation of the emperor) or individual confessional formulas composed by Reformation theologians, doctrine today emerges from a more corporate sense of the mutual accountability of Christians. The focus is on God's activity or praxis in the world, not our own.[14]

The God-walk of the black churches in America during the civil rights struggle certainly shaped new doctrinal understandings and new ways of Christian ministry, as has the God-walk of feminists. The God-walk of Third World Christians has identified apartheid as a heresy, poverty as anathema, and nuclear weapons as sinful.

The common beginning point for these diverse practical theologians is in God's justice struggle in Jesus. Christopraxis, rather than Christology, dominates the thinking of those who have sought to enter into God's solidarity and suffering with the "non-persons" of the world. Historically, "non-persons" have not had a place in dogmatics. As Herzog notes:

> Nicea and Chalcedon did not let Jesus the refugee, the homeless one, the "non-person," through their lofty christological grid. In the dogmatic tradition Jesus hardly appears as a particular human being, but rather as an impersonal being (as in the old doctrinal notion of *enhypostasia*). Nicea and Chalcedon dealt with the divinity of Jesus,

but not with the "humanity of God" in the streets—God in solidarity with the poor, wretched human being.[15]

In the face of those who have been impoverished, scorned, and oppressed, the Divine face appears. The incognito Christ may appear in the homeless, the hungry, and the faceless of this world. The practical theologian approaches people in the spirit of Cardinal Roncalli, before he became known as Pope John XXIII. Once, when he was devoted to rescuing Jewish children from the Nazis, his sister scolded him because he had spent his life with the "nobodies" of society. His simple reply was: "The reward for the past forty years is the past forty years." No one is a "nobody" or "non-person" in the kingdom of God.

Orthopraxy is not unrelated to the practical theologian's personal life. Discipleship includes not only participation in public life, but also the cultivation of the devotional arts, prayer, Bible reading, and authentic piety. These practices do not become ends in themselves, but means by which the practical theologian nurtures a deeper awareness of the Divine and a greater resource of spirit to encounter the ambiguities of life and leadership.

Preparation for ministry requires not only the acquisition of knowledge but also spiritual formation. As George Herbert once suggested "the greatest and hardest preparation is within."[16] There are no panaceas for developing sufficient personal spiritual depth in ministry to overcome automatically the temptations of dishonesty, the feelings of despair, the weariness of failure, and the symptoms of burnout. Faith for the practical theologian is God-walk, not simply God-talk.

The church has always hoped for its leaders to live up to its ideals. As Jacob of Voragine pointed out in the thirteenth century, "those who preach in word while their lives do not correspond, fish with broken nets." Words used to describe Lutheran expectations of pastors also reflect what post-denominational Christians look for in their leaders—namely, persons who follow

the practices commended to those who would live in God's presence: confession of sin to God, use of Scripture for personal nourishment, seeking out the guidance of the Holy Spirit, living with a sense of daily forgiveness, receiving Holy Communion regularly, and showing that the mission of Christ has first priority. This list strikingly recalls Luther's daily baptismal cycle of dying to sin and rising again to new life in Christ. When [persons] hear the Word of God proclaimed, they want to hear it from one who from daily contact knows the one proclaimed.[17]

Hermeneutics of Suspicion and Recollection

The commitment to critical reflection in ministry distinguishes the practical theologian from many other types of ministry. The practical theologian is not just an apologist or evangelist of the faith, without regard to the problems of communicating or receiving the *kerygma* in the contemporary culture. Further the practical theologian is not simply an activist or builder of community, bent on social action or structural achievements, without recognizing the ambiguities of social existence or changing trends in the society.

Praxis, or action, stems from a commitment to reflective decision making, which prompts an openness to new truth, a sensitivity to persons, a respect for tradition, and a willingness to consider alternative perspectives. The heuristic stance of the practical theologian prompts one to act on the basis of the best information and insight one can muster at the moment of decision, but living with a freedom to decide differently tomorrow if new truth emerges. This heuristic stance is not the straight posture of the rigid literalist or the ethical purist, who are always certain they know *a priori* the correct truth or moral decision in every case or context. Rather it is the bended posture of the person who knows how sin distorts reason, how culturally conditioned even the saints have been, and how fallible all human yearnings and decisions tend to be.

Within this reflective frame of mind, the practical theologian is open to the hermeneutics of suspicion and recollection.[18] In contrast, the non-reflective minister assumes that what the biblical text says is what it says. No hidden meanings, historical differences, or cultural biases interrupt communication between the text and the reader. Theological doctrines and social teachings are accepted in whatever version they are received, as if this is the final message from God. Never mind that, historically, councils or conferences have spoken in contradictory manners. Pay no attention to the fact that some development in thought emerged only in recent centuries or decades. What has been given has been set in the concrete of that person's mind, and critical reflection seldom is a lively option. Christian ministers of this genre are often the champions of cultural Christianity and civil religion, unable and unwilling to challenge the political powers or social mores that protect or promote oppression and discrimination.

French philosopher Paul Ricoeur coined the terms *hermeneutics of suspicion* and *hermeneutics of recollection*.[19] Despite our inflated self-confidence within the Christian community that we can easily discern God's will in the scriptures, philosophers like Ricoeur have demonstrated the complexity of the interpretive task. This often prompts a polarized response—some persons are dogmatic that proclamations from text can be clearly and easily interpreted, with others despairing completely, believing that all must be demythologized and reduced to illusion. *But suspicion need not lead to skepticism.* The practical theologian chooses neither alternative, believing it is impossible not to be critical, but that does negate the possibility of finding meaning and significance in authoritative sacred texts.

To understand God's Word for contemporary times, it is essential to begin with a hermeneutics of suspicion. When I finished my doctoral studies in Christian social ethics in 1969, I felt that I had been exposed uniquely at Harvard University and Boston University to the critical *avant garde* ethical issues facing church and society. What a shock within a few years to realize my education had been deficient in awareness about the ecological crisis, feminist theology and ethics, the gay liberation movement, and other issues.

Those in positions of power and authority seldom are the first to understand how interpretations, and consequent policies, are slanted. The bishops of the church originally did not perceive (and some still do not!) how women were experiencing discrimination within the life of the church. Male seminary faculty were not quick to note how patriarchal interpretations of scripture affected women negatively. Many laity and clergy continue to be bewildered by inclusive language, failing to understand how sexist language, including God-talk, reflects, reinforces, and creates reality. The hermeneutical task of suspicion has been primarily the burden and the glory of women who cared enough to open the church to new meanings and ministries.

The hermeneutics of suspicion is also employed by others who have found themselves in the margins of church and society. It is incredible how long the United States tolerated slavery, then segregation, and now racism. I remember in my own lifetime when Christians sought to justify segregation and racism by appeals to the scripture. Today similar claims are used to discriminate against homosexual persons, though scholars using the hermeneutics of suspicion are raising serious questions about the legitimacy of the church's historic homophobia.[20]

Practical theologians, unlike many of their colleagues in the life of the church in the world, will be alert to illusions of cultural superiority, economic arrogance, and moral self-righteousness that may be embedded in the church's texts, policies, doctrines, and the traditional interpretations given to them. The preaching, teaching, counseling, administration, and political activism of the practical theologian are likely to be different because of this willingness to reflect critically.

The hermeneutics of suspicion ultimately yields to the hermeneutics of recollection. Criticism bows to construction. The practical theologian attempts to free a text or a context from its bias in order to discover God's intent or will. Delwin Brown contends that "the text is enabled to speak to us most powerfully when we have questioned it, and our favored interpretations of it, most radically."[21] This "critical function" of interpretation, says Ricoeur

> does not turn [us] away from its appropriative function; I should say, rather, that it makes it more authentic. . . . Thus, the time of restoration is not a different time from that of criticism; we are in every way children of criticism, and we seek to go beyond criticism by means of criticism.[22]

Reflective ministry is post-critical. The maxim of the "hermeneutic circle" of believing and understanding, is: "Believe in order to understand, understand in order to believe."[23] A new rapport is established with the text because one has lovingly explored the scholarship available, unearthed the deceptions, considered alternative readings, deciphered new meanings, and possibly substituted new metaphors for distorted ones. In the context of praxis the Christian likewise adjusts his or her horizons to be more inclusive and yet more receptive to God's voice. The practical theologian believes with Emil Brunner that "the church must learn to combine Biblical faith with Biblical criticism."[24]

Implications for Teaching and Preaching

Throughout this discussion of the image of the practical theologian, care has been given not to relegate this metaphor only to the clergy or just to the internal life of the church. Too often in the past, practical theology has been reduced to pastoral theology and techniques confused with theologizing. Yet at the same time it is of value to focus on two roles of particular importance in the Christian community: teaching and preaching. Though preaching is associated more with clergy, the impact of lay preachers around the globe is inestimable to the vitality and outreach of the church.

Whatever else practical theologians may be, they are teachers. The reflective critical quest for new truth and the spirit of intellectual engagement that characterize ministers who are practical theologians almost inevitably result in teaching/learning situations. They speak with authority not because of their ecclesial office or institutional powers, but because they speak from a post-critical base of knowledge and understanding that wins respect and invites creative response.

Jesus was viewed as a "rabbi" or teacher. His reputation prompted the Gospel of John to present him as a teacher *par excellence* (John 3:2; 13:13). Large blocks of the Gospels are devoted to his teachings. Orthodox Jewish scholar Pinchas Lapide says that the Sermon on the Mount ought to be called the Instruction on the Mount. In the tradition of Moses, Jesus climbed a mount, sat with his disciples gathered around him, and taught in classic rabbinic style.[25] Though little is known of how Christianity was taught in the early church, the New Testament record is clear that Paul did teach in synagogues and homes (Acts 18:4-7; 19:8-9). The office of teacher is cited in the Pauline and post-Pauline Letters (I Cor. 12:28-29; Eph. 4:11) as well as the pastoral Letters (I Tim. 4:6, 11, 16; 6:2-3). Christians through the centuries have sought to emulate this model.

A dialogic approach characterized much of Jesus' teaching. Unlike other great teachers—such as Socrates, whose dialogues tended to be abstract and intellectual—Jesus appears to have taught at both a cognitive and an emotive level. Focusing on the people's needs, he sought to meet them with spiritual insights and resources. It was not teaching for the sake of erudition but of eternity. He was sensitive to special needs and even unspoken issues. To the man by Siloam for whom illness had become a life-style (John 5:6 ff.) and to the woman who sparred verbally with him at the well (John 4:7 ff.), Jesus perceived the critical questions and persisted in meeting them. This dialogic approach included the ability to confront people and issues that others tried to avoid. He confronted the ambitious sons of Zebedee (Mark 10:35) and Peter on more than one occasion (Mark

8:33 and 14:30, 37) as well as the disciples (Matt. 17:17; Matt 19:14; and Mark 4:40). This confrontation was aimed not at destroying others but at instructing, correcting, stimulating, and reassuring.[26]

Whenever the teaching office has been neglected, the church has suffered. One of the great opportunities of the laity is to provide Christian education courses. The Sunday school movements in the United States have been major methods of Christian nurture and church growth. Churches with pastors who regularly teach Bible classes and offer other types of instruction tend to be among those who demonstrate the most vitality.

The recovery of the teaching office can have a major impact on the ministry and mission of the church. Biblical illiteracy and theological ignorance can be overcome as practical theologians, both lay and clergy, renew educational efforts within the life of the church in the world.

Preaching is at the heart of a practical theologian's activity. In contrast to the academic theologian, reflective practitioners in ministry find the pulpit an important forum for communicating and educating. Proclamation of the Word is at the core of praxis and is approached as a high priority for ministry. Daring to interpret God's Word in contemporary idiom is an awesome task that commands the best intellectual and spiritual resources a person can muster. Critical reflection on the scriptural text and the pastoral context is required.

Far from being simply an intellectual transfer of information via lecture, the practical theologian realizes that in preaching a sermon one is struggling with ineffable mysteries of life and death. The practical theologian can easily identify with the situation and words of the Roman Catholic archbishop portrayed in Thornton Wilder's book *The Eighth Day.* The archbishop is imprisoned along with four priests and six nuns in a southern Chinese province. Communication was forbidden among them, but the archbishop developed a scheme of tapping between cells using a homemade version of the Morse code. The system worked well, transmitting news and hope from one isolated prisoner to another. But then one member died and was replaced by a Portuguese-speaking prisoner who could in no way understand the messages. This captive realized, however, the importance of the tapping to the others, so he faithfully executed the noises between cells. Commenting upon this, the archbishop declared: "Life is surrounded by mysteries beyond the comprehension of our limited minds. . . you and I have seen them. We transmit fairer things than we can fully grasp."[27] Without fully realizing, a preacher often taps out messages of hope far more sublime and spiritual than the words on the page.

Preaching, as understood theologically by the Protestant Reformers, is the work of the Holy Spirit. In Martin Luther's words: "God speaks through the preacher. When we preach *[lehren]* we are passive rather than active. God is speaking through us and it is a divine working [that is happening].[28] Since practical theologians are keenly aware of their own shortcomings in terms of their intellectual grasp, public speaking abilities, and spiritual maturity, they find consolation in the ancient Catholic church's teaching *(character dominicus)* that the gospel is communicated efficaciously by Word or Sacrament regardless of the condition of the communicator.

Few tasks are more demanding than preaching, particularly on a weekly basis. One cannot minimize the pressures of meeting the expectations and needs of a congregation. No one can always be inspiring; yet no one has a right to preach so as to send one's hearers away on "flat tyres."[29] Preachers who fail to plan ahead, using the lectionary or some other systematic approach, inevitably find themselves trapped in time crunches. The "unexpected" and the "interruption" are constant companions of the parish clergy and will inevitably become twin thieves, stealing away time and energy needed for preparing both the preacher and the sermon. What so often happens is that the felons go uncaptured. Ultimately the preacher's well runs dry and sermons are more like crumbs than slices of the bread of life. Michael Farrell says that:

> Preachers may console themselves that no one is complaining. That's like the *Comedia dell' Arte* joke about the man who wanted to train his donkey to go without food. The donkey eventually died of starvation. "I have suffered a great loss," the man mourned. "Just when my donkey had learned the art of going without food, he died." Congregations like the donkey, may not be complaining. That does not mean they are being trained to mediocrity. They may be just dying away.[30]

The practical theologian does not minimize the power of preaching. Few platforms exist in this world that equal the pulpit. Any political party would be pleased to gain access to the pulpits of a nation; instead they have to be satisfied with thirty-second commercials and endless campaign stops in the hope of getting their philosophy across to the public. Excessive fascination with the media and small groups during the 1960s prompted preaching to be deemphasized in many seminaries, much to the later detriment of the church in the world. The gift of preaching and the freedom of the pulpit are incredibly valuable resources available to the practical theologian.

Reason During a Reign of Emotion

Rationality has been in short supply globally among the excessive, emotional religious movements in the latter years of the twentieth century. The rise of fundamentalism in Islam, the politics of the religious right in the United States, and the religious conflicts of Northern Ireland and India have all been discouraging omens on the horizon of human history. Sometimes practical theologians feel like voices crying in the wilderness, as cultural and community forces seem swept away in a sea of emotion. Yet the practical theologian insists on a reflective ministry, combining reason and faith in critical and creative ways.

The need for such learned laity and clergy cannot be overstated. Communities caught in conflicts over the curriculums of public schools need Christian leaders whose hermeneutical skills and scientific knowledge can dispute creationism and challenge censors. When law and order forces begin to dominate, practical theologians are needed to point to deep rooted social causes for crime as well as to strike notes for grace and rehabilitation. When military adventurism threatens new quagmires in Central America or the Middle East, peacemakers are needed in every vocation throughout the society as well as in the pulpit on Sunday. When the local church becomes isolated and forgetful of its transcultural and transnational nature, pioneers of the post-denominational community of faith must lift it beyond its parochialism and prejudice. When racism rears its ugly head, the practical theologian is called to slay the dragon.

The moral power and authority of an informed and reflective mind should never be underestimated. The Christian who thoughtfully attempts to relate theology to life, ethics to day-to-day existence, will generate respect from unexpected quarters. Even those who disagree with certain conclusions or decisions often will come to appreciate the integrity of the practical theologian. In a culture as complex and as educated as ours, there can be little doubt that both the church and society will turn to the reflective Christian practitioner for leadership and guidance.

Chapter Ten

A PUBLIC MINISTRY
IN A GLOBAL
VILLAGE

I simply argue that the Cross be raised again at the centre of the market place as well as on the steeple of the church. I am recovering the claim that Jesus was not crucified in a Cathedral between two candles, but on a Cross between two thieves; on the town garbage heap; on a crossroads so cosmopolitan that they had to write his title in Hebrew and Latin and in Greek; at the kind of place where cynics talk smut, and thieves curse, and soldiers gamble. Because that is where he died and that is what He died about. And that is where churchmen should be and what churchmen should be about.

GEORGE McCLOUD, *Only One Way Left*

When Reverend John Fife was on trial for aiding and harboring Central American refugees, his congregation in Tucson, Arizona, interviewed candidates for his position. Southside Presbyterian Church asked each prospective pastor whether they were willing to go to jail. As the first congregation in the country to declare itself a sanctuary for Central American refugees, it is clear in its expectation of what it means to have a public ministry in a global village. Having aided more than 3,000 refugees, the church was aware of the biblical command to aid the oppressed, as well as the government demand that it cease.

Convicted and given five years probation, Fife continues his work, saying:

> Living in the midst of life and death questions, helping people who are being hunted down, dealing with the grief and pain of people who have been tortured, people who have been forced to watch family members raped and killed, children who have seen their parents cut up into little pieces—it is a strain.

This is not exactly what Fife imagined his ministry would be like. "I grew up thinking that every Presbyterian minister lived the life of Peter

Marshall," says Fife, recalling the image of the famous chaplain of the United States Senate who was a friend of the rich and powerful.[1]

Christians are constantly forced to reevaluate their images of ministry. Times change, and we change. Yesterday's metaphor may no longer be appropriate or fulfilling. What a young person envisioned in seminary probably does not fit ten years later or into mid-career. God's call to ministry does not usually follow neat and predictable career patterns. If one looks and acts exactly like one did twenty years ago, then perhaps a period of reevaluation is past due. Is the Spirit leading, or is *rigor mortis* beginning to set in? Finding a new image for oneself may add vigor to one's vocation and new life to the church.

New metaphors have the power to create new realities. Old images sometimes lose their capacity to empower or to transform because they have lost their original vitality and novelty due to trivialization, habitual use, or cultural acceptance and assimilation. Illustrative is a Franz Kafka parable: "Leopards break into the temple and drink up the sacrificial wine; this is repeated over and over again; eventually it becomes predictable, and is incorporated into the ceremony."[2]

The purpose of this book has been to supplement, not supplant, the major historic metaphors of ministry by examining some contemporary images of ministry. By looking through paradoxical lenses, new focus has, it is hoped, been gained. By appropriating insights from both the old and the new, it is possible to grasp new vision. For example, the pastor could be understood as a wounded healer, the prophet as an enslaved liberator, the priest as a political mystic, the preacher as a practical theologian, and the administrator as a servant leader (or some other combination of the traditional and the contemporary images).

The Public Ministry of the Good Shepherd

The revitalization of ministerial images also occurs by reexamining some of the biblical metaphors that may have lost their intended impact over time. Take, for instance, the paradigm of the good shepherd (John 10:7-18). Many Christians have appropriated publicly this image without realizing its radical meaning. A metaphorical thinker, not a systematic theologian, Jesus knew the serendipitous art of creating the new by transforming the old. In daring fashion, he would creatively appropriate the contradictory or unexpected and reverse religious understandings. He understood the power of paradox and parable. With the metaphor of the good Shepherd, Jesus was offering an oxymoron.[3]

An oxymoron occurs when a combination of contradictory words or incongruous thoughts are combined together. Some samples include authentic reproduction, down escalator, jumbo shrimp, postal service, and military intelligence. The value of this type of speech is that it jars the reader to new awareness or startles the listener to new understandings. In the hands of an artist, an oxymoron like "thunderous silence" paints an unforgettable word portrait.

For us there is little that is jarring, startling, or daring when we hear Jesus declare: "I am the good Shepherd." The shepherd image typically projects to us a positive and peaceful pastoral picture of a person who cares for the sheep. The image engenders within us warm feelings, as we think of shepherds loving their flocks, calling them individually by name, searching for the lost, and risking life and limb to protect lambs from predators. But as noted earlier in this book, the shepherd model for ministry seems to many like a "dead" metaphor, haplessly outdated and hopelessly rural in a modern, urban age.

The shocking good news of the gospel is missed if we do not understand its oxmoronic quality. When Jesus was criticized for hanging out with "tax collectors and sinners" (Mark 2:16; Matt. 11:19; Luke 15:1), or simply "sinners" (Mark 2:17; Luke 7:37, 39; 15:2; 19:7), that reference, Joachim Jeremias says, was not only used for those disreputable persons "who notoriously failed to observe the commandments of God," but also was a specific term applied to "those engaged in despised trades."[4] Far from being a noble profession, the job of shepherd in first-century Palestine was one of the most despised trades, along with gamblers, usurers, and publicans.

Contrary to our romantic images, shepherds were generally considered to be thieves. Far from being viewed as reliable and responsible, they were habitually known to graze on other people's lands and to pilfer the produce of the herd. Their societal and religious status would not be much higher than pimps and drug pushers in our day. They, like the publicans and tax collectors, therefore, were deprived of their civil rights. They could not fulfill a judicial office or be witnesses in court. It was forbidden to buy wool, milk, or a kid from a shepherd because it was widely assumed that it would be stolen property. One ancient writing reports that "no position in the world is so despised as that of the shepherd."[5]

Pause for a moment and imagine what might be the most upsetting or mind-boggling image to be employed today. Of course, it depends on your commitments and prejudices. "I am the good Sandinista" or "I am the good politician" or "I am the good gay" would enrage the Pharisees of most congregations. "I am the good Contra" or "I am the good bomb-maker" or "I am the good religious Right" would alienate others. It is no wonder then that after Jesus called himself the "good Shepherd" the Gospel of John reports, "there was again a division among the Jews because of these words" (John 10:19).

The public ministry Jesus projected may have been pastoral, but it also was fraught with conflict and controversy. By deliberately choosing a despicable trade like that of the shepherd, Jesus was standing with the acknowledged "sinners" and outcasts of his culture. What outraged the religious people was not his message of God's love, but his insistence on inclusiveness—no one was beyond the pale of God's grace. Particularly outrageous was his custom of having "table-fellowship" with the pariahs of his society. The religious custom was that the host would bless the bread, breaking it and sharing the blessing with all those who shared in the food. Such table-fellowship meant fellowship before God. In other words, this was not just unusual hospitality or generosity but participation in an eschatalogical feast, pointing to an end time when God would gather all the beloved. As Joachim Jeremias suggests: "The inclusion of sinners in the community of salvation, achieved in table-fellowship, is the most meaningful expression of the message of the redeeming love of God."[6]

Jesus deliberately modified the shepherd image with the adjective *good*, just as he described the despised Samaritan as "good." He contrasted the "good Shepherd" who owns the sheep with the "hireling" who is employed to take care of them. He claims that the "good Shepherd" will lay down life for the sake of the sheep, while the paid employee flees in the face of wolves "and cares nothing for the sheep."

The ever-present danger is that Christian clergy and laity will adopt the mentality of hirelings who do the minimum required by their job descriptions. Parenting becomes more a burdensome task than a joyful opportunity. Grudgingly, we spend time with our spouses or children. Our careers become more self-centered than concerned for the welfare of others. Like hirelings, we become paid functionaries, more concerned with employee benefits and potential advancement than with the public good. When it comes to critical public policy

173

questions, we often run away from controversy, like the hireling from the sheep, forgetting that the good Shepherd cares not only for our own flock but for others not of the immediate fold as well.

Public ministry today requires more good shepherds in the mold of John Fife than in the manner of Peter Marshall. Too often we so yearn for places or pulpits of prestige that we become self-protective as hirelings, unwilling to risk life or career or popularity. The good shepherd is willing to face conflict and controversy for the gospel's sake, while the hireling, remembering who provides the paycheck, muffles the prophetic trumpet notes of the good news.

In his novel *But Your Land Is Beautiful,* South African writer Alan Paton tells the story of the Holy Church of Zion, in which the ritual of foot washing precedes Holy Communion. The black pastor invited Judge Oliver to come to the church on Maundy Thursday to wash the feet of Martha Fortuin, the black woman who had raised and cared for the judge's children. A white man of moral character and principles, he accepted the invitation. After washing Martha Fortuin's feet, the judge remembered how she had often kissed the feet of his children. So after washing her feet in the ritual, he bent over and kissed them. Tears filled the eyes of other worshipers in the small church.

Somehow the press learned of the event and gave it wide publicity. In the light of the apartheid of South Africa, it is not surprising that shortly thereafter Judge Oliver was denied the chief judgeship he had been promised.

A few days later the pastor called on Judge Oliver to ask his forgiveness for involving him in an act that destroyed his professional advancement. The judge replied: "But taking part in your service on Thursday is to me more important than the Chief Judgeship. Think no more about it." And that is why the people of the Holy Church of Zion renamed their church "The Church of the Washing of Feet." And one can almost hear the voice of Jesus saying, "I am the good shepherd."[7]

Imagining a Global Village

The image of the earth as a global village is almost a cliché, as we have become accustomed to seeing pictures beamed back from outer space and hearing of the economic, cultural, technical, and military bonds that crisscross national boundaries. Yet we tend to think and act parochially, living in little denominational tents and waving partisan flags. An unknown author has written that:

> If the world were a global village of 100 residents,
>   6 of them would be Americans.
> These 6 would have half of the village's entire income;
>   the other 94 would exist on the other half.
>
> How would the wealthy 6 live "in peace" with their
>   neighbors?
> Surely they would be driven to arm themselves against
>   the other 94 . . .
> perhaps even to spend, as we do,
>   more per person on military "defense"
>   than the total per person incomes of the others.

In John Drinkwater's *Lincoln, The World Emancipator* a dialogue occurs between Lincoln and a woman who is a zealot for the Northern cause. A blind fanatic, she is against everything about the South. When she asks President Lincoln for news of the war, he replies: "Yes, there is news of victory. They lost 2,700 men and we lost 800!" The woman is ecstatic, responding "How splendid!" Stunned, Lincoln registers deep dismay, again saying slowly: "Thirty-five hundred human lives lost." But the woman interrupts, "Oh, you must not talk like that, Mr. President. There were only 800 that mattered." With drooping shoulders, Lincoln's tear-rimmed eyes flash, as he says with measured emphasis, "Madam, the world is larger than your heart."[8]

As good shepherds—or enslaved liberators or political mystics or whatever image one chooses—we are called to have enlarged global hearts, for Christians are concerned not only with their own flocks but care also for the sheep of other folds. The gospel of grace is for *all* people. In Christ there is no north or south, no east or west, no Protestant or Catholic, no First or Third World, but just one great fellowship of love throughout the whole wide earth. Or as Jesus said, "So there shall be one flock, one shepherd" (John 10:16).

The images of the Christian church presented in this book have sought to be co-extensive with this global village. No attempt has been made to provide a complete ecclesial doctrine or to be certain that all dimensions of the church—"truly catholic, truly reformed, truly evangelical"—have been fully expressed. This absence does not signify unconcern or imply unimportance. Rather the basic insistence has been to root ministry in the community of faith, in contrast to the individualistic professional tendencies of the current age.

In doing so, an effort has been made to envision the church in more normative than descriptive categories, using contemporary terms to express meanings richly embedded in traditional and biblical metaphors of the church, such as people of God and body of Christ. The Community of the Compassionate, the Servant Church, the Prophetic Community, the Rainbow Church, and the Post-denominational Church are visions that can become realities when Christians catch a global vision. Ecumenism means more than church cooperation or even organic unity. It is derived from the Greek word *oikoumene* meaning "the whole inhabited earth."

On occasion public ministry in this global village is enacted in the spotlight of the world's media. A 6'7" bearded Anglican layperson, Terry Waite, risks his life to rescue hostages in the Middle East. A frail, gnarled-faced Roman Catholic nun, Mother Teresa, creates orphanages for India's starving children and hospices for America's abandoned AIDS victims. But most of the time clergy and laity minister quietly in the footlights, serving as missionaries in distant lands or doing battle for peace and justice at their own doorsteps. Engagement in a public and global ministry does not require hopscotching around the world, but can begin by affirming the slogan seen on a billboard: "Love thy neighborhood."

Unfortunately, a public ministry with a global vision ranks low on the priorities of many laity and clergy. With few notable exceptions, most Christians view controversial social and political involvement either as ancillary to their calling or as an anachronism of a previous era.[9] Many are like the invalid Jesus described lying by the Sheep Gate pool (John 5:2-9). They are waiting, watching, and hoping for just the right break to get into the swim of life where dynamic ministry flows or into a church that will be a catalyst for change in community and society.

Paralyzed by apathy or antipathy, crippled by past experiences or limitations of the present, lame because of inadequate preparation or cynical despair, and blind due to excuse-making and fear of the unknown, Christians linger by the pool. Richard A. Goodling, speaking of the "pervasive unease" within the clergy ranks, argues that in part this is true because "of a felt sense of professional inadequacy and ineffectiveness, in short, the frustrating and demoralizing experience of being powerless or impotent."[10]

The man beside the Sheep Gate pool apparently had both the desire and the potential to act, but his performance had been inadequate and ineffective, resulting in some thirty-eight years of frustration, defeat, and demoralization. James E. Dittes asks:

> How much of a day, how much of a career is spent watching from a distance, perhaps great, perhaps tormentingly small, while others seem to be fully immersed in significant ministry? How many of those years are spent waiting with the rueful sense of separation between oneself and the significant currents of events in God's world. . . ?[11]

But Jesus' question remains the same today as it did many yesterdays ago in Jerusalem: "Do we want to be healed?" Do we want a public ministry in a global village? Do we want to sense healing and wholeness in our lives? Do we want to experience new power in our ministry? Do we want to become strategically involved in the great issues and crises of our time and church? Do we want to face the ambiguities and the anxieties, the conflicts and the controversies, the anger and the anguish, and the risks and the responsibilities of Christian leadership? Or do we want to continue to lie beside the troubled water and cry that we are too overburdened or complain that no one has yet come by and carried us into the surging waters of dynamic ministry or blame others for climbing into the pool's steps of success faster?

If our response is to be healed personally, to become empowered vocationally, then we need to try on some new images of ministry, accepting anew the invitation Jesus offered twenty centuries ago: "Rise, take up your pallet and walk." The creative and restorative forces of life are not always somewhere else. We are already in the midst of God's creative and redeeming power. The renewal of our ministry comes from within, in the place where we think we ought to be. The breakthroughs for social justice, evangelism, church growth, and increased civility in human life will come not by everyone's trading places, but by everyone's, in each and every place, rising up, speaking out, and walking forward into the heartaches and headaches, the storms and stresses of life.

Lest I be misunderstood, seizing the opportunity for healing, empowerment, involvement, and effectiveness in ministry does not mean that life will be easy or that one will be successful. There are no pills that we can pop and suddenly become charismatic, and there are no panaceas we can quickly adopt to change stubborn churches into serving communities of faith.

Clergy have more power potentially than they are usually ready to acknowledge or to accept. This represents not only personal gifts and graces, or professional knowledge and skills, but also the symbolic and organizational power of the church they represent. To be ordained is to be entrusted with authority and responsibility. To be identified as ministers of the gospel of Jesus Christ is to function in the public realm with authority and responsibility that is more than just a sum of one's personal and professional attributes.

Far from having to lie passively beside the pool while contemporary crises erupt within and around the church, each of us, thanks to God's grace, can become more effective public ministers in a global village. Far from having to blame others for not getting us into the swim of health and history, we can claim our own destiny as laity and clergy committed to social justice and civility in a global community.

Strategic Christian Involvement

To do so, obviously, involves many elements, but this closing chapter will focus on but two major dimensions. First, four steps for strategic Christian involvement will be outlined. Then, six imperative ministries of faithfulness and effectiveness will be underscored.

As the Christian becomes involved in the critical issues and problems of society, it is imperative for that person to remember that the task is that of enabling the whole body of Christ in every place to struggle for social justice and reconciliation. Clergy have both the right and the responsibility for involvement. Their leadership is often critical. Yet the theology of the ministry of the laity cannot be overstressed. Laypersons normally have an even greater stake in the health and welfare of the church and the community than do the itinerant clergy. In addition, laity often can witness more effectively for social justice and civility because they know the channels for penetrating power structures, cultural subgroups, parochial preju-dices, and provincial traditions.

All are involved in strategic social action at one level or another. Christian social action is the response of a Christian to an unmet human need in the light of one's theological and ethical convictions. It is planned, purposeful involvement in decision making processes that influence policies and institutions. Unfortunately, many have come to think of social action as simply being synonymous with demonstrations and confrontations—events such as trying to stop the "nuclear train" as it moves across the United States. But in reality, a complete typology of social action would have to include such diverse activities as praying for a city council meeting, leading a church to study the nuclear predicament, writing letters to legislators, or being personally involved in politics. Not every person will stand in a picket line or march in a demonstration. Expecting everyone to do so is to lose a valuable resource because of a narrow perspective. Just as Paul speaks about "the varieties of gifts" in the church, so also we must recognize a variety of gifts for public ministry.

If we want to become more sensitively and strategically involved in a public ministry, we can learn from four theoretical insights, succinctly stated by Robert H. Bonthius: exposure, intervention, collaboration, and organization.[12] Let me elaborate briefly on each.

First, one's perceptions and actions are shaped by life's experiences and exposures. Until a problem is identified, there is little chance of solving it. A basic theoretical foundation in the social sciences is the Thomas theorem that if persons ". . . define situations as real, they are real in their consequences."[13] This can hardly be stressed too much because it is so critical regarding the crises the global village is facing today.

During his presidency, Ronald Reagan repeatedly went on television and portrayed as vividly as he could the worldwide dangers posed by the Soviet Union and the need to escalate the military budget. He attempted to define the situation militarily to justify the consequences of a 1.9 trillion dollar defense buildup. He asked ministers to spread his anti-nuclear freeze message from their pulpits. The president understood that if persons define situations as real, they are real in their consequences. He succeeded in escalating the budget almost beyond belief and in persuading the American public to accept astronomical levels of national debt.

When AIDS first appeared in the early 1980s, little government concern or funding was made available. The public in general was uninformed and uninterested. Because the deadly disease was confined to the new "lepers" of society—homosexual men, drug users, and Haitian immigrants—homophobia and racial prejudice blinded perceptions and limited exposure to the primary victims. Early perceptual failures resulted in a disastrous global problem. The consequence has been years of delay in finding treatment and a cure, plus untold thousands of fatalities. Prejudice breeds death.[14]

If Christian ministers are exposed to human conditions crying out for justice and become sensitized to human problems, they are more likely to become change-agents for Christ. Ministers who are wounded healers reach out to the broken people Jesus came to save. A primary reason most of us lack understanding and compassion for people who are of a different race or nationality or religion or sexual orientation is that we simply have never had much opportunity to associate in meaningful ways with those who are different from ourselves.

Experience is essential in the process of exposure, but it is imperative that data be derived from a variety of sources. Besides meeting and talking with the victims, change-agents, powers, and experts involved in a particular problem, it is necessary to cross-check this oral data with written accounts published in newspapers, books, and surveys. It is critical to know, for example, that during the period of the Vietnam War, 58,000 American soldiers died in combat overseas while 17,000 American women died at home in acts of domestic violence or to know that 50,000 official reports of sexual abuse of children are made each year in the United States, with only an estimated 10 percent of the cases reported. Christians must be exposed to the facts: "Every *two* minutes a woman is raped. Every *eighteen seconds* a woman is beaten by the man she lives with. Every *five* minutes a child is molested. Every *thirty* minutes a daughter is molested by her father."[15]

Then comes our critical reflection upon this information in the light of our knowledge, moral outrage about the situation, theoretical input regarding the possibilities and limitations of social change, and consideration of the constraints and convictions of the Christian faith. Scriptural insights and traditional theological teachings provide normative guidance. Practical theology is not an abstraction, but an absolute necessity as the Christian is involved in public ministry.

A *second step in this process is intervention.* Fact-finding is but the prolegomena to direct action. Research into any issue will provide a plethora of perceptions, problems, and possibilities. Out of the multitude of concerns, specific plans must be outlined, and proposals must be reduced to operational dimensions. Goals must be realistic. Attainment of ends sought must be a real possibility. Resolutions urging mutually verifiable arms reductions have a chance for success; unilateral disarmament proposals are utopian impossibilities.

Personal theological understandings influence one's social and political ministry. A theology excessively dominated by a pessimistic view of one's ability to change the world will not produce political mystics or enslaved liberators willing to contribute abundant energy, time, and talent in social action causes. Christian realism that stresses human sinfulness and the penultimate nature of nation, class, and ideology, but is imbued with a real vision of the future, is a theology of hope. Therefore, it provides a framework for political and social involvement.

Once we know our goal, as Christian ministers we need to select methods that cohere with our chosen ends. If freedom is a goal, for example, then one ought not to use methods that rob others of their right of decision. If respect for persons is a basic ethical principle, then in conflict situations one must seek to back an opponent into a corner with an open door; in other words, help those with whom we disagree to change position without losing their dignity.

Theology should stimulate, inform, and correct our social action. Persons engaged in training clergy for action discover, however, that *"people more frequently act their way into a new way of thinking than think their way into a new way of acting."*[16] In other words, our theology develops in response to an empirical situation. In response to unmet human needs, servant leaders discover new scriptural insights and resources. In trying to influence the policies of human institutions, political mystics are likely to understand Paul's references concerning the evils of "principalities." In meeting conflict and defeat, pride and self-confidence are likely to be shaken, prompting humility, and perhaps holiness, to emerge.

Strategizing must include not only theological and ethical reflection, but also an assessment of costs and resources, plus a deploying of necessary energies for achieving goals. In designing plans it is necessary that Christian ministers select the issues carefully, weighing their relatedness and evaluating the group's realistic power. Throughout the stage of intervention, strategy must be heuristic, since effective social action takes into account the revising of goals, the changing of personnel and social situations, the shifting of alternatives, and so on.

No religious professional operates prophetically exclusive of other concerns. If one is providing pastoral leadership to a local church, then one has many other responsibilities. One, therefore, must balance social action contributions with other pastoral duties. The pastor who alienates his or her church because of neglecting basic pastoral tasks also usually fails to be effective in social action. The basic dilemma facing every pastor in social action is how to be a moral leader without alienating those whom you are trying to influence. Lay opposition to pastoral action is often based on rational grounds; other times the "flak" is irrational. Loving, caring pastoral concern has a therapeutic effect in such situations and often reduces the anger, if not the disagreements.

The preacher who enters the pulpit to preach on controversial issues needs to have a grieving heart, full of what Abraham J. Heschel would have called the "pathos" of God.[17] Political mystics stand not above but with their people, not in detached judgment but involved with them for justice's sake. In the words of Martin Luther King, Jr., "Whom you would change you must first love." Pastors will never have an effective public ministry for social justice, reconciliation, and civility in human life if they do not truly embrace with love and care the people in their churches whom they are called to serve and to change. As George A. Buttrick said in his Lyman Beecher lecture:

> The wise preacher of the social gospel is always ahead of his people, but always tied to them in loyalty and understanding love. If their minister has been with them in stress of joy and sorrow, in overcoming and failure, they will not question too strongly his right to speak the whole truth as he sees it in Christ.[18]

The enslaved liberator involved in the controversial social action, of course, has no sure-fire formulas for success and can make as many mistakes as any other. The person of faith, however, recognizes that God's love means mercy and forgiveness. Intervention involves choices. To remain neutral and not act really means to take a side and to choose. Life is always a choice of values, sometimes of choosing between lesser evils. Theology is never more practical than when we bow before the Cross and seek God's forgiveness.

Collaboration is a third step for a public ministry in a global village. Church leaders cannot initiate or sustain social action by themselves. Christian laity and clergy are, therefore, urged to collaborate with a variety of people and groups. Ministry is always collegial and not individualistic. Tentative alliances with groups of diverse purposes and functions must be formed for effective social action on a particular issue. Once a problem is pinpointed, it is essential to note how much support already exists for solution of the problem. Christians in social action should develop working relationships with (1) church hierarchies, (2) a network of consultants, (3) community change-agents, (4) a circle of supportive persons, and (5) the local congregation. Let me briefly note why each is important.

Everyone has what is called a "reference group" in sociology. These reference groups have normative or comparative influence on us. Theological professors often look to graduate school mentors or professional organizations, such as the American Academy of Religion and the Society of Biblical Literature. Students may be influenced by professors. The professional clergy reference group are usually clergy colleagues who set formal or informal standards of behavior and provide a frame of comparison by which we can evaluate ourselves. Laypersons have similar mentors in their professions or occupations. If they expect or approve of our public ministry, then it is easier for us to endure the conflict and controversy that inevitably arise around significant projects.

Pastors need to keep their church leaders informed of their activities. Churches with a strong hierarchical structure can be especially helpful to a pastor who is involved in social action. Other churches have similar organizational mechanisms. Church groups and leaders provide sources of legitimization for ministry as well as being possible resources of money, persons, and facilities.

Collaboration must also continue with a network of consultants. The victims of social injustice and those persons who are intimately acquainted with the problems must be continually contacted for purposes of information, exposure, and evaluation. Church groups traveling to Nicaragua and other Central American nations make contact with people for whom diplomats and generals have little knowledge or concern. Consultation with these "non-persons," the forgotten victims of war, sheds a radically different perspective on events and policies.

Community change-agents—those persons in every place who have power to enact change at various levels—are valuable persons for enabling public ministry. They can provide leadership, expertise, and resources for information and assistance. Political leaders, for example, are responsive to the interests of campaign donors, public supporters, and public opinion. They can be reached personally or through mutual friends who have ready access. If a Christian minister seeks to be an enslaved liberator, then deliberate time and effort must be set aside for getting to the power brokers. Frankly, this can have a two-fold impact. The powers themselves are persons, often hurting and needing the care of a compassionate, wounded healing ministry. Second, it creates the condition for future influence on public policy issues.

Those in public ministry especially need the collaboration of a circle of supportive persons, including wives, husbands, lovers, like-minded professional colleagues, and kindred community spirits. These persons provide services of commiseration and cross-criticism.[19] They are important reference systems for those in public ministry. Christians whose spouses disapprove of their public praxis will find it difficult to continue their involvement.

A final reference group with a major impact on ministers is the local congregation. Pastors are deeply influenced by what their people expect of them. While denominational officials tell clerics to be prophets in word and deed, what they often mean is to engage in a public ministry without unnecessarily upsetting the church program, budget, or people. In their classic study of Little Rock clergy during the racial crisis over schools, Campbell and Pettigrew discovered that the local congregation was the most important reference group prohibiting meaningful social action.[20] Fear of alienating one's congregation and thus losing friends and possibly position is a major force operating to keep pastors from being political mystics, enslaved liberators, or servant leaders.

This fear closely correlates to a person's tolerance for ambiguity, compromise, and conflict. As Seward Hiltner once noted, "A minister who cannot tolerate ambiguity cannot tolerate a local church."[21] Consensus-oriented persons take fewer risks than Christians who can live comfortably with more conflict. But as the great black leader Frederick Douglass asserted:

> If there is no struggle, there is no progress. Those who profess to favor freedom, and yet deprecate agitation, are men who want crops without plowing up the ground. They want rain without thunder and lightning. . . . This struggle may be a physical one or it may be both moral and physical, but there must be a struggle.

In a study of clergy, Francine Carol Juhasz discovered that "a person's ability to manage social conflict is a predictor" of "effectiveness in bringing about social change." The portrait of a successful pastor in social action that emerged from this study indicates that such persons:

—have a positive attitude toward social conflict
—view conflict as a means, not an obstacle;
—work cooperatively with others;
—refuse to be threatened by conflict;
—see conflict as a challenge, not as a defeat;
—are able to maintain a sense of humor; and
—do not blame themselves for the occurrence of conflict. [22]

An effective public ministry in a global village is inhibited if controversy and conflict are avoided. If, as someone has said, fear is the darkroom where negatives are developed, it is imperative for ministers to overcome this personality hangup if they expect to be servant leaders for social justice.

Change seldom comes rapidly or without persistence—organization is imperative. A church that has not been regularly educating and sensitizing its people to critical issues facing the church and society will always be at a disadvantage to organized forces that seek to undermine the church and to discredit its leadership.

Subrosa power structures in boards of directors or organizations can stymie individual efforts for change. Early in my ministry, I met defeat in an effort to reform a private child care agency because I discovered too late the hidden interlocking relationships of board members who were also members of a fraternal order and directors of a particular bank, which held that agency's funds and investments. I spoke with a prophetic voice! But I got booted off the board! All because I did not properly study the total system and organize support before I went into battle. Since then I have sought to select issues carefully, trying to determine the depth of opposition, weighing carefully the possibilities of victory, and moving forward into controversy with a more realistic understanding of what "powers" and "principalities" I was facing.

Impoverished social issue campaigns characteristically suffer from the neglect of the details of morale-building, finances, equipment, and public relations. The art of administration is critical; without it one can expect unnecessary failures in a public ministry. When you operate in public, nothing becomes more visible than poor organization.

Obviously, these four theoretical axioms—exposure, intervention, collaboration, and organization—provide but a rough sketch of what it means to "rise, take up your pallet, and walk," into a public ministry. But perhaps they provide at least some clues as to what is necessary both personally and vocationally if we are to model effectively and faithfully the contemporary images of Christian ministry in this book.

Ministries of Faithfulness and Effectiveness

This leads to highlighting what a public ministry of faithfulness and effectiveness would be in our time. *First, it would be a ministry of reminding.* Clearly one responsibility is to remind our church and society of higher values than are the "common coin of the realm." The Church must be the conscience of the nation. In an age of alarming militarism, pressing economic needs, world hunger, and oppressed human rights, the exigencies of global life make imperative a renewed role of reminding for the Christian church and its ministers.

Some years ago Michael Harrington reminded us that the poor in the United States are invisible. Tragically, hunger is again on the rise in this country. One out of seven Americans—mostly women and their children, the elderly, and the unemployed—lack resources to feed themselves and their families properly. The percentage of children in poverty has been climbing. For most church people in the United States, global poverty in the Third and Fourth Worlds is even more invisible. We who are committed to a faith that has a clear bias toward the poor, therefore, must remember that ours is always a ministry of reminding, of calling attention to forgotten people, to hurting victims of life's tragedies and systems, and to transcendent norms that summon us to repentance and renewal.

Second, ours should be a ministry of interpretation. Much of our ministry is done in the interruptions of life. Until the *Readers' Digest* and "60 Minutes" launched attacks in the 1980s few clergy had planned to spend time interpreting the National Council of Churches or the World Council of Churches to their people. Certainly before the 1980s few Christians struggled with the practical theological questions of homosexuality and ordination. Yet now we find ourselves in that role, and we know that in the future other agendas will press in upon us. We will be called to be faithful interpreters of the Word in relation to the needs of the World. It has been noted that the ancient prophets discerned and interpreted the signs of the times. Our task is no less. We are called to discern the moral meaning of the present situation and so interpret it that eyes are opened, hearts moved, and political will redirected.[23]

Third, ours must be a ministry of protest. There are simply times when we must say no. As Christians, we have to draw ethical lines and raise probing moral questions. It has been said that three of the greatest social movements of our time have involved saying no: (1) "no" to segregation; (2) "no" to the war in Vietnam; and (3) "no" to male chauvinism. Getting persons to just say no to drugs and other addictive habits remains a great challenge. By declaring ourselves in protest to policies, procedures, and programs that dehumanize persons, we begin to be catalysts for Christ in our churches and communities.

The conscientious Christian has to define, at least personally, what are the moral limits—the "here I stand, I can do no other" points—the violation of which would undermine all the good one seeks. Learning what these limits are may be the beginning point of our public ministry. "Negative starting points" are easier to identify sometimes than positive programs. But as Peter L. Berger has suggested, we must begin by saying:

> No to children living in garbage, *no* to exploitation and hunger, *no* to terror and totalitarianism, *no* to anomie and the mindless destruction of human beings. . . . From these concrete instances of saying *no* one may then move ahead to the painstaking task of finding alternatives which will not only be morally acceptable, but which will work.[24]

Illustrative are Christians who are beginning to say no to more and more nuclear weapons, believing they rob the poor, endanger the planet, and must be questioned not only in terms of deployment but even whether they should be manufactured as well. Opposition is changing to resistance, non-support to non-cooperation. New forms of a public ministry are beginning to emerge around the globe.

Fourth, ours must be a ministry of advocacy. Few persons and professionals in American society have the freedom and the opportunity to speak as advocates without being accused of self-interest. Yet the clergy can be advocates of what Jesus called "the least of these" in our society. The church, said Walter Rauschenbusch, must fight for the "underdog" since "the strong have ample means of defending their interests and usually enough power left to guard their unjust interests also."[25]

Enslaved liberators take a clue from Jesus' relationships with the discouraged and downtrodden of his society, along with the thundering prophetic voices of the Old Testament against injustice and insensitivity to the needs of the poor. Contemporary Christian theology and ethics have a decided leaning toward what the Latin Americans call a "preferential option for the poor." God does not love the victims of society more than others, but because Yahweh is a righteous God, Divine concern reaches out especially for persons, races, classes, and nations in need. Theologian Karl Barth said:

> The Church is witness of the fact that the Son of God came to seek and to save the lost. And this implies that—casting all false impartiality aside—the Church must concentrate first on the lower and lowest levels of human society. The poor, the socially and economically weak and threatened, will always be the object of its primary and particular concern, and it will always insist on the state's special responsibility for those weaker members of society.[26]

Truly, our vocational calling as laity and clergy is a ministry of advocacy!

Fifth, ours must be a ministry of envisioning. Without a vision, the people perish; that is a cornerstone of prophetic understanding. Visions have way of defining reality, and, like the Thomas theorem suggests, visions have consequences. Because Martin Luther King, Jr., had a "dream," America is different today than when he proclaimed his dream in Washington, D.C., in 1963. Because Pope John XXIII had a dream of a renewed church, not only is Catholicism different today, but so is all Christendom as well.

Dreamers run risks. Visionaries are often persecuted. Not all dreams become reality. But to use the words of John F. Kennedy, we must become "idealists without illusions." Just as voices from mainstream Protestantism in the 1970s finally helped bring an end to the Vietnam War, so also it may be that in the 1980s the bishops of the Roman Catholic and The United Methodist Churches helped provide the needed impetus for the United States, at least, to reconsider the consequences of the nuclear arms race.

Dreaming impossible dreams, seeing beyond the usual, envisioning a new way or a new world—flows from the very essence of the Christian faith. Because the church's commitments transcend parochial and national self-interest, and because the values affirmed inspire greater compassion, justice and equality for all persons, Christians should dare to be involved in a public ministry in order to transform dreams into reality. Our dreams can become our destiny.

To think of the church as the conscience of the nation may seem like a romantic dream—"tilting at windmills"—yet it represents America's, if not the world's, greatest and best hope. *Time* correspondent L. Bruce van Voorst, writing in *Foreign Affairs*, argues that "because of their enormous memberships, organization, and dedication, the role of the churches will become critical in determining the political impact and outcome of the 'nuclear movement' in the United States."[27] Far from being impotent, the church can be a powerful force. As theologian Jürgen Moltmann noted, "Hope alone is to be called 'realistic,' because it alone takes seriously the possibilities with which all reality is fraught."[28]

And, finally, our ministry must be a ministry of reconciliation. Love must be the norm and style of our life as clergy and laity. Our calling demands nothing less. Our Christ demonstrated nothing more.

In the struggles of controversy, it is easy to forget the commands to love neighbor—and enemy. Let there be room in debates on homosexuality, war and peace, ecumenism, or whatever, for the conscientious objector—for the person who takes a stand diametrically opposite to our own. Let us humanize our polarizations, remembering that none of us is certain we have God-given answers to social questions and issues. Christians need to hear and to heed the voice of the Vietnamese poet and Zen Buddhist monk, Thich Nhat Hanh.

> In the peace movement, there is a lot of anger, frustration and misunderstanding today. The people in the movement can write very good protest letters, but they are not yet able to write love letters. We need to learn to write to the Congress and to the President of the United States letters that they will not put in the trash can. We need to write the kind of letter that they will like to receive. The way you speak, the kind of language you use, and the kind of understanding you express should not turn people off. Because the people you write to are also persons like all of us.[29]

All stand in the need of God's grace and forgiveness. In public ministry, all should stand boldly and bravely for their beliefs, but simultaneously love intensely those with whom they disagree and who work in opposite directions. If God can see the good in each of us and love us as we are, then surely we can see the good in those with whom we disagree. What Robert Kennedy spontaneously spoke in a black neighborhood in Indianapolis the night Martin Luther King, Jr., was assassinated needs to be reheard again.

> What we need . . . is not division; what we need . . . is not hatred; what we need . . . is not violence or lawlessness, but love and wisdom, and compassion toward one another, and the feeling of justice toward those who still suffer . . . , whether they be white or they be black. . . .
>
> Let us dedicate ourselves to what the Greeks wrote so many years ago: "to tame the savageness of man, make gentle the life of this world."[30]

The value of examining historical metaphors and exploring contemporary images of Christian ministry lies not in particular labels or titles but in the possibility that by revisioning the ministry it may have a new identity and vitality. The church, understanding itself as a global ministering community, will do much to "tame the savageness" and "make gentle the life of this world." Let this be our prayer and our practice.

Notes

Introduction

1. See Donald E. Messer, "It's Three O'clock in the Morning," *The Christian Ministry* (January 1983): 13-16.
2. The six practitioner roles cited are adapted from Samuel W. Blizzard, "The Minister's Dilemma," *The Christian Century* (April 25, 1956): 508.

1. The Art of Imaging

1. Avery Dulles, *Models of the Church* (Garden City, N.Y.: Doubleday/Image Books, 1978), p. 170.
2. See especially Sallie McFague, *Metaphorical Theology* (Philadelphia: Fortress Press, 1982), pp. 14 ff.
3. Ibid., p. 26. See also George Lakoff and Mark Johnson, *Metaphors We Live By* (Chicago: University of Chicago Press, 1980).
4. Leonard I. Sweet, "The Rainbow Church," *The Christian Ministry* (March 1986): 6.
5. Paul Minear, *Images of the Church in the New Testament* (Philadelphia: The Westminster Press, 1960), p. 23.
6. F. W. Dillistone, *Christianity and Symbolism* (London: William Collins, 1955), p. 161.
7. James H. Cone, "The Story Content of Black Theology," *Theology Today* 32 (1975): 145. See also p. 150.
8. Susan Brooks Thistlethwaite, *Metaphors for the Contemporary Church* (New York: The Pilgrim Press, 1983), p. 12.
9. John Shea, *Stories of God: An Unauthorized Biography* (Chicago: Thomas More, 1978), p. 56.
10. Douglas Bland, "Storytelling as Grief Ministry," *The Christian Century* (September 1982): 33.
11. Jacob Bronowski, *The Visionary Eye: Essays in the Arts, Literature, and Science*, ed. Piero E. Ariotti (Cambridge, Mass.: M.I.T. Press, 1978), p. 28.
12. McFague, *Metaphorical Theology*, p. 16.
13. Thistlethwaite, *Metaphors of the Contemporary Church*, p. 18.
14. Sheldon B. Kopp, *If You Meet the Buddha on the Road, Kill Him! The Pilgrimage of Psychotherapy Patients* (New York: Bantam Books, 1981), p. 21.
15. McFague, *Metaphorical Theology*, p. 20.
16. See my book *Christian Ethics and Political Action* (Valley Forge: Judson Press, 1984) for a more detailed discussion of this imperative.

17. Fred B. Craddock, *Overhearing the Gospel* (Nashville: Abingdon Press, 1978), p. 24.

18. Beverly Roberts Gaventa, "The Scandal of Vocation," *The Christian Ministry* (July, 1983): 24.

19. Dulles, *Models of the Church*, pp. 167-68.

20. *Baptism, Eucharist, and Ministry*. Faith and Order Paper No. 111, World Council of Churches, Geneva Switzerland, 1982, p. 24.

21. Lynn Rhodes, *Co-Creating: A Feminist Vision of Ministry* (Philadelphia: The Westminster Press, 1987), p. 51.

2. Shifting Historical Images of Ministry

1. See Urban T. Holmes III, *The Future Shape of Ministry* (New York: The Seabury Press, 1971) p. 32.

2. See Kenneth Underwood, *The Church, the University, and Social Policy* (Middleton, Conn.: Wesleyan University Press, 1969), vol. I, p. 84.

3. See Eusebius, *Ecclesiastical History* 5.24.3.

4. For more details, see John Knox, "The Ministry in the Primitive Church," and George H. Williams, "The Ministry of the Ante-Nicene Church" (c. 125–325), in *The Ministry in Historical Perspectives*, eds. H. Richard Niebuhr and Daniel D. Williams (New York: Harper and Brothers, 1956).

5. George H. Williams, "The Ministry in the Later Patristic Period (314–451)," in ibid., p. 61.

6. Roland H. Bainton, "The Ministry in the Middle Ages," in ibid., p. 91.

7. Ibid., p. 107.

8. Martin Luther, *The Babylonian Captivity of the Church*, 1520, WA 6, 407, pp. 22 ff, or LW 44, pp. 127-28.

9. Wilhelm Pauck, "The Ministry in the Time of the Continental Reformation," in Niebuhr and Williams, *The Ministry in Historical Perspectives*, p. 116.

10. Karl Barth, *The Word of God and the Word of Man* (New York: Harper Torchbooks, 1957), p. 114.

11. Martin Luther, cited in Niebuhr and Williams, *The Ministry in Historical Perspectives*, p. 115.

12. See Winthrop S. Hudson, "The Ministry in the Puritan Age," and Edward Rochie Hardy, Jr., "Priestly Ministries in the Modern Church," in Niebuhr and Williams, *The Ministry in Historical Perspectives*.

13. See Pauck, ibid., p. 146.

14. See Sidney E. Mead, "The Rise of the Evangelical Conception of the Ministry in America," ibid., p. 229.

15. Vincent Harding, *There Is a River: The Black Struggle for Freedom in America* (New York: Harcourt Brace Jovanovich, 1981), p. 111.

16. See C. Howard Hopkins, *The Rise of the Social Gospel in American Protestantism, 1865-1915* (New Haven, Conn. Yale University Press, 1940), p. 9.

17. P. T. Forsyth, *Positive Preaching and the Modern Mind* (Grand Rapids: Wm. B. Eerdman's, 1907), p. 60.

18. Holmes, *The Future Shape of Ministry*, pp. 140-41.

19. See Urban T. Holmes III, *Ministry and Imagination* (New York: The Seabury Press, 1976), pp. 222 ff. James C. Fenhagen develops "the ministry of enablement" in *Mutual Ministry, New Vitality for the Local Church* (New York: The Seabury Press, 1977). Michael E. Cavanagh speaks of "ministers as facilitators of growth," in *The Effective Minister: Psychological and Social Considerations* (San Francisco: Harper & Row, 1986). Elton Trueblood proposed the "player coach" model in *The Incendiary Fellowship* (New York: Harper & Row, 1967).

20. H. Richard Niebuhr, *The Purpose of the Church and Its Ministry* (New York: Harper and Brothers., 1956), pp. 79 ff.

3. The Divine Madness of Ministry

1. Elie Wiesel, *Zalmen or the Madness of God*, adapted by Marion Wiesel, trans. Nathan Edleman (New York: Random House, 1975), p.vii.

2. Ibid., pp.79-80.

3. Gary W. Charles, "The Divine Madness of Ministry," *The Christian Century* (April 20, 1983): 360.

4. Hans Küng, *The Church* (New York: Sheed and Ward, 1968), p. 438.

5. Franz Kafka, *Parables and Paradoxes* (New York: Schocken Books, 1946), p. 81.

6. Colbert S. Cartwright, "The Minister: An Impossible Figure," *The Christian Ministry* (July 1982): 28.

7. Bill C. Davis, *Mass Appeal* (New York: Avon Books, 1981), p. 42.

8. See Asbury's Journal for May 29, 1774. Also note R. Benjamin Garrison, *Portrait of the Church: Warts and All* (Nashville: Abingdon Press, 1964), pp.15-25.

9. Cited in Robert Moats Miller, *How Shall They Hear Without a Preacher: The Life of Ernest Fremont Tittle* (Chapel Hill: University of North Carolina Press, 1971), p. 209.

10. Cited in Stanley Hauerwas, *Truthfulness and Tragedy: Further Investigations in Christian Ethics*, (Notre Dame, Ind.: University of Notre Dame Press, 1977), p. 206, footnote 14.

11. See Joan Zimmerman, *Thank God It's Tuesday! A Positive Theology of Sexuality* (six cassettes).

12. Charles Merrill Smith, *How to Become a Bishop Without Being Religious* (Garden City, N.Y.: Doubleday, 1965), pp. 24-25.

13. Urban T. Holmes III, *The Priest in Community: Exploring the Roots of Ministry* (New York: Seabury Press, 1978), p. 78.

14. See David S. Schuller, "Basic Issues in Defining Ministry, in *Ministry in America*, eds. David S. Schuller, Merton P. Strommen, and Milo L. Brekke (San Francisco: Harper & Row, 1980), pp. 18-20. See also David O. Aleshire, "Eleven Major Areas of Ministry." Ibid, pp. 49-50.

15. David E. Richards, "Anglican-Episcopal Churches." Ibid, p. 240.

16. George Barna and William Paul McKay, *Vital Signs: Emerging Social Trends and the Future of American Christianity* (Westchester, Ill.: Crossway Books, 1984), p. 61.

17. Martin Marty, *Context*, vol. 16, no. 21, (December, 1984): 5.

18. Barna and McKay, *Vital Signs*, pp. 11-12.

19. Michael E. Cavanagh, *The Effective Minister: Psychological and Social Considerations* (San Francisco: Harper & Row, 1986), pp. 30-31.

20. See Merton P. Strommen, "Models of Ministry," in Schuller, Strommen, and Brekke, *Ministry in America*, pp. 76-77.

21. Gary L. Harbaugh, *Pastor as Person: Maintaining Personal Integrity in the Choices and Challenges of Ministry* (Minneapolis: Augsburg Publishing House), p. 47. See also Donald P. Smith, *Clergy in the Cross Fire* (Philadelphia: The Westminster Press, 1973), pp. 62-63.

22. James L. Waits, "The Education of Ministers and Divines." Inaugural address as a Griggs Candler Professor of Divinity on September 6, 1984. Published as a pamphlet.

23. Stanley Hauerwas, "Clerical Character: Reflecting on Ministerial Morality," *Word and World* vol. VI, No. 2, (Spring, 1986): 183.

24. Harvey Cox, *The Seduction of the Spirit* (New York: Simon and Schuster, 1973), p. 86.

25. Urban T. Holmes III, *The Future Shape of Ministry* (New York: Seabury Press, 1971), pp. 246-47.

26. Holmes, *The Priest in Community*, p. 98.

27. William K. McElvaney, *The People of God in Ministry* (Nashville: Abingdon Press, 1981), p. 40.

28. Jeffrey Archer, *First Among Equals* (New York: Simon and Schuster, 1984), p. 84. Archer himself was forced to leave public office in Great Britain because of this dilemma.

29. Stephen B. Oates, *Let the Trumpet Sound: The Life of Martin Luther King, Jr.* (New York: Harper & Row, 1982), pp. 282-83.

30. Holmes, *The Priest in Community*, pp. 158-59.

31. Mimeographed remarks by Governor Mario M. Cuomo at Saint John the Divine, New York City, November 27, 1983, p. 3.

32. "An Exclusive Telephone Conversation with Frederick Buechner," *Just Looking* (March 1984): 2.

33. H. Richard Niebuhr, *The Purpose of the Church and Its Ministry* New York: Harper and Brothers, 1956), p. 54.

4. A Theology of Ministry

1. Edward Farley, *Theologia: the Fragmentation and Unity of Theological Education* (Philadelphia: Fortress Press, 1983), p. 127. An excellent example of pastoral theology is Thomas C. Oden, *Pastoral Theology: Essentials of Ministry* (San Francisco: Harper & Row, 1982).

2. Avery Dulles, *Models of the Church* (Garden City, N.Y.: Doubleday/Image Books 1978), pp. 178-79.

3. Henry Sloane Coffin, *In a Day of Social Rebuilding* (New Haven: Yale University Press, 1918), pp. 192-93.

4. Colin Morris, *Include Me Out! Confessions of an Ecclesiastical Coward* (Nashville: Abingdon Press, 1968), p. 14.

5. *Baptism, Eucharist and Ministry*, Faith and Order Paper No. 111, (Geneva: World Council of Churches, 1982), p. 20.

6. Francis O. Ayres, *The Ministry of the Laity: A Biblical Exposition* (Philadelphia: The Westminster Press, 1962), p. 37. See also Hendrick Kraemer, *A Theology of the Laity*, (Philadelphia: The Westminster Press, 1958); Yves Congar, *Lay People in the Church: A Study for a Theology of the Laity*, trans. Donald Attwater (London: Bloomsbury Publishing Company, 1957); and James D. Anderson and Ezra Earl Jones, *Ministry of the Laity* (San Franciso: Harper & Row, 1986).

7. Martin Luther, *Church Postil*, 1522. Cited in Wilhelm Pauck, "The Ministry in the Time of the Continental Reformation," in *The Ministry in Historical Perspectives*, eds. H. Richard Niebuhr and Daniel Day Williams (New York: Harper and Brothers, 1956), p. 113.

8. Martin Luther, *Tischreden (Table-Talk)*, vol. 16, p. 62. 1.5 cited in Niebuhr and Williams, *The Ministry in Historical Perspectives*, p. 112.

9. Robert C. Mackie et al., eds. *Layman Extraordinary, John R. Mott: 1865-1955* (New York: Association Press, 1965), p. 118.

10. See Waldron Scott, *Bring Forth Justice* (Grand Rapids: Wm. B. Eerdman's, 1980), p. 145. For more details, see David Bouton, *The Grease Machine* (New York: Harper & Row, 1978).

11. Dietrich Bonhoeffer, *Life Together* (New York: Harper and Brothers, 1954).

12. See James M. Gustafson, "Professions as 'Callings,' " *Social Service Review* (December 1982). H. Richard Niebuhr, *The Purpose of the Church and Its Ministry* (New York: Harper and Brothers, 1956), p. 64, adds a prior call "to be a Christian."

13. James M. Hoppin, *The Office and Work of the Ministry* (New York, 1869), p. 423.

14. *The Book of Discipline of The United Methodist Church*, (Nashville: The United Methodist Publishing House, 1984), par. 402, p. 189.

15. Martin Luther, "An Appeal to the Ruling Class (1520)," cited in Lewis W. Spitz, *The Protestant Reformation* (Englewood Cliffs, N.J.: Prentice-Hall, 1966), p. 54.

16. Urban T. Holmes III, *The Priest in Community: Exploring the Roots of Ministry* (New York: The Seabury Press, 1978), p. 160.

17. Daniel O. Aleshire, "Eleven Major Areas of Ministry," in *Ministry in America*, eds. David S. Schuller, Merton P. Strommen, and Milo L. Brekke (New York: Harper & Row, 1980), p. 37.

18. Jackson W. Carroll, "Some Issues in Clergy Authority," *Review of Religious Research*, vol. 23, no. 2 (December 1981): 104-5.

19. For a more detailed discussion, see Merton P. Strommen, "Models of Ministry," in Schuller, Strommen, and Brekke, *Ministry in America*, pp. 81 ff.

20. See Jackson W. Carroll, "Some Issues in Clergy Authority," *Review of Religious Research*, vol. 23, no. 2 (December 1981): 106-7.

21. James Forbes, cited in Holmes, *The Priest in Community*, p. 118.

22. Address to Anglo-Catholic Congress of 1923, cited in H. Maynard Smith, *Frank, Bishop of Zanzibar* (London, 1926), p. 302; also quoted in Edward Rochie Hardy, Jr., "Priestly Ministries in the Modern Church," in Niebuhr and Williams, *The Ministry in Historical Perspectives*, p. 174.

23. See Merton P. Strommen, "Models of Ministry," in Schuller, Strommen, and Brekke, *Ministry in America*, p. 84.

24. Loren Eiseley, *The Immense Journey* (New York: Random House, 1957), p. 175.

25. Reinhold Niebuhr, *Leaves from the Notebook of a Tamed Cynic* (Cleveland: The World Publishing Company, 1929), p. 42.

26. James D. Glasse, *Profession: Minister* (Nashville: Abingdon Press, 1968), p. 18.

27. See Thomas C. Oden, *Pastoral Theology: Essentials of Ministry* (San Francisco: Harper & Row, 1983), pp. 4-5, and Alastair V. Campbell, *Professionalism and Pastoral Care* (Philadelphia: Fortress Press, 1985).

28. William K. McElvaney, *The People of God in Ministry* (Nashville: Abingdon Press, 1981), p. 94.

29. Darrell Reeck, *Ethics for the Professions: A Christian Perspective* (Minneapolis: Augsburg Publishing House, 1982), p. 18. The italics have been removed.

30. James Gustafson, quoted in "The Professional Model of Ministry—Is It Worth Saving?" *Theological Education* (Spring 1985): 42.

31. Carl. E. Braaten, *Eschatology and Ethics: Essays on the Theology and Ethics of the Kingdom of God* (Minneapolis: Augsburg Publishing House, 1974), p. 147.

5. Wounded Healers in a Community of the Compassionate

1. Avery Dulles, *Models of the Church* (Garden City, N.Y.: Doubleday/Image Books, 1978), p. 67.

2. See Joachim Jeremias, *New Testament Theology* (New York: Charles Scribner's Sons, 1971), vol. 1, pp. 115-16, 121; Gunter Bornkamm, *Jesus of Nazareth*, trans. Irene and Fraser McLuskey with James Robinson (New York: Harper & Row, 1967), pp. 102, 107. See also Sallie McFague, *Metaphorical Theology* (Philadelphia: Fortress Press, 1982), p. 180.

3. Cited in George H. Williams, "The Ministry of the Ante-Nicene Church," in *The*

Ministry in Historical Perspectives, eds. H. Richard Niebuhr and Daniel D. Williams (New York: Harper and Brothers, 1956), p. 31.

4. See Robert Inchausti, "Interpreting Mother Teresa," *The Christian Century* (October 16, 1985): 920.

5. Matthew Fox, *A Spirituality Named Compassion and the Healing of the Global Village* (Minneapolis: Winston Press, 1979), p. 27.

6. Mary Pellauer, "Violence Against Women: The Theological Dimension," *Christianity and Crisis* (May 30, 1983): 210.

7. Thomas à Kempis, *The Imitation of Christ,* trans. John Rooney (Springfield, Ill.: Templegate, 1980), p. 42.

8. Henri J. M. Nouwen, *The Wounded Healer* (New York: Doubleday/Image Books, 1972), p. xvi. This section is adapted from Donald E. Messer, "It's Three O'Clock in the Morning," *The Christian Ministry* (January 1983).

9. Norman Cousins, *Anatomy of an Illness as Perceived by the Patient: Reflections on Healing and Regeneration* (New York: W. W. Norton and Company, 1979), p. 153.

10. Dorothee Soelle, *Suffering,* trans. Everett R. Kalin (Philadelphia: Fortress Press, 1975).

11. James D. Glasse, *Profession: Minister* (Nashville: Abingdon Press, 1968), p. 65.

12. See Ernest Hemingway, *A Farewell to Arms.*

13. F. Scott Fitzgerald, "The Crack-Up," *Esquire* (February 1982): 78.

14. Ibid., p. 80.

15. Karin Granberg Michalson, "Until the Very Desert Blooms," *Sojourners* (October 1977): 27.

16. Phyllis Battelle, "12 Women Who Most Impress Barbara Walters," *The Sunday Denver Post,* Contemporary (October 2, 1983): 24.

17. John Osborne, *Luther* (New York: Criterion Books, 1961), p. 125.

18. Richard Wright, *Black Boy* (New York: World Publishing Company, 1945), p. 150.

19. Nouwen, p. 72.

20. Ibid., p. 94.

21. Paul Tillich, *The Shaking of the Foundations* (New York: Charles Scribner's Sons, 1948), pp. 161-62.

22. See C. W. Brister, James L. Cooper, and J. David Fite, *Beginning Your Ministry* (Nashville: Abingdon Press, 1981), p. 35.

23. See Richard John Neuhaus, *Freedom for Ministry* (Harper & Row, 1976), p. 13.

24. Jonathan Schell, *The Fate of the Earth* (New York: Alfred A. Knopf, 1982), p. 65.

25. Walter Wink, "Faith and Nuclear Paralysis," *The Christian Century* (March 3, 1981): 234-35.

26. Garfield Owens, *All God's Chillun: Meditations on Negro Spirituals* (Nashville: Abingdon Press, 1971), p. 138.

6. Servant Leaders in a Servant Church

1. Avery Dulles, *Models of the Church* (Garden City, N.Y.: Doubleday/Image Books, 1978), p. 26.

2. John Naisbitt, *Megatrends: Ten New Directions Transforming Our Lives* (New York: Warner Books, 1982), p. 209.

3. Robert Greenleaf, *Servant Leadership* (New York: Paulist Press, 1977), pp. 7 and 10.

4. Neill Q. Hamilton, *Maturing in the Christian Life* (Philadelphia: The Geneva Press, 1984), pp. 23-24.

5. Stanley S. Harakas, "The Orthodox Priest as Leader in the Divine Liturgy," *The Greek Orthodox Theological Review,* vol. 21, no. 2 (Summer 1976): 163-76.

6. George A. Buttrick, *Interpreter's Bible*, vol. 7 (New York: Abingdon-Cokesbury Press, 1951), p. 496.

7. Dietrich Bonhoeffer, *Letters and Papers from Prison* (New York: Macmillan, 1971), p. 203.

8. Jürgen Moltmann, *The Crucified God* (New York: Harper & Row, 1974), p. 40.

9. Paul D. Hanson, "The Servant Dimension of Pastoral Ministry in Biblical Perspective," in *The Pastor As Servant*, eds. Earl E. Shelp and Ronald H. Sunderland (New York: The Pilgrim Press, 1986), p. 19.

10. Jim Wallis in a lecture at The Iliff School of Theology, April 10, 1984.

11. James H. Cone, "The Servant Church," in Shelp and Sunderland, *The Pastor As Servant*, p. 76.

12. See *Newscope*, February 25, 1983.

13. Ludwig Marcuse, *Soldier of the Church* (New York: Simon and Schuster, 1939), p. 220.

14. Martin Luther King, Jr. Quoted on a postcard distributed by the Martin Luther King Center, Atlanta, Georgia.

15. David E. Richards, "Anglican-Episcopal Churches," in Schuller, Strommen, and Brekke, *Ministry in America*, p. 244.

16. See A. James Armstrong, *Telling Truth: The Foolishness of Preaching in a Real World* (Waco, Tex.: Word, 1977), p. 109.

17. Langdon Gilkey, "Plurality, Our New Situation," in Shelp and Sunderland, *The Pastor As Servant*, pp. 113-14.

18. See *Context*, vol. 16, no. 19 (November 1, 1964): 5.

19. William Temple, *The Hope of a New World* (New York: Macmillan, 1943), p. 20.

20. William H. Willimon, *The Service of God: Christian Work and Worship* (Nashville: Abingdon Press, 1983), p. 42.

21. Edward Schillebeeckx, *Ministry: Leadership in the Community of Jesus Christ* (New York: Crossroad Publishing Company, 1981), p. 37.

22. Mark O. Hatfield, *Between a Rock and a Hard Place* (Waco, Tex.: Word, 1976), p. 27.

23. Thomas J. Peters and Robert H. Waterman, Jr., *In Search of Excellence* (New York: Harper & Row, 1982), p. 239.

24. Martin E. Marty, *The Fire We Can Light* (Garden City, N.Y.: Doubleday, 1973), p. 165.

25. Greenleaf, *Servant Leadership*, p. 20.

26. Ibid. p. 21.

27. For historical and contemporary descriptions of these functions, see William A. Clebsch and Charles R. Jaekle, *Pastoral Care in Historical Perspective* (Englewood Cliffs, N.J.: Prentice-Hall, 1964), and Howard J. Clinebell, Jr., *Basic Types of Pastoral Counseling* (Nashville: Abingdon Press, 1966).

28. James McGregor Burns, *Leadership* (New York: Harper & Row, 1978), p. 4.

29. Lee Iacocca with William Novak, *Iacocca: An Autobiography* (New York: Bantam Books, 1984), pp. 229-30.

30. Joseph C. Hough, Jr., and John B. Cobb, Jr., *Christian Identity and Theological Education* (Chico, Calif.: Scholar's Press, 1985), p. 80.

31. "One of the Last Tycoons," *Time* (March 24, 1975): 37.

32. James P. Shannon, "The Pilgrim Church," *Minneapolis Tribune* (March 30, 1975): 13A.

33. "An Address to the Clergy," *The Works of John Wesley*, vol. X (London: Wesleyan-Methodist Book Room), p. 487.

7. Political Mystics in a Prophetic Community

1. Allister Sparks, "Bishop Tutu's Delicate Balance," *The Washington Post* (August 19, 1985): 15.
2. Matthew Fox, *On Becoming a Musical, Mystical Bear* (New York: Paulist Books, 1976), pp. x-xi.
3. See James D. Smart, *The Rebirth of Ministry: A Study of the Biblical Character of the Church's Ministry* (Philadelphia: The Westminster Press, 1960), pp. 56-57.
4. Martin E. Marty, "Mysticism and the Religious Quest for Freedom," *The Christian Century*, March 16, 1983, p. 243.
5. Ibid., p. 242.
6. James D. Glasse, *Putting It Together in the Parish* (Nashville: Abingdon Press, 1972), pp. 55-56.
7. Urban T. Holmes III, *The Priest in Community* (New York: The Seabury Press, 1978), p. 67.
8. Wallace M. Alston, Jr., in *The Church* (John Knox Press), cited in *Context* 17, 8 (April 15, 1985).
9. Gustavo Gutierrez, "A Spirituality for Liberation," *The Other Side* (April/May, 1985): 43.
10. Waldron Scott, *Bring Forth Justice* (Grand Rapids: William B. Eerdmans, 1980), p. 65.
11. Jose Porfirio Miranda, *Marx and the Bible*, trans. John Eagleson (Maryknoll: Orbis Books, 1974), p. 48.
12. Henri J. M. Nouwen, *The Wounded Healer* (Garden City, N.Y.: Doubleday/Image Books, 1979), p. 19.
13. Jürgen Moltmann, *Theology of Hope* (New York: Harper & Row, 1967), p. 21.
14. Susan Brooks Thistlethwaite, *Metaphors for the Contemporary Church* (New York: Pilgrim Press, 1983), p. 124.
15. For an excellent synoptic understanding, see Robert R. Wilson's "Prophet," in *Harper's Bible Dictionary*, ed. Paul J. Achtemeier (San Francisco: Harper & Row, 1985), pp. 826-30.
16. Robert N. Bellah, Richard Madsen, William M. Sullivan, Ann Swidler, and Steven M. Tipton, *Habits of the Heart* (Berkeley: University of California Press, 1985), p. 246.
17. For an in-depth understanding, see Martin E. Marty, *The Public Church: Mainline—Evangelical—Catholic* (New York: The Crossroad Publishing Company, 1981).
18. Parker J. Palmer, *The Company of Strangers: Christians and the Renewal of America's Public Life* (New York: The Crossroad Publishing Company, 1981), p. 56.
19. Dennis J. Geaney, *The Prophetic Parish: A Center for Peace and Justice* (Minneapolis: Winston Press, 1983), p. 5.
20. The United Methodist Council of Bishops, *In Defense of Creation: the Nuclear Crisis and a Just Peace*, Foundation Document (Nashville: Graded Press, 1986), pp. 84 and 88.
21. Robert Coles, lecture at Dakota Wesleyan University, March 5, 1980.
22. Geaney, *The Prophetic Parish*, p. 35.
23. See William Johnston, *Christian Mysticism Today* (San Francisco: Harper & Row, 1984).
24. Marty, "Mysticism and the Religious Quest for Freedom," p. 243.
25. Walter G. Muelder, "Communitarian Christian Ethics: A Personal Statement and a Response," in *Toward a Discipline of Social Ethics: Essays in Honor of Walter George Muelder*, ed. Paul Deats, Jr. (Boston: Boston University Press, 1972), p. 297.

26. Sean O'Casey, *Rose and Crown* (New York: Macmillan, 1961).

27. Fox, *On Becoming a Musical, Mystical Bear*, p. xv.

28. James Baldwin, *The Fire Next Time* (New York: Dell, 1962), p. 104.

29. Contemporary literature in spiritual development is abundant. Three excellent books are Tilden H. Edwards, *Spiritual Friend* (New York: Paulist Press, 1980); Kenneth Leech, *Soul Friend: The Practice of Christian Spirituality* (San Francisco: Harper & Row, 1980); and Urban T. Holmes III, *Spirituality for Ministry* (San Francisco: Harper & Row, 1982).

30. Fred B. Craddock, *Overhearing the Gospel* (Nashville: Abingdon Press, 1978), p. 43.

31. See Gustavo Gutierrez, "Where Hunger Is, God Is Not," *The Witness* (April 1977): 4.

32. See *When Prayer Makes News*, eds. Allan A. Boesak and Charles Villa-Vicencio (Philadelphia: The Westminster Press, 1986), p. 5.

33. Sheldon B. Kopp, *If You Meet the Buddha on the Road, Kill Him! The Pilgrimage of Psychotherapy Patients* (New York: Bantam Books, 1981), p. 91.

8. Enslaved Liberators of the Rainbow Church

1. Thomas P. McDonnell, ed., *A Thomas Merton Reader* (Garden City, N.Y.: Doubleday/Image Books, 1974), p. 16.

2. Delwin Brown, *To Set at Liberty: Christian Faith and Human Freedom* (Maryknoll, N.Y.: Orbis Books, 1981), p. 81.

3. Ernst Troeltsch, *The Social Teaching of the Christian Churches*, vol. 2 (New York: Harper & Row, 1960), p. 1013.

4. Parker J. Palmer, *The Promise of Paradox: A Celebration of Contradictions in the Christian Life* (Notre Dame, Ind.: Ave Maria Press, 1980), pp. 18-19.

5. John Howard Yoder, *The Politics of Jesus* (Grand Rapids: William B. Eerdman's, 1972), p. 39.

6. Robert McAfee Brown, *Unexpected News: Reading the Bible with Third World Eyes* (Philadelphia: The Westminster Press, 1984), p. 81.

7. Elsa Tamaz, *Bible of the Oppressed* (Maryknoll, N.Y.: Orbis Books, 1982), p. 68.

8. Gustavo Gutierrez, *A Theology of Liberation* (Maryknoll, N.Y.: Orbis Books, 1973), p. 208.

9. References from *The Gospel in Art by the Peasants of Solentiname*, eds. Philip and Sally Scharper (Maryknoll, N.Y.: Orbis Books, 1984) pp. 6, 8, 60.

10. Commentaries based on the four volumes of Ernest Cardenal, *The Gospel in Solentiname* (Maryknoll, N.Y.: Orbis Books, 1976-82).

11. Walter Brueggemann, *The Prophetic Imagination* (Philadelphia: Fortress Press, 1978), p. 13. The italics have been removed.

12. Ibid.

13. Ibid., p. 14.

14. Brown, *To Set At Liberty: Christian Faith and Human Freedom*, p. 92.

15. Helmut Thielicke, *How the World Began: Man in the First Chapters of the Bible* (Philadelphia: Muhlenberg Press, 1961), pp. 287-99.

16. Leonard I. Sweet, "The Rainbow Church," *The Christian Ministry* (March 1986): 6.

17. Arthur Waskow, "Noah and the Nuclear Rainbow," *Worldview* (October 1983): 18.

18. Anders Nygren, *The Gospel of God* (Philadelphia: Westminster Press, 1951), p. 21.

19. D. T. Niles, *That They May Have Life* (New York: Harper and Brothers, 1951), p. 96.

20. Jose Miguez Bonino, *International Review of Mission*, 73, 289 (January 1984): 113.

21. Article 5, cited in C. Peter Wagner, *Church Growth and the Whole Gospel* (San Francisco: Harper & Row, 1981), p. 14.

22. This phrase is attributed to George Hunter, "Can United Methodists Recover Evangelism?" *Church Growth Bulletin*, 13, no. 4 (March 1977): 111-12.

23. Dietrich Bonhoeffer, *Prisoner for God* (New York : Macmillan, 1954), p. 169.

24. Johannes Verkuyl, "Emilio Castro: Servant of World Mission and Evangelism," *International Review of Mission*, 73, 289 (January 1984): 107.

25. "The Faith of Children," *Sojourners* (May 1982): 14.

26. *Global 2000 Report* (Washington, D.C., for sale by Superintendent of Documents, U.S.G.P.O, 1980–1981).

27. *The New York Times* (August 10, 1984): 12.

28. Robert McAfee Brown, *Theology in a New Key: Responding to Liberation Themes* (Philadelphia: The Westminster Press, 1978), p.62.

29. K. H. Ting, "Christian Witness in China Today," The Neesima Lectures (Kyoto, Japan: Doshisha University Press, 1985), p. 32.

30. See Robert McAfee Brown, *Makers of Contemporary Theology: Gustavo Gutierrez* (Atlanta: John Knox Press, 1980), p. 41.

31. Joseph C. Hough, Jr., and John B. Cobb, Jr., *Christian Identity and Theological Education* (Chico, Calif.: Scholars Press, 1985), p. 60.

32. "In the Court of Public Opinion, Lawyers Rank Low," *The Washington Post National Weekly Edition* (September 1, 1986), 38.

9. Practical Theologians in a Post–Denominational Church

1. See *Practical Theology: the Emerging Field in Theology, Church and World* , ed. Don S. Browning (San Fransisco: Harper & Row, 1983); James N. Poling and Donald E. Miller, *Foundations for a Practical Theology of Ministry* (Nashville: Abingdon Press, 1985); Joseph C. Hough, Jr., and John B. Cobb, Jr., *Christian Identity and Theological Education* (Chico, Calif.: Scholars Press, 1985); James D. Whitehead and Evelyn Eaton Whitehead, *Method in Ministry: Theological Reflection and Christian Ministry* (New York: The Seabury Press, 1980); Friedrich Schleiermacher, *Christian Caring: Selections from Practical Theology*, eds. James O. Duke and Howard Stone (Philadelphia: Fortress Press, 1988).

2. See Edward Farley, "Theology and Practice Outside the Clerical Paradigm," in Browning, *Practical Theology*, p. 26. See also Edward Farley, *Theologia: The Fragmentation and Unity of Theological Education* (Philadelphia: Fortress Press, 1983).

3. John Deschner, "What Does Practical Theology Study?" *Perkins Journal* (Summer 1982): 9.

4. Browning, *Practical Theology*, p. 11.

5. See Ronald F. Thiemann, "Making Theology Central in Theological Education," *The Christian Century* (February 4-11, 1987).

6. Hough and Cobb, *Christian Identity and Theological Education* , p. 118.

7. Alfred N. Whitehead, *Adventures of Ideas* (New York: Macmillan, 1933), pp. 27-28.

8. Paul Tillich, *Systematic Theology* (Chicago: The University of Chicago Press, 1951), vol. I, p. 3.

9. Paul Minear, *Images of the Church in the New Testament* (Philadelphia: The Westminster Press, 1960), pp. 66-220.

10. Wang Shengcai, "Tear Down and Build Up," *China News Update* (January 1987):2.

11. H. Richard Niebuhr, *The Social Sources of Denominationalism* (Cleveland: The World Publishing Company), p. 25.

12. See *Context* 16, 19 (November 1, 1984): 6.

13. D. Elton Trueblood, *Quarterly Yoke Letter;* 29, 2 (June 1987): 1.

14. Frederick Herzog, "A New Spirituality: Shaping Doctrine at the Grass Roots," *The Christian Century* (July 30–August 6, 1986): 680-81.

15. Ibid., p. 681.

16. See Winthrop S. Hudson, "The Ministry in the Puritan Age," in *The Ministry in Historical Perspectives* , eds. H. Richard Niebuhr and Daniel D. Williams (New York: Harper and Brothers, 1956), p. 205.

17. Milo L. Brekke, Merton P. Strommen, and Dorothy L. Williams, *Ten Faces of Ministry* (Minneapolis: Augsburg Publishing House, 1979), p. 28.

18. I am indebted to my colleagues, Dr. Delwin Brown and Dr. Sheila Davaney at The Iliff School of Theology, for introducing me to literature in this field.

19. See Paul Ricoeur, *Freud and Philosophy: An Essay on Interpretation* (New Haven, Conn.: Yale University Press, 1970), pp. 20-37.

20. See Victor Paul Furnish, *The Moral Teaching of Paul* (Nashville: Abingdon Press, 1979); John Boswell, *Christianity, Social Tolerance, and Homosexuality* (Chicago: The University of Chicago Press, 1980); James B. Nelson, *Embodiment* (Minneapolis: Augsburg Publishing House, 1978); Letha Scanzoni and Virginia Ramey Mollenkott, *Is The Homosexual My Neighbor?* (New York: Harper & Row, 1978); Robin Scroggs, *The New Testament and Homosexuality: Contextual Background for Contemporary Debate* (Philadelphia: Fortress Press, 1983); and John Linscheid, "Our Story in God's Story: Reading the Bible with Gay Eyes," *The Other Side* (July/August, 1987).

21. Delwin Brown, unpublished manuscript, July 13, 1987.

22. Paul Ricoeur, *The Symbolism of Evil* (New York: Harper & Row, 1967), p. 350.

23. See Ricoeur, *Freud and Philosophy*, p. 28.

24. Emil Brunner, *Reason and Revelation* (Philadelphia: The Westminster Press, 1946), p. 276.

25. Pinchas Lapide, *The Sermon on the Mount* (Maryknoll, N.Y.: Orbis Books, 1986), pp. 11-13.

26. See J. T. Holland, "Jesus, A Model For Ministry," *The Journal of Pastoral Care* 36,4 (1982): 255-64.

27. Thornton Wilder, *The Eighth Day* (New York: Harper & Row, 1967), pp. 248-50.

28. See Wilhelm Pauck, "The Ministry in the Time of the Continental Reformation," in *The Ministry in Historical Perspectives* , eds. H. Richard Niebuhr and Daniel D. Williams (New York: Harper and Brothers, 1956), pp. 114-15.

29. See *Context*, 16, 12 (June 15, 1984): 5.

30. Michael Farrell quoted from the *National Catholic Reporter* in *Context* 16, 12 (June 15, 1986):6.

10. A Public Ministry in a Global Village

1. Virginia Culver, "Sanctuary Minister Undaunted by Trial," *The Denver Post* (June 6, 1987).

2. Franz Kafka, "Leopard in the Temple," in *Parables and Paradoxes*, trans. Ernest Kaiser and Eithne Wilkins (New York: Schocken Books, 1961), p. 93.

3. This section is adapted from Donald E. Messer, "The Good Shepherd: An Oxymoron," *Circuit Rider* (December 1987–January 1988): 4-5.

4. Joachim Jeremias, *New Testament Theology* (New York: Charles Scribner's Sons, 1971), p. 109.

5. Cited in footnote of Kittel's *Theological Dictionary of the New Testament*, vol. VI, p. 489.

6. Jeremias, *New Testament Theology*, p. 116.

7. Alan Paton, *But Your Land Is Beautiful* (New York: Scribner's, 1982).

8. John Drinkwater, *Lincoln, The World Emancipator* (Boston: Houghton Mifflin Company, 1920).

9. The remainder of this chapter is an adaption of an essay entitled "A Christian Ministry of Social and Political Action," *The Iliff Review* (Fall 1983).

10. Richard A. Goodling, "The Clergy and the Problem of Professional Impotency," *The Duke Divinity School Review* (Fall 1980): 31.

11. James E. Dittes, *Minister on the Spot* (Philadelphia: Pilgrim Press, 1970), p. 2.

12. See Robert H. Bonthius, "Getting Into Social Action—And Staying With it," *Theological Education* 6, 2 (Winter 1970): 102. See also Donald E. Messer, "Social Action Blueprint for Parish Pastors," *Christian Advocate* (November 12, 1970): 7-8.

13. See Robert K. Merton, *Social Theory and Social Structure* (New York: The Free Press, 1957), p. 421.

14. Documentation for these assertions can be found in Randy Shilts, *And the Band Played On* (New York: St. Martin's Press, 1987).

15. Mary Pellauer, "Violence Against Women: The Theological Dimension," *Christianity and Crisis* (May 30, 1983): 206.

16. Quoted from a group called TRUST by Robert H. Bonthius in "Action Training: What Is It?" p. 92.

17. See Abraham J. Heschel, *The Prophets* (New York: Harper & Row, 1962), p. 224.

18. See Lovett Hayes Weems, Jr., "Pastoral Care and Social Controversy," *The Christian Ministry* (March 1983): 20.

19. Robert H. Bonthius, "Getting Into Social Action—And Staying With It," p. 105.

20. See Ernest Q. Campbell and Thomas F. Pettigrew, *Christians in Racial Crisis: A Study of Little Rock's Ministry* (Washington, D.C.: Public Affairs Press, 1959), p. 87.

21. Seward Hiltner, *Ferment in the Ministry* (Nashville: Abingdon Press, 1969) p. 22.

22. Francine Carol Juhasz, "Management of Social Conflict as a Predictor of Effectiveness in Social Action," Ph.D. dissertation (Cleveland: Case Western Reserve University, 1969), pp. 10-11.

23. The first five of these ministries are adapted from the listing found in "Identifying a Food Policy Agenda for the 1980's: A Working Paper," Interreligious Task Force on U.S. Policy, 1980, pp. 8-9.

24. Peter L. Berger, *Pyramids of Sacrifice: Political Ethics and Social Change* (New York: Basic Books, 1974), pp. 227-28.

25. Walter Rauschenbusch, *Christian and the Social Crisis*, ed. Robert D. Cross (New York: Harper & Row, 1965) p. 361; first published in 1907.

26. Karl Barth, "The Christian Community and the Civil Community," in *Against the Stream* (London: S.C.M. Press, 1934), p. 37.

27. L. Bruce van Voorst, "The Churches and Nuclear Deterrence," *Foreign Affairs* (Spring 1983): 830.

28. Jürgen Moltmann, *Theology of Hope* (New York: Harper & Row, 1967), p. 103.

29. Thich Nhat Hanh, "Being Peace: Thoughts for Peace Workers and Others," *Fellowship/Reconciliation International* (July/August 1986).

30. Robert F. Kennedy, cited in Arthur M. Schlesinger, Jr., *Robert Kennedy and His Times* (Boston: Houghton Mifflin Company, 1978), p. 914.

Index